THE COLD WAR IN THE THIRD WORLD

NATIONAL HISTORY CENTER

REINTERPRETING HISTORY
Wm. Roger Louis, *series editor*

Historiography is the art of conveying the ways in which the interpretation of history changes over time. The series Reinterpreting History is dedicated to the historian's craft of challenging assumptions, examining new evidence, and placing topics of significance in historiographical context. The vigorous and systematic revision of history is at the heart of the discipline.

Reinterpreting History is an initiative of the National History Center, which was created by the American Historical Association in 2002 to advance historical knowledge and to convey to the public at large the context of present-day issues. The books in the series usually have their origins in sessions organized by the National History Center at the annual meetings of the AHA.

THE COLD WAR IN THE THIRD WORLD

EDITED BY

Robert J. McMahon

OXFORD
UNIVERSITY PRESS

OXFORD
UNIVERSITY PRESS

Oxford University Press is a department of the University of Oxford.
It furthers the University's objective of excellence in research, scholarship,
and education by publishing worldwide.

Oxford   New York
Auckland   Cape Town   Dar es Salaam   Hong Kong   Karachi
Kuala Lumpur   Madrid   Melbourne   Mexico City   Nairobi
New Delhi   Shanghai   Taipei   Toronto

With offices in
Argentina   Austria   Brazil   Chile   Czech Republic   France   Greece
Guatemala   Hungary   Italy   Japan   Poland   Portugal   Singapore
South Korea   Switzerland   Thailand   Turkey   Ukraine   Vietnam

Oxford is a registered trademark of Oxford University Press
in the UK and certain other countries.

Published in the United States of America by
Oxford University Press
198 Madison Avenue, New York, NY 10016

Library of Congress Cataloging-in-Publication Data
The Cold War in the Third World / edited by Robert J. McMahon.
pages cm.—(Reinterpreting history)
ISBN 978–0–19–976868–4 (alk. paper)—ISBN 978–0–19–976869–1 (alk. paper)
1. Developing countries—History, Military—20th century.
2. Developing countries—Politics and government—20th century.   3. Developing
countries—Foreign relations.   4. United States—Relations—Developing countries.
5. Soviet Union—Relations—Developing countries.   6. Cold War.
I. McMahon, Robert J.
D883.C65 2013
909'.097240825—dc23
2012041777

CONTENTS

CONTRIBUTORS

CAROL ANDERSON is an associate professor of African-American studies and history at Emory University. She is the author of *Eyes Off the Prize: The United Nations and the African American Struggle for Human Rights, 1944–1955* (2003).

JEFFREY JAMES BYRNE is an assistant professor of history at the University of British Columbia. He has written articles on the international history of the developing world for the *International Journal of Middle East Studies*, *Diplomatic History*, and other journals. His first book, *Mecca of Revolution: Algeria, Decolonization, and the Global Third World Project* is forthcoming from Oxford University Press.

CHEN JIAN holds the Michael J. Zak Chair in the History of U.S.-China Relations at Cornell University. Among his many publications are *China's Road to the Korean War* (1994) and *Mao's China and the Cold War* (2000).

NICK CULLATHER is a professor of history at Indiana University. He is the author, among other works, of *Illusions of Influence: The Political Economy of United States–Philippines Relations, 1942–1960* (1994) and *The Hungry World: America's Cold War Battle against Poverty in Asia* (2010).

DAVID C. ENGERMAN is a professor of history at Brandeis University. After completing two books on the USSR in American intellectual life, he is currently researching a history of superpower aid competition in Cold War India.

GREG GRANDIN is a professor of history at New York University and a member of the American Academy of Arts and Sciences. He is the author of a number of books, including *Blood of Guatemela: A History of Race and Nation* (2000), which won the Latin American Studies Association's Bryce Wood Award; *Fordlandia: The Rise and Fall of Henry Ford's Forgotten Jungle City* (2009), which was a finalist for the Pulitzer Prize, the National Book Award, and the National Book Critics Circle Award. Most recently, he has been the Gilder Lehrman Fellow at the New York Public Library's Cullman Center for Scholars and Writers.

MARK ATWOOD LAWRENCE is an associate professor of history at the University of Texas at Austin. He is the author of *Assuming the Burden: The American Commitment to War in Vietnam* (2005) and *The Vietnam War: A Concise International History* (2008). He has also published numerous essays on the history of the Cold War and is now at work on a study of U.S. policymaking toward the Third World during the 1960s and early 1970s.

ROBERT J. MCMAHON is the Ralph Mershon Distinguished Professor in the History Department and the Mershon Center for International Security Studies at Ohio State University. He has also taught at the University of Florida and held visiting professorships at the University of Virginia, University College Dublin, and the Free University (Berlin). Among McMahon's books are *The Cold War on the Periphery: The United States, India, and Pakistan* (1994), *The Limits of Empire: The United States and Southeast Asia since World War II* (1999), and *Dean Acheson and the Creation of an American World Order* (2009).

JASON C. PARKER is an associate professor of history and the Rothrock Faculty Research Fellow at Texas A&M University. He is the author of *Brother's Keeper: The United States, Race, and Empire in the British Caribbean, 1937–1962* (2008), which was awarded the Bernath Book Prize by the Society for Historians of American Foreign Relations. He has also published articles in the *Journal of American History*, *Diplomatic History*, the *Journal of African American History*, and the *International History Review* and is currently writing a book that analyzes U.S. Cold War public diplomacy in the Third World.

ANDREW J. ROTTER is the Charles A. Dana Professor of History at Colgate University. He is the author, most recently, of *Hiroshima: The World's Bomb* (2008) and *Comrades at Odds: The United States and India, 1947–1964 (2000)*.

BRADLEY R. SIMPSON is an associate professor of history and Asian studies at the University of Connecticut. The author of *Economists with Guns: Authoritarian Development and U.S.-Indonesian Relations, 1960–1968* (2008), he is currently writing a global history of the idea of self-determination, and a history of U.S.-Indonesian relations during the reign of General Suharto (1966–1998).

ODD ARNE WESTAD is a professor of history at the London School of Economics and the author of numerous books on international history. His latest work, *Restless Empire: China and the World since 1750*, was published in 2012. An earlier book, *The Global Cold War: Third World Interventions and the Making of Our Times* (2005) won the Bancroft Prize.

SALIM YAQUB is an associate professor of history at the University of California, Santa Barbara. His first book, *Containing Arab Nationalism: The Eisenhower Doctrine and the Middle East* was published in 2004. He is now writing a book on U.S.-Arab relations in the 1970s.

ACKNOWLEDGMENTS

I am extremely grateful to Wm. Roger Louis for first suggesting this project to me, and for his steady support and wise counsel throughout. It has been a sheer delight to work with Susan Ferber at Oxford University Press. From the very inception of this project, she has been wonderfully supportive. I have benefited enormously from her experience, commitment, and advice.

Ohio State University's Mershon Center for International Security Studies made it possible for me to bring many of the contributors to Columbus for a stimulating and productive two-day mini-conference in February 2010. I am deeply appreciative of the Mershon Center's support. I thank, in particular, my colleague Richard Herrmann, the center's former director, not just for enthusiastically supporting this book project but for all that he has done to make the center an exciting venue for interdisciplinary research and interaction. I am grateful to Ann Powers for her characteristically excellent work with conference planning and logistics.

Several scholars from inside and outside Ohio State contributed significantly to this volume's development by participating actively in the conference and offering critical feedback and advice to the essayists. For their valuable assistance and constructive suggestions, I thank Peter Hahn, Ted Hopf, Mitch Lerner, Jonathan Winkler, Molly Wood, and Judy Wu.

Finally, I am indebted to Oxford's two anonymous reviewers, each of whom provided very helpful advice during this manuscript's final stage of development, and to Drew Herrick for expert computer assistance.

THE COLD WAR IN THE THIRD WORLD

INTRODUCTION

The second half of the twentieth century came to be dominated by two distinct, if overlapping and intertwined, historical phenomena: the Cold War and the emergence of the Third World. In the immediate aftermath of World War II, an epic struggle for power, influence, and ideological supremacy erupted between the United States, the Soviet Union, and their respective allies that would place an indelible shape on the international history of that era. The superpower competition dragged on for four-and-a-half decades, encompassing virtually every corner of the globe and blurring, in the process, traditional distinctions between core and peripheral areas. It left few states and societies unaffected, either in the industrialized world or in the developing world. Although we know now that the Cold War ended peacefully, with the retrenchment and eventual implosion of the Soviet Union, its dangers cannot be minimized. The Soviet-American contest edged the world, on several occasions, to the very brink of a nuclear exchange that would have brought death, destruction, and environmental degradation to the planet on an unimaginable scale.

The rise of a decolonized Third World—or what contemporary analysts often label the global South—constitutes a historical force of perhaps equal weight and consequence. In the two decades that followed the end of World War II, Western colonial empires were dismantled across Asia, Africa, the Middle East, and the Caribbean. Some forty new nation-states were born during those years alone, forever changing the scope of the global community and the nature of international diplomacy, norms, and discourse. The newly emerging areas threw off the shackles of colonialism and neocolonialism during the latter half of the twentieth century, boldly articulated their own national aspirations, strove to achieve economic as well as political independence, and became increasingly influential agents of their own destinies. The Third World's coalescence as a vibrant new force in international affairs posed the most fundamental challenge to Western global dominance of the modern era.

It posed a fundamental challenge as well to the aspirations and designs of the two superpowers. Washington and Moscow were competing ferociously with each other for the position of preeminent world power at the very moment that the international community itself was rapidly changing—not least in terms of its sheer number of active participants. Throughout the non-Western world, decolonization struggles and state-building efforts unfolded against the backdrop of a bipolar, geopolitical conflict, a conflict that in the broadest sense was also a contest "for the very soul of mankind."[1] The far-reaching political, economic, and social upheavals wracking the global South from the mid-1940s onward sent shock waves through the international system as a whole. Profound reconfigurations of power, especially on the Asian and African continents, opened enticing opportunities and also daunting problems for each of the superpowers.

The stakes at play in the Third World seemed unusually high to both. American and Soviet strategists alike identified vital interests there, appraising the developing areas as critical to the achievement of important strategic, economic, and political goals. The vast resources and mineral wealth located in the Southern Hemisphere made those regions potentially vital contributors to the economic and military strength of each of the rival Cold War camps. Policymakers in the Kremlin and the White House, moreover, saw the ultimate politico-economic orientation of those areas as a crucial marker in the ideological competition between capitalism and socialism.

Americans and Soviets each subscribed to a set of deeply held, if diametrically opposed, convictions about the proper path toward development and modernity—indeed, about the very direction of history. Third World states could help validate one or the other of those rival ideologies when they opted to embrace either democratic capitalism or Soviet-style socialism as the true path to modernist transformation. At various moments in the Cold War, leaders in each capital celebrated—or bemoaned—the direction in which the developing world seemed to be moving. The "revolutionary struggle of the working people has never before known such sweep," announced an ebullient Leonid Brezhnev in 1965. "Socialist ideas are conquering the minds of the liberated peoples more and more," the Soviet leader asserted. "Many states in Asia and Africa are entering on the path of socialist reforms....They see that communists are the vanguard of the revolutionary struggle."[2]

For a mélange of reasons, consequently, Soviets and Americans alike came to envisage vast stretches of the Third World as more than just instrumental in maintaining the overall balance of military, economic, and political power in the international arena. They also came to see in the dominant trends throughout the developing regions a litmus test of their core ideas about the nature and direction of historical change. "What was at stake," suggests political scientist Robert Jervis, "was nothing less than each side's view of the rightness of its cause, the universalism of its values, and the answer to the question of whose side history was on."[3]

It bears emphasizing that the very term "Third World" is a Cold War construction. In the early 1950s, French journalists began referring to the developing areas as "le tier monde." The term took hold following the landmark Bandung Conference of the Afro-Asian nations in April 1955. A convenient political catchphrase that rather loosely lumped together the predominantly poor, nonwhite, and uncommitted areas of the globe, "Third World" originally connoted an arena of contestation between West and East, the so-called First and Second worlds. Many Asian and African statesmen themselves embraced the concept; as historian Chen Jian makes clear, even so committed a Communist as Mao Zedong proclaimed with pride that revolutionary China belonged to the Third World and not with the "rich" countries of the Western and Eastern blocs.

This volume highlights the manifold interconnections between the Cold War and the Third World's rise. It explores two distinct but closely interrelated sets of questions. First, how did the Third World influence the course of the Cold War and the international behavior and priorities of the two superpowers? In other words, how did perceptions of, rivalry over, and events within the global South shape the overall Soviet-American contest for global dominance? And, second, what impact did the Cold War exert on the developing states and societies of Asia, Africa, the Middle East, and Latin America? What difference did it make, in sum, *within* the Third World?

The first generation of Cold War scholarship remained overwhelmingly Eurocentric, concentrating on the Soviet-American confrontation in the heart of Europe while paying but cursory attention to most Third World areas. From the 1970s onward, historians and political scientists began to devote much more sustained attention to the global dimensions of the Cold War. In so doing, they focused especially on many of the key flashpoints of superpower confrontation in the global South: the Suez, Taiwan Strait, Congo, and Cuban missile crises; the Korean and Vietnam wars; the U.S.-instigated coups in Guatemala and Iran; and the Soviet intervention in Afghanistan—each of these generated a substantial historical literature.

Yet much of that early work hewed to a narrow interpretive paradigm that privileged the actions and motivations of policymakers in Washington and Moscow, treating Third World actors—at least by implication—more as objects of manipulation than as active agents shaping their own fate.[4]

In recent years, international and imperial scholars have joined area-studies specialists to trumpet the importance of Third World areas *and* Third World actors. Their pioneering work, often rooted in careful investigations of non-Western sources and evidence, has helped forge a rare scholarly consensus on at least two crucial points: that the Cold War constituted a truly global contest, in which the Third World served as a critical theater, and that it was an event in which non-Western actors assumed a large and substantive role. Over the past two decades, there has been an explosion of new scholarship on the Cold War in the Third World. The upsurge of interest in such "hot" topics as decolonization, development, sovereignty, state-formation, and human rights has helped move the Third World from periphery to center stage in several disciplines and subfields, fueling a burgeoning scholarship on the global South during the postwar era. Similarly, the cultural turn in the humanities and social sciences, with its insistence on the critical importance of race, gender, identity, religion, emotion, and language has also proved to be a powerful spur for Third World–oriented scholarship, as historian Andrew Rotter demonstrates in much of his own pathbreaking work.[5]

Many of the authors featured in this volume, like Rotter, have contributed in significant ways to the new scholarship on the Third World's Cold War. Their chapters herein aim to synthesize, build on, critique, and extend the fruits of recent scholarly work while also pointing toward issues and themes that warrant further investigation.

Divided between six regionally focused and five thematically focused essays, with an epilogue by one of the world's foremost international historians, this book seeks to introduce scholars, students, and general readers to one of the most significant and challenging topics in twentieth-century history. Although the emphasis of most contributors lies with the international political dimensions of the Cold War in the Third World, many also explore the complex ways in which an all-encompassing East-West conflict affected social, political, and economic processes within Third World regions and societies. "U.S. and Soviet interventionisms to a very large extent shaped both the international and the domestic framework within which political, social, and cultural changes in Third World countries took place," notes Odd Arne Westad in his award-winning book, *The Global Cold War*. "Without the Cold War, Africa, Asia, and possibly also Latin

America would have been very different regions today."[6] One of the aims of this volume is to examine the implications of Westad's provocative assertion while paying careful attention to important disparities across different regions, states, and populations.

The sudden appearance on the world stage of a vibrant group of newly independent states marked, on one level, a triumph of hope and idealism. It served to validate the principle of self-determination enshrined in the Atlantic Charter and UN Charter as a basic norm of the new postwar order. The transition from empire to indigenous rule helped rejuvenate and give hope to a world community traumatized by the ever-present prospects of nuclear war. The dizzying pace of decolonization not only gave birth to dozens of new countries, but also brought forth a number of stirring and charismatic nonwhite statesmen. Their very emergence served as a stern rebuke to long-held notions of Western racial superiority.

Transnational racial solidarities bound populations in the Third World with those in the West, as Carol Anderson's chapter emphasizes; those bonds both influenced and were influenced by the proliferating number of nonwhite states. The rising tide of color, she reminds us, inspired great idealism and a palpable sense of world-historical transformation among Third World actors and their supporters and admirers in the United States, Europe, and elsewhere. The African-American struggle against segregation and oppression in the United States fed this powerful stream, as Jason Parker's contribution stresses, turning such signal local battles as the Montgomery Bus Boycott and the Little Rock school desegregation showdown into portentous events of international scope and import. American civil rights activists and colonial nationalists followed each other's struggles closely. They took inspiration from and found connections between national movements for racial equality and freedom and their global counterparts, creating a genuinely transnational assault on embedded structures of white supremacy.

The Bandung Conference of 1955, which echoed with calls for racial solidarity, social justice, and an end to all forms of imperial control, showcased those interconnections. "This is the first intercontinental conference of coloured peoples in the history of mankind!" exclaimed Indonesian president Sukarno. In his eloquent opening address to the assembled delegates, Sukarno declared that "we, the peoples of Asia and Africa, 1,400,000,000 strong," represent "half the human population of the world.... We can demonstrate to the minority of the world which lives on the other continents that we, the majority, are for peace, not war, and that whatever strength we have will always be thrown on to the side of peace."[7] The celebrated African-American writer and activist Richard Wright, who reported brilliantly on the Bandung sessions for a mostly Western readership, heartily concurred. Following that gathering, Sukarno joined with Indian prime minister Jawaharlal Nehru, Egyptian president Gamal Abdel Nasser, and like-minded leaders (including Yugoslavia's Josef Broz Tito) to create the Non-Aligned Movement. It aimed to preserve the neutrality and freedom of maneuver of those states disinclined, for practical or moral reasons, to choose sides in the East-West struggle. Nonalignment, as Mark Lawrence elucidates, proved a powerful force that altered the dynamics of the Cold War in profound ways.

The superpower conflict infiltrated the regions of the global South at different times and with varying degrees of intensity. Asia became the first non-Western area fully entangled in the Cold War. That stemmed from the convergence of several galvanizing factors: the region's lead role in the decolonizing process, the early emergence of indigenous, Communist-led insurgencies in Southeast Asia and China, the triumph of Mao Zedong's Communists in China's Civil War, and the Sino-Soviet alliance forged shortly thereafter by Mao and Stalin. The outbreak of open hostilities between Soviet- and Chinese-supported North Korea and U.S.-supported South Korea, in June 1950, led to a superpower proxy war that raged for close to three years and that wound up enveloping much of the Asian continent in a Cold War now turned dangerously hot.

The Middle East also became an early site of Cold War competition, its unmatched oil riches, coveted military bases, and prime geostrategic location ensuring the region's inevitable if unenviable role as a cockpit of great-power competition—from the Iranian Crisis of 1946 onward. Latin America and sub-Saharan Africa became embroiled in the Cold War later, though the impact exerted by the superpower struggle on the states and peoples of those areas may have been just as profound as in the Middle East. Indeed, the newly independent—and exceptionally brittle—nations of Africa may have been the ones who suffered the deeper and more long-lasting societal disruptions from their collisions with the East-West struggle.

In the most basic—and tragic—sense, of course, the Cold War brought violent human conflict to multiple parts of the Third World. Tellingly, every one of the wars of the Cold War era was fought in the Third World. Most of the East-West crises of the era, further, occurred in the developing regions, including nearly all of those that threatened to escalate into direct U.S.-Soviet confrontations. The only clashes of arms involving U.S., Soviet, or Chinese military forces during this period, moreover, took place there as well. Indeed, one of the paradoxes of the Cold War is that it ushered in the longest sustained period of peace in modern European history at the very time that Asia, Africa, the Middle East, and parts of Latin

America were convulsed by unprecedented violence and conflict. All but 200,000 of the estimated twenty million people who died in wars fought between 1945 and 1990 lost their lives in the conflicts that raged across various parts of the Third World. In other words, only about 1 percent of the total war-induced casualties of the Cold War era occurred in the Northern Hemisphere, 99 percent in the Southern Hemisphere.[8]

If Europe's "Long Peace" can be directly attributable to the structure of stability imposed by the East-West standoff, then we must ask to what extent the logic and structure of the Cold War encouraged, ignited, or exacerbated the Third World conflicts of the Cold War epoch. Several of the chapters in this volume directly tackle that important question, exploring the links connecting the Cold War to the Third World's hot wars—whether interstate or civil in character. Few, if any, of the conflicts waged throughout the global South during the 1945–1990 period can be directly attributable to the Cold War, to be sure, at least not in causative terms. Decolonization and its contentious aftermath, local and regional rivalries, simmering border disputes, ethnic and religious tensions, internal contests for power, struggles over resources, conflicts stemming from the role of foreign-owned corporations—all exerted a more significant impact on the genesis of hostilities than did the Cold War per se. In nearly every important case, however, the Cold War played a galvanizing role, either by offering opportunities to, or setting limits on, local actors; by intensifying, prolonging, internationalizing, or foreshortening conflicts after they commenced; or by facilitating diplomatic settlements. Those connections are ubiquitous: from the early anticolonial insurrections in French Indochina, the Dutch East Indies, and British Malaya, to the later independence struggles in Algeria, the Congo, and Angola; and from the superpower interventions in the Korean and Vietnamese civil wars, far and away the bloodiest of the era, to the Suez Crisis of 1956, the Soviet-Afghan War of the 1980s, and the covert interventions by the United States in Iran, Guatemala, Indonesia, Cuba, El Salvador, Nicaragua, and elsewhere.[9]

The formation of new, postcolonial states throughout much of Asia, Africa, the Middle East, and parts of the Caribbean also played out against the backdrop of the Cold War. The complex and multifaceted interconnections between those two historical processes constitute core concerns of this volume. The shape, cohesion, and vitality of those new states as well as the internal configurations of power within them were affected significantly by the Cold War. So, too, was their ability to command international attention and prestige and their leaders' prospects for securing external resources, capital, and technical assistance to meet economic development priorities or for garnering military assistance to bolster defense needs. Consequently, the story of post–World War II state formation in the Third World—like the history of decolonization and of Third World conflicts—simply cannot be written without careful, systematic attention to that key variable.

In the essentially bipolar world that all Third World independence movements from the mid-1940s through to the mid-1970s faced, the pressure to line up with one or the other ideological camp-cum-military alliance system was hard to deflect—especially since concrete benefits could flow, or be blocked, as a result of the choice made. The more contested the bid for independence, the greater the need of the independence-seekers to gain support from one or the other of the two blocs. When anticolonial coalitions fractured, moreover, such as in the Congo in 1960 and Angola in 1974–1975, the temptation for competing factions to attract different superpower patrons proved irresistible. The particular visions that nationalist leaders had for the future, which often encompassed far-reaching socioeconomic transformations within their native lands, further complicated the choices forced on them by the pressures of the East-West conflict. Joining the Western power bloc, with its deep-seated suspicions of those inclined to march to a socialist drumbeat, could constrict certain domestic political and development paths, compromising the freedom of choice that founding national elites invariably crave. Committing to the socialist bloc, on the other hand, would almost surely minimize, if not preclude entirely, the option of coaxing dollars and support from the world's richest and most powerful nation.

With independence, newly established Third World states faced an equally acute set of dilemmas. Some actively sought alignment with the United States because a formal commitment to the West seemed to comport best with key domestic needs. Others sought alignment with the Sino-Soviet bloc to serve different domestic needs. The strategy of studied nonalignment appealed to another group of Third World leaders, those who believed that important national goals could be more effectively advanced by eschewing a formal commitment to either West or East.

Indonesia's Sukarno, Egypt's Gamal Abdel Nasser, India's Jawaharlal Nehru, and Ghana's Kwame Nkrumah, among others, consciously strove for a position of independence for their nations from both of the Cold War blocs. "It is not indifference that leads to a policy of non-alignment," explained Nkrumah in a 1958 speech in New York, one year after Ghana had become the first of Britain's African colonies to gain independence. "It is our belief that international blocs and rivalries exacerbate and do not solve disputes and that we must be free to judge issues on their merits and to look for solutions that are just and peaceful, irrespective of the powers involved. We do not wish to be in the position of condoning imperialism or aggression from any quarter."[10] Much to the consternation of American and Soviet Cold Warriors, who frequently exhibited a you-are-with-us-or-you-are-against-us mentality, Washington and Moscow were each compelled to compete for— all the while seeking to convert—the neutral nations of the Third World.

Recognizing the agency of Third World actors, the chapters in this volume highlight the ways in which many of those actors labored quite consciously to harness the dominant international reality of their age, the Cold War, to maximize potential benefits, or at least to minimize potential damages. The collection also emphasizes, however, that many of the Cold War's consequences for Third World peoples and societies proved as profoundly disruptive—even, in some cases, catastrophic—as they were beyond the control of *any* local actors. In that regard, it is worth recalling that the Third World emerged as early as 1950 as the Cold War's principal battlefield. Conflicts with local roots—from Korea, the Congo, and Vietnam to Angola, Afghanistan, and Nicaragua—became exponentially more costly because the superpower conflict became superimposed upon them. From the Korean Peninsula to Cuba, moreover, some of those Cold War–fueled conflicts linger well into the twenty-first century. Long after the Cold War's demise and the collapse of the Soviet Union, the aftershocks of the superpower conflict still reverberate across the global South.

NOTES

1. The phrase is from former president George H. W. Bush. See George H. W. Bush, "Introduction," in Thomas C. Reed, *At the Abyss: An Insider's History of the Cold War* (New York: Ballantine Books, 2004), 1.

2. Quoted in Melvyn P. Leffler, *For the Soul of Mankind: The United States, the Soviet Union, and the Cold War* (New York: Hill and Wang, 2007), 233.

3. Robert Jervis, "Identity and the Cold War," in *The Cambridge History of the Cold War, II, Crises and Détente*, ed. Melvyn P. Leffler and Odd Arne Westad (Cambridge: Cambridge University Press, 2010), 33.

4. There are numerous, excellent surveys of the evolving literature on various Third World areas and the Cold War. Particularly useful are the following chapters in *America in the World: The Historiography of American Foreign Relations since 1941*, ed. Michael J. Hogan (New York: Cambridge University Press, 1995): Gary R. Hess, "The Unending Debate: Historians and the Vietnam War," 358–394; Mark T. Gilderhus, "An Emerging Synthesis? U.S.-Latin American Relations since the Second World War," 424–462; Douglas Little, "Gideon's Band: America and the

Middle East since 1945," 462–500; and Robert J. McMahon, "The Cold War in Asia: The Elusive Synthesis," 501–535. See also Mark Philip Bradley and Marilyn Young, *Making Sense of the Vietnam Wars: Local, National, and Transnational Perspectives* (New York: Oxford University Press, 2008); David C. Engerman, "The Second World's 'Third World,'" *Kritika* 12 (Spring 2011), 183–211; and Prasenjit Duara, "The Cold War as a Historical Period: An Interpretive Essay," *Journal of Global History* 6 (November 2011), 475–80.

5. See especially Andrew J. Rotter, *Comrades at Odds: The United States and India, 1947–1964* (Ithaca, NY: Cornell University Press, 2000), as well as his essay in this volume.

6. Odd Arne Westad, *The Global Cold War: Third World Interventions and the Making of Our Times* (New York: Cambridge University Press, 2005), 3.

7. Quoted in George McTurnan Kahin, *The Asian-African Conference: Bandung, Indonesia, April 1955* (Ithaca, NY: Cornell University Press, 1956).

8. David S. Painter, "Explaining U.S. Relations with the Third World," *Diplomatic History* 19 (Summer 1995), 525.

9. For an extended discussion of the relationship between the Cold War and the Third World's hot wars, see Robert J. McMahon, "Heiße Kriege im Kalten Krieg" (Hot wars in the Cold War), in *Heiße Kriege im Kalten Krieg*, ed. Bernd Greiner, Christian Th. Muller, and Dierk Walter (Hamburg: Hamburger Edition, 2006), 16–34.

10. Quoted in *The Cold War: A History in Documents and Eyewitness Accounts*, ed. Jussi M. Hanhimäki and Odd Arne Westad (New York: Oxford University Press, 2003), 355.

1

THE COLD WAR AND THE MIDDLE EAST

SALIM YAQUB

For four-and-a-half decades after the end of World War II, the great powers of the world struggled to shape the geopolitical destiny of the Middle East. They did so mainly because of the region's vast mineral resources and vital strategic location. The Middle East held 60 percent of the world's known oil reserves, access to which was essential to global industrial development in the postwar era. The region was situated at the crossroads of Europe, Africa, and Asia and was adjacent to the Soviet Union. In 1945 Britain still dominated the Middle East, but over the following decade it was largely supplanted by the United States, while the Soviet Union gained consider-able influence as well. For the remainder of the Cold War era, the two super-powers were the main outside parties to the struggle for the Middle East.

All three powers—along with lesser players like France, Communist China, and some Eastern European countries—had to contend with indige-nous nationalist movements, which were primarily secular in the early post-war decades and increasingly religious (mostly Islamist) thereafter. Middle Eastern nationalists were generally indifferent to the merits of the Cold War struggle. They instead sought to achieve or maintain national independence, to attract support from outside powers while avoiding domination by them, to develop their own resources, and to gain advantage in local conflicts. In many of these conflicts, the superpowers lined up behind the opposing parties. Thus, in disputes pitting Israel against the Arab states, Iran against Iraq, and conservative versus radical Arab regimes, the Americans generally supported the first set of antagonists and the Soviets the second.

To some extent, then, the Cold War further polarized the region. In the 1950s, U.S. support for conservative states like Saudi Arabia, Jordan, and Iraq combined with Soviet support for Egypt and Syria to exacerbate an existing inter-Arab split. From the late 1960s on, Cold War rivalries were increasingly mapped onto the Arab-Israeli and Iranian-Iraqi disputes, intensifying each. In all of these situations, however, the antagonists needed little encouragement and, in the case of the Arab-Israeli conflict, often resisted their patrons' efforts to restrain them. It is possible, too, that the Cold War impeded democracy in the Middle East, as the historian Rashid Khalidi argues.[1] Both superpowers helped authoritarian regimes gain or keep power with little evident popular support. But except in a very small number of cases, most prominently that of Iran in 1953, it is not clear that Middle Eastern societies were heading toward democracy or constitutionalism on their own, only to be stymied by outside intervention.

The Cold War in the Middle East was never a contest between equals. The Western powers always enjoyed a decisive advantage. Although they could not, over the long term, retain outright control over the region's oil reserves and strategic positions, they succeeded in preserving access to them, mainly by cultivating cooperative local regimes. The general unpopularity of these regimes, combined with Arab bitterness over Western support for Israel, gave the Soviet Union numerous opportunities to enhance its own position in the region. But Moscow had limited ability to exploit these openings, on account of its relative weakness, its outsider position, and its lack of appeal to ordinary Middle Easterners, especially devout Muslims who disdained the atheism of Communist doctrine. The Soviets never came close to dislodging the Western powers and exhausted themselves in the effort. Indeed, it can be said that the Cold War ended a decade early in the Middle East. As the 1980s began, the Soviet Union presented hardly any impediments to the extension of U.S. power in the region. The main resistance came from local actors, especially Islamists, as it would continue to do in the post–Cold War era.

In the interwar period, much of the Middle East was under Western European domination. Following its defeat in World War I, the Ottoman Empire lost its non-Turkish holdings and reemerged as the modern republic of Turkey, mostly confined to Anatolia. The League of Nations awarded France a single mandate over Syria and Lebanon and gave Britain separate mandates over Iraq, Transjordan, and Palestine. Egypt, though not part of the Mandate system, remained subject to British military occupation, as it had been since 1882. Much of North Africa was under French colonial rule, and Britain had protectorates on the Arabian Peninsula. Saudi Arabia and Iran were formally independent, though the former was subject to heavy-handed British guidance and the latter to economic, military, and diplomatic pressure from both Britain and the Soviet Union. Throughout the interwar Middle East, the experience of European domination aroused powerful nationalist sentiments, which grew even stronger during and after World War II.[2]

From late 1941 to mid-1945, when they were allied against the common Nazi foe, Britain, the United States, and the Soviet Union cooperated in the Middle East in ways that prefigured their postwar rivalry. The Allies agreed on the vital strategic importance of the region for two main reasons: it contained enormous oil reserves, and it abutted the Soviet Union. The Middle East's oil had to be kept accessible to the Allies and denied to the Axis powers. Its territory was prized as a transit route for the shipment of U.S.-supplied war materiel from the Persian Gulf to the Soviet Union. Together and individually, London, Washington, and Moscow labored to ensure that Middle Eastern governments supported or acquiesced in the Allied war effort. Britain forcibly removed pro-Axis cabinets in Egypt and Iraq. The United States extended Lend-Lease aid to Iran and Saudi Arabia. British, U.S., and Soviet troops jointly occupied Iran so that Russia could be supplied via the "Persian Corridor."[3]

After 1945 the three powers continued to value the Middle East's crucial importance, again because of its massive oil wealth and its proximity to Soviet territory. Yet now these features were points of conflict, rather than cooperation, between the Soviets on the one hand and the Anglo-Americans on the other. At war's end, most of the oil Americans consumed came from the Western Hemisphere. But the economic recovery of Britain and the rest of Western Europe, in which the United States had a vital stake, overwhelmingly depended on continued access to Middle Eastern oil. European recovery also entailed the revival of Germany's industrial zone, a project anathema to the Soviet Union. Geographically, whereas during the war the Middle East had been an avenue of sustenance for the Soviet Union, it now became a staging area for potential attack. As intercontinental ballistic missiles had not yet been developed, Anglo-U.S. war plans relied on the ability to conduct short- and medium-range bombing raids against enemy targets. Britain's numerous airbases in the Middle East, along with some American ones, gave both countries the capability to strike Soviet territory.[4] In short, Britain and the United States wanted to tap Middle Eastern oil for postwar recovery and to use the region's territory to threaten the Soviet Union. The Soviets sought to disrupt these plans.

Although the main zone of Cold War contention lay in Europe, some of the earliest Cold War crises occurred in the Middle East. These erupted when Joseph Stalin, the Soviet leader, attempted to create buffer zones between Soviet territory and areas controlled by hostile adversaries, much as he was already doing in Eastern Europe. At the end of World War II, the Soviet Union refused to withdraw its troops from northern Iran, demanded disputed territories on the Soviet-Turkish border, and pressed for partial Soviet control over the Turkish Straits. With U.S. and British diplomatic backing, Iran and Turkey resisted the Soviet demands. In early 1947 the United States assumed financial responsibility for the Turkish and Greek governments (the latter was battling a leftist insurgency), after Britain gave notice that it could no longer bear this burden. In a statement that became known as the Truman Doctrine, President Harry S. Truman declared, "[I]t must be the policy of the United States to support free peoples who are resisting attempted subjugation by armed minorities or by outside pressures." Moscow, which had already withdrawn its troops from Iran, subsequently eased its pressure on Turkey, which in 1951 joined the newly formed North Atlantic Treaty Organization.[5]

Having failed to secure a Middle Eastern periphery, Stalin resigned himself to the presence of hostile forces on his southwestern borders. But fears of a resumption of Soviet adventurism, combined with suspicion of local nationalism, kept Anglo-U.S. officials in a state of exaggerated vigilance, as a second Iranian crisis made clear. In 1951 the Iranian parliament nationalized the Anglo-Iranian Oil Company (AIOC) and awarded the premiership to Mohammed Mossadeq, who began a power struggle with the country's pro-Western monarch, Mohammed Reza Shah Pahlavi. In 1953, fearing that Mossadeq was paving the way for a Soviet takeover, U.S. and British intelligence agencies orchestrated an Iranian military coup that unseated Mossadeq and granted the shah unquestioned authority.[6]

Confirmed in power, the shah visited a corrupt and repressive reign on his country, supported by a succession of U.S. administrations preoccupied with oil and geopolitics. "American policy between 1953 and 1978," writes the Iran scholar James A. Bill, "emphasized a special relationship with the shah and his political elite while largely ignoring the needs and demands of the Iranian masses."[7] On both the secular Left and the religious Right, these circumstances created a mood of simmering resentment toward the shah and his American patrons that would erupt in revolution in the late 1970s.

If the full potential of Iranian nationalism took a quarter-century to reveal itself, the power of Arab nationalism was already evident in the 1950s. Much of that power grew out of the Arab world's experience with Western domination, which had been more direct and heavy-handed than that endured by non-Arab countries like Turkey and Iran. Arabs were also traumatized by the establishment of the state of Israel in 1948, at the expense of a settled Palestinian Arab society. Although Moscow had joined Washington in supporting Israel's creation, in the early 1950s the Soviets began endorsing Arab positions in the Arab-Israeli dispute (while still supporting Israel's existence), and Israel gravitated toward the Western camp.[8] These facts, combined with the memory of Britain's support for Zionism during and shortly after World War I, reinforced the Arab tendency to see Zionism as another form of Western imperialism.

Such sentiments posed a formidable challenge to Anglo-U.S. attempts to enlist the Middle East in the Cold War, while offering the Soviets a golden opportunity to expand their influence in the region. In the early to mid-1950s, Britain and the United States tried to organize an anti-Soviet Middle East defense pact to complement similar initiatives in Western Europe and East Asia. The effort ran afoul of Egypt's charismatic leader, Gamal Abdel Nasser. Though strongly opposed to local Communism, Nasser insisted that the Arab states refrain from aligning with either of the two Cold War blocs and instead pursue productive relations with both. In 1955 Egypt concluded a barter agreement with the Soviet Union (via Czechoslovakia), acquiring over $200 million worth of sophisticated weapons in exchange for surplus cotton.[9] Over the next three-and-a-half decades, Moscow would conclude numerous other arms and aid agreements with left-leaning (but almost always non-Communist) Arab regimes.

The Nasserist challenge opened a rift between Britain and the United States and helped draw the two superpowers more deeply into Middle Eastern affairs. In 1956, after Nasser nationalized the largely British-owned Suez Canal Company, Britain joined France and Israel in a military assault on Egypt.[10] Though hostile to Nasser, President Dwight D. Eisenhower saw the attack as a politically disastrous throwback to the age of European imperialism. In a remarkable spectacle, the United States and the Soviet Union simultaneously condemned the intervention. Eisenhower then placed intense diplomatic and economic pressure on Britain, France, and Israel, forcing them to halt their attack on Egypt.

The Suez Crisis showed that Britain could no longer be considered the primary Western power in the Middle East. Britain would continue for some years to dominate Iraq and portions of the Arabian Peninsula, but its ability to call the shots in a more general sense was severely diminished. The United States and the Soviet Union, by contrast, gained considerable regional prestige for opposing the attack on Egypt. Over the next quarter-century, the two superpowers would be the primary outside actors in Middle Eastern affairs. Nasser was an even greater beneficiary of the crisis. Having defiantly withstood an attack by great powers, he now emerged as the standard-bearer of pan-Arab nationalism.[11]

Seizing the mantle of Western leadership in the Middle East, in 1957 and 1958 Eisenhower pursued a policy, known as the Eisenhower Doctrine, aimed at discrediting Nasser's neutralist program by forging a coalition of conservative Arab regimes willing to side openly with the United States in the Cold War. Although such a coalition did briefly emerge, it soon collapsed under the weight of Nasserist sentiment in the region. In July 1958 Iraq's pro-Western monarchy was overthrown by nationalist army officers. Eisenhower sent 14,000 U.S. marines to occupy Lebanon, which seemed in danger of succumbing to a Nasserist rebellion. No sooner had the marines waded ashore, however, than Eisenhower quietly abandoned his doctrine in favor of a less confrontational approach. "The people are on Nasser's side," he privately confessed. Unexpectedly, Nasser soon began feuding with the Soviets, whom he accused of meddling in internal Arab affairs. Seeing that Nasserism could function as a barrier to, rather than merely an avenue of, Soviet encroachment on the region, Washington enjoyed a modest rapprochement with Cairo.[12]

In the early 1960s, Cold War tensions in the Middle East were relatively muted. Preoccupied with crises elsewhere, especially the standoffs over Berlin and Cuba, the superpowers showed little interest in confronting each other in the Middle East. They also worked to improve relations with regional powers they had previously shunned. Thus President John F. Kennedy sought closer ties to Egypt and like-minded Arab states, while the Soviets mended fences with Turkey and Iran. By decade's end, however, the pattern had been inverted. Even as the superpowers pursued global détente, their rivalry intensified in the Middle East. Washington and Moscow were enmeshed in the region's politics to an unprecedented degree, and their involvement seemed certain to grow in the future.

To some extent, this rising activism resulted from decisions made outside the region. In 1962, after a bloody eight-year war, France abandoned its colony in Algeria, and in 1967 it stopped serving as Israel's primary arms supplier. That same year Britain pulled out of the Aden protectorate in southern Yemen, and in 1968 London announced it would complete its withdrawal from the Persian Gulf region in 1971. These retractions of European power presented Washington and Moscow with opportunities—obligations, they would say—to expand their own involvement in the Middle East, at a time of escalating global demand for the region's oil.

A greater catalyst for superpower involvement was the persistence of local disputes that followed a logic of their own but destabilized the region in ways that invited outside intervention. A case in point was what the political scientist Malcolm Kerr calls the "Arab Cold War," which pitted

U.S.-allied conservative regimes (like Saudi Arabia and Jordan) against self-proclaimed "radical" regimes (like Egypt, Syria, and Iraq) that were formally nonaligned but increasingly dependent on Soviet support.[13] One effect of the Arab Cold War was to push each camp closer to its superpower patron, especially in arms purchases. Another was to make the Arab states as a whole increasingly reckless in their dealings with Israel. The result was a brief but cataclysmic war in 1967 that transformed the geopolitical landscape of the Middle East and drew the superpowers more deeply into the region.

By the mid-1960s the Arab Cold War largely amounted to an anti-Zionist bidding war, with each camp seeking to outdo the other in its menacing gestures toward Israel. In 1966 a new, more radical Syrian regime raised the stakes, encouraging Palestinian guerrillas to launch raids into Israel from Syrian territory. The Israelis furthered the escalation by conducting disproportionate reprisals against Syria and Jordan (from which Palestinians were also staging attacks, against the wishes of the Jordanian government) and by seeking to gain possession of three demilitarized zones along the Israeli-Syrian armistice line. Under growing pan-Arab pressure to enter the fray, and presented with (faulty) intelligence that Israel was preparing to invade Syria, in May 1967 Nasser requested the withdrawal of United Nations' peacekeeping forces stationed in the Sinai Peninsula and announced the closure of the Strait of Tiran to Israeli shipping. In early June Israel launched a devastating strike against Egypt, moving next against Jordan and Syria when they entered the war on Egypt's side. In six days, Israel seized the Sinai Peninsula and Gaza Strip from Egypt, the West Bank from Jordan, and the Golan Heights from Syria. The Arabs, Kerr notes, had used Israel as a political football only to discover that the football could kick back.[14]

The 1967 war was a crushing defeat for Nasserist pan-Arabism. Previous Arab setbacks could be blamed on effete politicians who had allegedly betrayed the Arab cause on behalf of Western patrons. This war had been lost by fiery Arab nationalists. It was a blow from which Nasserism never fully recovered, and the movement was further diminished by Nasser's death in 1970. Nasserism's decline left a vacuum in Arab politics that would be filled by two previously marginalized tendencies: Palestinian nationalism, which sprang up almost immediately after the 1967 war, and political Islam, which gathered force more gradually, not emerging into full view until the 1980s.[15]

After 1967, the superpowers became much more closely identified with the contending parties in the Arab-Israeli conflict. The Soviet Union rebuilt Egypt's and Syria's shattered militaries, an enormous undertaking involving the dispatching of thousands of military advisers and technicians. The United States replaced France as Israel's primary arms supplier, providing Israel with state-of-the-art aircraft. Both superpowers justified arms transfers as confidence-building measures that would induce greater diplomatic flexibility. All too often, however, the availability of arms encouraged the parties to shun compromise and pursue their objectives through force.[16]

Another new element was the rise of Palestinian nationalism. In 1969 the Palestine Liberation Organization (PLO), which the Arab League had created in 1964 to provide a harmless outlet for mounting Palestinian frustration, emerged as an independent force. From bases in Jordan, Syria, and Lebanon, PLO groups launched guerrilla raids into Israel and staged spectacular terrorist attacks worldwide to draw attention to the Palestinian cause. Even as some Arab states grew increasingly willing to recognize Israel within its pre–June 1967 borders, the PLO called for the dismantling of Israel in favor of a "secular democratic state" in which Muslims, Christians, and Jews enjoyed equal political rights.[17]

By the early 1970s, Moscow was furnishing the PLO modest military aid. Still committed to Israel's existence, the Soviets had little use for the PLO's political program, but they were determined to expand their ties in the Arab world and to prevent their Communist Chinese rivals, who were aggressively courting Palestinian groups, from making further inroads into the region. The United States, by contrast, shunned the PLO as a lawless organization with unrealizable aspirations.[18] This was another way in which Cold War rivalries were mapped onto the Arab-Israeli dispute.

The Persian Gulf, too, was becoming an arena of greater superpower involvement. By the late 1960s the Soviets were concerned about their ability to produce enough oil. Most of the country's untapped reserves lay in frozen Siberia, accessible only at great trouble and expense. So Moscow moved closer to Baghdad, offering increased military and economic assistance in exchange for access to Iraqi crude. In January 1968 Britain announced that it would complete the withdrawal of its forces from the Persian Gulf region by December 1971, prompting speculation over who would fill the resulting vacuum. The shah of Iran was eager to step into the breach. Shrewdly highlighting Soviet support for his Iraqi rivals and for radical insurgencies operating in the area, he appealed to the United States for increased military assistance.[19]

The shah's regional ambitions dovetailed with emerging U.S. policy. By the late 1960s a relative decline in U.S. global power, combined with the debacle of Vietnam, pushed U.S. policymakers to place stricter limits on America's overseas commitments. In a July 1969 speech, President Richard

M. Nixon declared that, while the United States remained committed to its allies, the latter must play a larger role in their own defense.[20] The Nixon Doctrine, as this statement came to be called, provided the strategic justification for a reduction of U.S. forces overseas and for a greater reliance on client states in trouble spots around the globe. Accordingly, Nixon enthusiastically endorsed the shah's bid for regional hegemony, agreeing to sell him any conventional weapons he desired. U.S. officials paid little attention to the shah's dismal human-rights record and growing unpopularity at home.[21]

Another beneficiary of the Nixon Doctrine was Saudi Arabia. The late 1960s brought an end to the postwar oil glut, as global demand began to outstrip available supply, boosting the price of oil and the strategic leverage of oil-producing states. Holding one-fifth of the world's proven reserves, Saudi Arabia benefited hugely from this shift. In the early 1970s it spent tens of millions of dollars of its expanding oil revenues on U.S.-made weapons, especially in air defense. The Nixon administration warmly encouraged the sales, partly to promote the American defense industry, partly to retain Saudi friendship, and partly to empower Saudi Arabia to help Iran combat Soviet and radical influences in the Gulf region.[22]

By the early 1970s, then, both the United States and the Soviet Union were deeply entrenched in Middle Eastern geopolitics, lining up behind their respective proxies in Arab-Israeli, inter-Arab, and Iranian-Iraqi disputes. In all of these arenas, each superpower had to pursue two separate and often competing goals: retaining influence with its clients and preventing regional disputes from escalating in ways that damaged its own interests. In retrospect, it is clear that the United States played this game far more successfully than the Soviet Union did. Indeed, the events of the 1970s broke the back of Soviet influence in the Middle East. Although daunting obstacles remained in the path of U.S. hegemony into the 1980s, by then they were almost entirely indigenous.

The main driver of Moscow's undoing was the highly asymmetrical manner in which the Arab-Israeli conflict unfolded, both on the battlefield and at the negotiating table. As the 1970s began, Israel and its Arab neighbors remained deadlocked over the consequences of the 1967 war. Officially, both superpowers favored a settlement involving Israel's withdrawal from occupied land in exchange for Arab recognition of Israel. In practice, both abetted a drift toward renewed hostilities. After 1971 Nixon's national security adviser, Henry Kissinger, stymied the U.S. State Department's diplomatic initiatives, seeking to delay any settlement until key Arab countries reduced their ties to the Soviet Union. U.S. military aid to Israel dramatically increased, reinforcing Israel's inclination to sit on its gains. The Soviets continued to build up the arsenals of Egypt and Syria. Although Moscow worried that its clients might rush into another disastrous war, it seemed even more fearful of losing influence with them. This dilemma was evident in July 1972, when Nasser's successor, Anwar Sadat, expelled thousands of Soviet military personnel from Egypt, to protest Moscow's reluctance to furnish the best weapons in its arsenal. The Soviets hastened to conclude a more generous arms agreement.[23]

In October 1973 Egypt and Syria launched major offensives against Israeli positions in the Sinai Peninsula and Golan Heights. Although the Arabs did surprisingly well at first, Israel quickly gained the initiative and pushed the attackers back to the 1967 cease-fire lines, and even behind them in places. The three-week war was deeply unsettling to the international community. In retaliation for U.S. support for Israel, several oil-producing Arab states embargoed oil shipments to the West, damaging the global economy. The conflict also briefly exacerbated superpower tensions, prompting the United States to place its forces, including nuclear ones, on worldwide alert. As the cease-fire took hold, then, both Washington and Moscow seemed to agree that the Arab-Israeli status quo was untenable.[24]

And so Henry Kissinger, now secretary of state, launched his famous "shuttle diplomacy." Although international opinion favored a comprehensive settlement of the Arab-Israeli dispute, Kissinger believed a bilateral Egyptian-Israeli peace process would be more manageable. For this, he had an ally in Sadat, who was desperate to end Egypt's conflict with Israel and focus instead on pressing economic needs. Deftly sidelining the Soviets, Kissinger encouraged Israel to vacate portions of the Sinai as Egypt eased its belligerency against Israel. Kissinger left office in early 1977, but his diplomacy came to fruition with the Camp David process of 1978–1979, whereby Egypt, in exchange for Israel's withdrawal from the rest of the Sinai, recognized and made peace with the Jewish state. Israel continued to occupy the Golan Heights, the West Bank, and the Gaza Strip, but Egypt's removal from the conflict left the remaining Arab actors with few means to recover their lost territories. Egypt also ended its quasi-alliance with the Soviet Union and became a client of the United States, receiving nearly as much military and economic aid as Israel.[25]

Sadat's defection was a crippling blow to the Soviets. This fact was not immediately apparent, however, for in 1978–1979 Washington suffered two major reverses in the Middle East that gave Moscow hope of improving its regional position. One setback was the Arab world's angry rejection of the

Camp David peace process, which restored Egyptian territory while leaving other Arab lands under occupation. The Arab League moved its headquarters from Cairo to Tunis and imposed economic sanctions against Egypt. The anti-Egyptian campaign temporarily united Syria and Iraq, whose mutual enmity had frequently exasperated Soviet officials. Perhaps, these officials now hoped, the Damascus/Baghdad rapprochement could form the nucleus of a revived "anti-imperialist" Arab bloc. The other U.S. setback was the Iranian Revolution of 1978–1979. The collapse of the shah's regime weakened America's position in the Persian Gulf, and the subsequent hostage crisis damaged U.S. prestige.[26]

Still, Washington's travails afforded Moscow only limited advantage. Syria and Iraq soon resumed their feuding, frustrating Soviet hopes for a united anti-Western coalition. Iraq further irritated the Soviet Union by cracking down on the Iraqi Communist Party and skirmishing with the People's Democratic Republic of Yemen (also known as South Yemen), the only avowedly Marxist Arab regime. Despite the Arab world's nearly universal rejection of Camp David, the Soviets were incapable of launching a peace process of their own, largely because they had almost no leverage over Israel, having severed diplomatic relations with that country in 1967. The Iranian Revolution, meanwhile, proved as damaging to Soviet interests as it was to American ones. Iranian Communists did wield some influence in the early stages of the revolution, but soon Shia conservatives gained control of the new government, purged it of secular and leftist figures, and announced a policy of "equidistance" from the two superpowers—often a euphemism for extreme hostility to both. Worse still, the Revolution unleashed an Islamic messianism that threatened to spread to Muslim populations within the Soviet Union itself.[27]

This latter concern propelled Moscow toward disaster. In 1978, a Marxist regime had seized power in Afghanistan. The new government's clumsy imposition of economic and social reforms provoked a formidable Islamist rebellion that drew inspiration from the revolution unfolding in neighboring Iran. Alarmed by the specter of Islamist agitation in a nation bordering its own Central Asian republics, in December 1979 the Soviet Union sent 80,000 troops into Afghanistan to shore up the Marxist regime.[28]

The United States reacted extremely harshly to the invasion, interpreting it as the first step in a Soviet drive toward the Persian Gulf. Washington imposed economic sanctions against Moscow and provided military aid to the anti-Soviet rebels. President Jimmy Carter hyperbolically called the invasion "the greatest threat to peace since the Second World War," an act signaling Moscow's aggressive intent.[29]

Actually, the Soviets had plunged into a quagmire. Although Soviet forces held Afghanistan's urban centers, they could not pacify the country-side, where a fractious array of local Islamist insurgents, supported by the United States, Pakistan, Saudi Arabia, China, and other nations, harassed and bloodied the occupiers. Over the next decade, the commitment in Afghanistan would drain an already depleted Soviet treasury, hampering Moscow's ability to project power elsewhere. The war tarnished the Soviet Union's international image, especially in the Muslim world, and demoralized the Soviet citizenry.[30] To be sure, Afghan Islamism was a double-edged sword that would, in the 1990s, start slicing against the United States and its regional allies. During the lifespan of the Cold War, however, the Soviet Union was the principal victim of that phenomenon.

Thus, by 1980 the Soviets had embarked on a venture that would help to ensure their global defeat a decade later. In the Middle East, they had already lost the Cold War. Although Moscow continued to cultivate Middle Eastern clients into the 1980s, it grew less and less relevant to the region's politics. Despite continuing Arab disapproval, the Egyptian-Israeli agreement held, and the United States remained central to any future Arab-Israeli peacemaking. The Soviet Union could provide Arab states with arms and diplomatic support, but only the United States could compel Israel to withdraw from occupied territory. The 1980s also marked the resumption of direct U.S. military intervention in the Middle East, a practice generally avoided since the dispatching of marines to Lebanon in 1958. While these latter-day adventures entailed considerable risks, military intervention by the Soviet Union was almost never one of them. Rather, the United States was increasingly vexed by indigenous Middle Eastern adversaries, especially Iranian-backed Shia militants.

Events in and around Lebanon bear out these patterns. In June 1982 Israel invaded Lebanon to crush PLO forces based in that country, install a friendly government in Beirut, and weaken the Palestinian movement elsewhere in the region. The invasion brought Israel into confrontation with Syrian forces already occupying the country. The Israeli air force destroyed eighty-five Syrian planes without losing a single plane of its own. Moscow partially replenished these losses but otherwise took little action, allowing Washington to monopolize the diplomacy surrounding the crisis and to contribute marines to a multilateral peacekeeping force that excluded the Soviets. The U.S. intervention in Lebanon quickly soured. The marines became a target of some of the country's warring factions, especially Lebanese Shia who had borne the brunt of the Israeli invasion. In October 1983 a suicide bomber—apparently a Syrian-backed Lebanese Shia—drove a truck filled with explosives into the marines' headquarters, killing 241 servicemen. President Ronald Reagan withdrew the marines, but the United States' troubles in Lebanon continued. Over the next few years Iranian-supported Lebanese Shia factions abducted several American residents. Secretly, the Reagan administration sold arms to Iran to induce it to pressure its Lebanese allies to release the hostages. In 1986 the administration's covert dealings (which were bizarrely linked to Central American politics) came to light, causing considerable embarrassment in Washington.[31] These were striking reverses for the United States, but they had nothing to do with Moscow's actions and scarcely redounded to its gain.

Events elsewhere in the region further underscored and sometimes hastened the Soviets' decline. In 1986 Moscow stood by as the United States bombed Libya, a major recipient of Soviet military aid, on the claim that Libya was complicit in international terrorism. The Iran-Iraq War of 1980–1988—in which both superpowers generally tilted toward Iraq—diverted Arab governments' attention away from the Arab-Israeli conflict, easing Egypt's diplomatic isolation and further obstructing Soviet efforts to forge an anti-U.S. Arab coalition. Instead, the crisis drew conservative Arab Gulf states closer to the United States and permitted a vast expansion in the Gulf of U.S. naval forces, which in 1987–1988 skirmished openly with Iranian gunboats.[32]

By now, Soviet foreign policy was in a state of upheaval. Upon assuming leadership of the Soviet Union in 1985, Mikhail Gorbachev had pledged to redouble his government's efforts to keep and gain influence in the Third World, including the Middle East, but the deterioration of the Soviet economy made such a posture untenable. The Soviets had fewer resources to devote to Third World ventures, especially as the war in Afghanistan ground on. Gorbachev also realized that the surest route to economic relief was a reduction of Cold War tensions, as this would allow Moscow to spend less on arms and improve its trade relations with the West. One price of renewed détente was a scaling back of Soviet activism across the globe. In the late 1980s, Moscow began retreating from its Third World commitments, most prominently by withdrawing its troops from Afghanistan.[33]

In the Middle East, Gorbachev's "new thinking" amounted to near-total acquiescence in U.S. initiatives. After Iraq invaded Kuwait in August 1990, the Soviet Union abandoned its erstwhile client and sat on the sidelines as a U.S.-led coalition ejected Iraqi forces from Kuwait. In October 1991 the Soviet Union and the United States cosponsored an international conference in Madrid to pursue Arab-Israeli peace. Moscow had long championed a comprehensive Middle East settlement to be reached through multilateral negotiations, but the Madrid conference scarcely fulfilled those criteria. After a few days of public speeches, the conference broke up into a series of bilateral negotiations, dominated by the United States, in which the Israelis dealt separately with their Syrian, Jordanian, and Palestinian counterparts. These ground rules ensured minimal pressure on Israel to conduct a substantial withdrawal from occupied territory.[34] By year's end the Soviet Union had vanished into history. It thereafter remained for local actors—whether "rogue" states like Iraq and Iran or Islamist movements like Hizbollah and the emerging al-Qa'ida network—to mount the principal opposition to U.S. hegemony in the Middle East.

The Cold War accentuated existing patterns in Middle Eastern geopolitics. The great powers enhanced the ability of local actors to pursue rivalries they would have pursued anyway, occasionally restraining the antagonists when their conflicts threatened to spin out of control. Anglo-American support allowed conservative, oil-rich governments to cling to power (thus ensuring Western access to the region's petroleum reserves), while the Soviets offered a leg-up to secular, left-leaning nationalist regimes and movements. In the 1970s secular nationalism lost vitality, eventually giving way to Islamist forms. This phenomenon followed an internal logic of its own but was reinforced by the simultaneous decline of Soviet influence in the area. And so, a decade before the Soviet Union disintegrated, the post–Cold War era dawned over the Middle East. The United States began projecting power directly and unilaterally into the Middle East, facing little opposition from outside the region but no shortage of passionate resistance from within. This pattern has continued into the current era and seems likely to endure for years to come.

NOTES

1. Rashid Khalidi, *Sowing Crisis: The Cold War and American Dominance in the Middle East* (Boston: Beacon Press, 2009), 159–200.

2. Albert Hourani, *A History of the Arab Peoples* (Cambridge, MA: Harvard University Press, 1991), 315–332.

3. Thomas A. Bryson, *Seeds of Mideast Crisis: The United States Diplomatic Role in the Middle East during World War II* (Jefferson, NC: McFarland, 1981), 33–65.

4. David S. Painter, *Oil and the American Century: The Political Economy of U.S. Foreign Oil Policy, 1941–1954* (Baltimore: Johns Hopkins University Press, 1986), 153–160; Melvyn P. Leffler, "Strategy, Diplomacy, and the Cold War: The

United States, Turkey, and NATO, 1945–1952," *Journal of American History* 71:4 (March 1985), 813–814.

5. James A. Bill, *The Eagle and the Lion: The Tragedy of American-Iranian Relations* (New Haven, CT: Yale University Press, 1988), 31–38; Galia Golan, *Soviet Policies in the Middle East: From World War II to Gorbachev* (Cambridge: Cambridge University Press, 1990), 30–32; George S. Harris, *Troubled Alliance: Turkish-American Problems in Historical Perspective, 1945–1971* (Washington, DC: American Enterprise Institute, 1972), 15–44.

6. For an account of this event, see Mary Ann Heiss, *Empire and Nationhood: The United States, Great Britain, and Iranian Oil, 1950–1954* (New York: Columbia University Press, 1997). See also the following chapters in *Mohammad Mosaddeq and the 1953 Coup in Iran*, ed. Mark J. Gasiorowski and Malcolm Byrne (Syracuse, NY: Syracuse University Press, 2004): Wm. Roger Louis, "Britain and the Overthrow of the Mossadeq Government," 126–177; Malcolm Byrne, "The Road to Intervention: Factors Influencing U.S. Policy toward Iran, 1945–1953," 220–226; and Mark J. Gasiorowski, "The 1953 Coup d'État Against Mosaddeq," 227–260.

7. Bill, *Eagle and the Lion*, 92–97.

8. Ritchie Ovendale, *Origins of the Arab-Israeli Wars* (London: Longman, 1984), 29–71, 92–125; Golan, *Soviet Policies*, 34–43.

9. Steven Z. Freiberger, *Dawn over Suez: The Rise of American Power in the Middle East, 1953–1957* (Chicago: Ivan R. Dee, 1992), 83–100, 103–104.

10. For accounts of the *Suez* Crisis, see Keith Kyle, *Suez* (New York: St. Martin's Press, 1991); W. Scott Lucas, *Divided We Stand: Britain, the United States, and the Suez Crisis* (London: Hodder and Stoughton, 1991).

11. Salim Yaqub, *Containing Arab Nationalism: The Eisenhower Doctrine and the Middle East* (Chapel Hill: University of North Carolina Press, 2004), 61–65.

12. For an account of the Eisenhower Doctrine, see Yaqub, *Containing Arab Nationalism* (Eisenhower quoted on 228).

13. Malcolm H. Kerr, *The Arab Cold War: Gamal 'Abd al-Nasir and His Rivals, 1958–1970*, 3rd ed. (London: Oxford University Press, 1971).

14. Patrick Seale, *Asad of Syria: The Struggle for the Middle East* (London: I. B. Tauris, 1988), 118–121, 123–129; Kerr, *Arab Cold War*, 125–129.

15. Adeed Dawisha, *Arab Nationalism in the Twentieth Century: From Triumph to Despair* (Princeton, NJ: Princeton University Press, 2003), 251–259, 278–279.

16. William B. Quandt, *Peace Process: American Diplomacy and the Arab-Israeli Conflict Since 1967*, rev. ed. (Berkeley: University of California Press, 2001), 66, 70–72; Robert O. Freedman, *Soviet Policy toward the Middle East since 1970* (New York: Praeger, 1982), 31–33.

17. Helena Cobban, *The Palestine Liberation Organization: People, Power, and Politics* (Cambridge: Cambridge University Press, 1984), 28–29, 36–57.

18. Freedman, *Soviet Policy*, 38–39, 69–70; Roland Dannreuther, *The Soviet Union and the PLO* (London: Macmillan, 1998), 36–43.

19. Freedman, *Soviet Policy*, 35–36; Bill, *Eagle and the Lion*, 169–182.

20. Nixon quoted in Walter LaFeber, *The American Age: United States Foreign Policy at Home and Abroad*, 2nd ed., *1750 to the Present* (1989; New York: W. W. Norton, 1994), 638.

21. LaFeber, *American Age*, 640; Bill, *Eagle and the Lion*, 183–202.

22. Daniel Yergin, *The Prize: The Epic Quest for Oil, Money, and Power* (New York: Simon and Schuster, 1991), 567–568, 580–587; David Long, *The United States and Saudi Arabia: Ambivalent Allies* (Boulder, CO: Westview Press, 1985), 47–48.

23. Quandt, *Peace Process*, 92–104; Freedman, *Soviet Policy*, 73–75, 84–91.

24. Quandt, *Peace Process*, 105–124.

25. For an account of the Camp David process, see Quandt, *Camp David: Peacemaking and Politics* (Washington, DC: Brookings Institution, 1986).

26. Freedman, *Soviet Policy*, 346–352, 370–373; David Farber, *Taken Hostage: The Iran Hostage Crisis and America's First Encounter with Radical Islam* (Princeton, NJ: Princeton University Press, 2005), 72–180.

27. Golan, *Soviet Policies*, 107–109, 126–137, 170–173, 185–190; Freedman, *Soviet Policy*, 357–369; Oles M. Smolansky and Bettie M. Smolansky, *The USSR and Iraq: The Soviet Quest for Influence* (Durham, NC: Duke University Press, 1991), 127–140; John W. Parker, *Persian Dreams: Moscow and Tehran since the Fall of the Shah* (Washington, DC: Potomac Books, 2009), 5–10.

28. Odd Arne Westad, *The Global Cold War: Third World Interventions and the Making of Our Times* (Cambridge: Cambridge University Press, 2005), 299–326, 328.

29. Gaddis Smith, *Morality, Reason, and Power: American Diplomacy in the Carter Years* (New York: Hill and Wang, 1986), 224–230; Ronald E. Powaski, *The Cold War: The United States and the Soviet Union, 1917–1991* (New York: Oxford University Press, 1998), 223–224.

30. Henry S. Bradsher, *Afghan Communism and Soviet Intervention* (Oxford: Oxford University Press, 1999), 196–255.

31. Patrick Tyler, *A World of Trouble: The White House and the Middle East—from the Cold War to the War on Terror* (New York: Farrar Straus Giroux, 2009), 267–290, 290–302, 304–311, 328–333; Golan, *Soviet Policies*, 126–137.

32. Freedman, *Moscow and the Middle East: Soviet Policy since the Invasion of Afghanistan* (Cambridge: Cambridge University Press, 1991), 238–241, 267–276; Stephen Page, "'New Political Thinking' and Soviet Policy toward Regional Conflict in the Middle East," in *The Decline of the Soviet Union and the Transformation of the Middle East,* ed. David H. Goldberg and Paul Marantz (Boulder, CO: Westview Press, 1994), 30–36; Parker, *Persian Dreams*, 13–14; Golan, *Soviet Policies*, 195.

33. Westad, *Global Cold War*, 364–387.

34. Page, "New Political Thinking," 36–44; Kathleen Christison, *Perceptions of Palestine: Their Influence on U.S. Middle East Policy* (Berkeley: University of California Press, 1999), 265–273.

2

WHAT WAS CONTAINMENT?

Short and Long Answers from the Americas

GREG GRANDIN

The Containment of Latin America

There is no other area outside the United States and Europe where the trajectory of post–World War II history maps so evenly onto a traditional periodization of the Cold War as Latin America: The Latin American Cold War started in 1947 when a series of coups and conservative back-lashes fueled by rising anti-Communism closed a brief but consequential continent-wide democratic opening; its end can be dated to either the 1989 invasion of Panama (a month after the fall of the Berlin Wall) or the 1990 elections in Nicaragua that removed the revolutionary Sandinistas from power. In the intervening decades, a number of the Cold War's signal events took place: the CIA's 1954 coup against Guatemalan president Jacobo Arbenz, the 1959 Cuban Revolution, the 1961 Bay of Pigs invasion, the following year's missile crisis, John F. Kennedy's intervention to prevent Cheddi Jagan from coming to power in Guyana, Lyndon B. Johnson's 1965 invasion of the Dominican Republic, the 1973 overthrow of Chilean presi-dent Salvador Allende, and the Iran-Contra scandal of the 1980s.

Yet for this periodization to make any analytic sense it has to be set within a longer, more consequential epoch: Latin America's revolutionary twentieth century.[1] Starting with the Mexican Revolution of 1910 and run-ning through the insurgencies that took place in the Central American coun-tries of El Salvador, Nicaragua, and Guatemala in the 1970s and 1980s, this period was defined by sequential bids to move beyond what had become an unsustainable model of economics and politics that had taken shape beginning in the 1820s, after independence from Spain and Portugal. This model included exclusionary nationalism, restricted political institutions, persisting rural clientalism and forced labor, and dependent, export-based economic development.

The experience of each country's involvement in the cycle of twentieth-century insurgent politics was specific. Yet many shared familiar patterns of radicalization, followed by revolution, civil war, or state terror, with each successive attempt to transform society generating experiences that shaped subsequent efforts. The 1910 Mexican Revolution marked the first sustained assault on nineteenth-century authoritarian liberalism, putting agrarian reform and social rights fully on the policy agenda. In the 1930s and 1940s, populism in Brazil and Argentina, among other places, extended rights, superseded regional caudillo patronage relations with national institutions, and advanced a more inclusive national-popular identity. After World War II, socialists, nationalists, and social liberals tried to make good on the promise of antifascist social democracy. In the 1950s, a sharper nationalism gained ground, in Guatemala and Bolivia, for example, with a defined program of import-substitution meant to capitalize local industry.

By the late 1950s, the frustrations and radicalization that produced the Cuban Revolution could have, in fact, come to a head in a similar upheaval in any number of other countries, such as Guatemala, Colombia, or Peru. An overdetermined event in the fullest sense of the term, the Cuban Revolution both distilled decades of regional experience and linked that experience to a broader, global crisis of legitimacy that by 1968 had threatened to overwhelm both West and East alike. The revolution was the first in Latin America to fully understand itself as "world historical" and thus try to externalize itself, fracturing Latin America's already debilitated Old Left and spawning and supporting imitators throughout the Andes and Central America in the 1960s and the southern cone in the 1970s. It was consequential not only in this alone, but also because its success spawned insurgent *foco* theory (which emphasized small, isolated guerrilla units carrying out provocative military actions), with disastrous results in Venezuela, Peru, Bolivia, and Colombia; subsequently, New Left intellectuals and activists tried to transcend the revolution's limitations. Liberation theology; oppositional movements organized around nascent political identities that resisted vertical integration into reformist parties or bureaucratic corporatist states; Chile's Popular Unity coalition, which sought to achieve socialism without sacrificing political pluralism; and even new guerrilla organizations that hoped to avoid *foquismo*'s errors and build mass support through "pedagogy of the oppressed"–like consciousness raising: all were as much reactions to the Cuban Revolution as they were products of it. These elements came together in their fullest expression in the Central American insurgencies of the late 1970s and 1980s, conflicts coterminous with the Cold War's final decade.

The history of Washington's role in propelling Latin America's revolutionary century forward is well documented. It began with U.S. ambassador Henry Lane Wilson's involvement in the February 18, 1913, overthrow of Mexican president Francisco Madero, resulting in Madero's execution, which in turn provoked years of cataclysmic violence, and continued through President Ronald Reagan's patronage of Central American death squads in the 1980s.[2] In this sense, then, when Latin Americanists consider the term "containment," they usually define it not as a specific policy meant to check Soviet Communism associated with George F. Kennan's 1947 *Foreign Affairs* article, but as the New Left did, as a reactionary if not fully "counterrevolutionary" response to third-world nationalism, an opinion that, beginning in the mid-1960s, was held even by centrist scholars, such as that expressed by economic historian Robert Heilbroner, in an 1967 essay in *Commentary,* titled "Counter-revolutionary America."[3]

The Containment of the Americas: Bogotá 1948

In keeping with the spirit of the New Left approach, which tried to reveal the connections between domestic and foreign policy, it is worth expanding the concept of the Latin American Cold War into a fully American, or Western Hemispheric, one. In the United States, social and intellectual historians have identified a shift taking place between 1947 and 1948 from New Deal, or popular front, liberalism, to Cold War liberalism. Politically, the former was represented by the antifascist alliance of liberals and the left, including the Communist Party, manifest both within the Democratic Party and labor unions. Intellectually, it represented the last gasp of what political philosopher Judith Shklar has called a "liberalism of hope," with its faith in progress and reason and its analysis that the source of political conflict was economic exploitation.[4] The end of the liberal-left alliance was announced in 1947 by a series of well-known events, including the Taft-Hartley Act, which greatly circumscribed the ability of unions to organize, the Truman Doctrine, which, along with other executive-branch actions, formally declared that the purpose of U.S. diplomacy was to contain Soviet expansion, and the first rushes of the Red Scare, which purged the left from political influence.[5] These events, among others, prompted Henry Wallace, Franklin Delano Roosevelt's vice president during his first three terms, to break with the Democratic Party and to try to gather the disaffected left-wing of the New Deal coalition behind his 1948 third-party bid for the presidency.

Wallace's poor showing in that campaign could be taken as one marker of the ascendance of what Shklar calls the "liberalism of fear," where the evident cruelties of the twentieth century confirmed for many intellectuals that the best a government could do was to protect the individual from oppression—and from his own base passions and worst instincts. As Mark Kleinman argues in his intellectual biography of Henry Wallace and theologian Reinhold Niebuhr, who best represent the transition from the New Deal to the Cold War, optimism gave way to realism.[6] Particular Communists, and even whole national parties, might have been motivated by humane reasons and might have been, at certain moments, essential to achieving an expansion of democracy in any given country (including, in their advocacy of labor and civil rights, the United States). Yet at a fundamental and generalized level, an alliance with Communists would provide an opening for the darkness that lies within.[7] Beyond this, any refusal to stand "humble" before history and insist that an ever more perfect world could be achieved by public policy, especially policy that presumes to trespass on private property, would unleash forces that couldn't be controlled. "History is not a redeemer, promising to solve all human problems in time," Arthur Schlesinger, Jr., cautioned in a 1949 *Partisan Review* essay nominally about the Civil War but really a brief for containment (both of the Soviet Union and the New Deal); it is rather a "tragedy in which we are all involved, whose keynote is anxiety and frustration."[8] Others like Richard Hofstadter and Niebuhr invoked the force of instinct and passion in mass society as something of a deus ex machina to stress history's tragic dimensions. The notion that evil did not "proceed from a cruel system"—that is, a system that could be rigged to produce ever more virtue—but from man's "dark and tangled aspects," as Schlesinger interpreted Niebuhr, helped transform liberalism from a politics of hope to one of fear. On an existential level, then, "tough liberals" knew the world needed to be policed. Containment of the Soviet Union was justified by this ethic, and served as its concrete manifestation.[9]

Scholars of Latin America do not generally use the categories "New Deal liberalism" or "Cold War liberalism" to describe the rise of Cold War anti-Communism that overcame most Latin American countries, beginning in 1947. Historians tend to present Latin American "liberalism" as exhausted by midcentury; instead, they use terms such as "agrarianism," "socialism," or "populism" to describe political efforts to democratize extremely hierarchal societies. There is not much research on the "popular front" in Latin America, at least not as American studies scholar Michael Denning understands the period: not as a Comintern-mandated alliance between Communist parties and liberals, but as a profound cultural revolution that created an organic American nationalism, an alternative to, on the one hand, elite WASP identity and, on the other, southern white supremacy.[10] Yet by tuning out the categorical dissonance that prevents relating the New Deal and popular front to early twentieth-century Latin American democracy movements, we will be able to gain a new, more panoramic perspective on the Cold War in the Americas and the meaning of containment.[11]

It is difficult, of course, to date the start of any historical period as subject to interpretation as the Cold War, particularly in Latin America, where Soviet influence was negligible. But as good a date as any would be April 9, 1948, the day Jorge Eliécer Gaitán, leader of Colombia's Liberal Party, was assassinated, a history-heavy moment that crystallized the hemisphere's political, economic, and intellectual currents and contours.

April 9, 1948, was a Friday, and Bogotá was hosting the ninth International Conference of American States, a meeting that would result in the founding of the Organization of American States (OAS) and signal the formal switch in the wartime pan-American alliance from fighting fascism to containing Communism. Preparations for the Bogotá conference took place in the wake of the March 1947 Truman Doctrine and in the shadow of the White House's multibillion dollar "rearmament" budget request; the region's political elites, having drawn close to the United States during World War II, maneuvered to show support for Washington's stance against the Soviet Union as the summit approached. Brazil had outlawed its Communist Party the previous May. In January, Chilean president Gabriel González Videla, elected in 1946 with strong support from the Communist Party (Pablo Neruda, then a Communist senator representing a nitrate-rich northern state, served as his campaign manager), violently suppressed a miners strike. In February, Venezuela's Acción Democrática expelled leftists from its affiliated national oil workers' union. In Mexico, just a few months before the Bogotá conference, the labor leader Vicente Lombardo Toledano—described by the U.S. embassy the year before as "our country's most dangerous enemy in Mexico...a bitter and dangerous enemy"—was expelled from the Confederación de Trabajadores de México.[12] Other countries similarly signaled their backing for a strong anti-Soviet, pro-stability hemispheric policy. In exchange, the governments of these countries wanted something more than World Bank loans and technical support of the kind

President Harry S. Truman would soon offer in his 1949 Point IV speech. They expected their own Marshall Plan.

In the weeks prior to the arrival of Secretary of State George C. Marshall, Latin American nations demanded clarification about the kind of capital and credit the region could expect from the United States. Carlos Sanz de Santamaria, a respected Colombian politician (he had served both as defense and finance minister) then taking a degree in economics at Georgetown, stated the problem succinctly:

> It is necessary for our Latin American countries to bring closer together the present difference in the value of their exports and imports. That is true mainly because now they have to pay for manufactured merchandise, produced with labor receiving from $2 to $3 an hour, by selling raw materials, and eventually semi-manufactured products and agricultural products, the last of which is cultivated with wages of $1 a day.... That imbalance must be remedied in some way to pave the way for economic cooperation in the hemisphere.[13]

For its part, Chile advocated for import restrictions and quotas to protect fledgling industries. Just a month before the Bogotá conference, in February, this program for rectifying underdevelopment—a stretching of the logic of Keynesianism to cover the global political economy—found an institutional home with the establishment of the United Nations' Economic Commission for Latin America and the Caribbean, based in Santiago, Chile, and headed by Argentine economist Raúl Prebisch. In the years to come this commission would be the intellectual home of many of the economists and sociologists who presided over the radicalization of developmentalist thought and elaborated what would become known as "dependency theory."

But it had become clear, months before the conference, that the Truman administration would not subsidize the capitalization of Latin American industry. In February 1948, the National Foreign Trade Council and the Council for Inter-American Cooperation, two powerful business lobbies, provided a long, detailed report that stressed the need to promote a hemispheric economic diplomacy based on "private risk capital." Latin American countries needed to create a "healthy investment climate" by foreswearing nationalization and guaranteeing private property, low tax rates, and profit repatriation.[14] Marshall largely followed this program after arriving in Bogotá in late March. On April 1, he gave a long speech urging Latin Americans to "remove barriers to private capital investment." "The rewards of freedom are economic as well as political," he said; only such freedom could "give full rein to individual initiative."[15]

It was a hard sell, especially since the U.S. Congress was exactly at that moment discussing, and would pass the next day, the act that authorized the Marshall Plan for Western Europe. So Latin American delegates greeted Marshall's speech with silence.[16] To concerns that the massive public funding of European industrialization would cement in place the kind of imbalance described by Sanz, the U.S. Secretary of State said that increased demand for Latin American goods generated by aid to Europe would ease their dollar crunch and help spur industrialization.[17] Bowing somewhat to pressure, on April 8, one day before Jorge Gaitán's murder, Marshall announced, in a press conference held with great fanfare, a half billion dollars in direct aid. Again, his words were met with silence. "There was not," observed one reporter, "a single handclap"; the secretary "sat in uncomfortable silence as the session ended." With Latin American economists estimating they needed twenty times what the United States was offering to industrialize, the event was deemed a "fiasco."[18]

When Gaitán was executed the next day outside his downtown law office, Bogotá erupted. Crowds grabbed his assassin, Juan Roa Sierra, who was mentally unstable and had vague fascist sympathies and shadowy ties to security forces, and beat him to death. Stores were looted, buildings burned, and police stations sacked. Gaitán was the leader of the historic Liberal Party, which had recently governed Colombia for sixteen years but was then in opposition to the Conservative government. As a lawyer who had built a base of support by defending workers and peasants in court, and leading a public campaign against agrarian violence and dispossession carried out by Colombia's landed oligarchy, Gaitán was enormously popular; he can best be thought of as representing the socialization of liberalism that had taken place throughout Latin America in the early twentieth century, a move away from a positivist focus on order and progress to a promotion of land reform, workers' rights, and a definition of democracy that understood individual freedom as predicated on some degree of economic security, if not equality. Liberal political leaders blamed the Conservative government for his murder, but the *gaitanista* rank-and-file held elites of both parties responsible. By the next morning, most of downtown Bogotá was destroyed and thousands of lives were lost. Representatives of the Liberal and Conservative parties eventually worked out a temporary truce and, after a few days, restored order. Yet historians date the *Bogotazo*, as the riot is called, as the beginning of *La violencia*, a decade-long civil war that left hundreds of thousands dead.

Taking place less than two months after the installation of a Communist government in Czechoslovakia, as Italian Communists were running strong in upcoming elections, the U.S, State Department seamlessly folded the uprising into its emerging Cold War narrative. Marshall blamed the riot on "international Communism." The press followed suit, reporting rumors of a Communist coup in Paraguay and "waves of revolt" sweeping across Latin America. The *Los Angeles Times* described events in Colombia as a "red masterpiece," the "crowning achievement of the master craftsmen of discord," designed to sabotage the Pan-American Conference. There is no evidence that Communists were behind Gaitán's execution (a Scotland Yard investigation on the execution was suppressed, and to this day, rumors of CIA involvement abound). Donald Jackson, a Republican representative from California attending the Bogotá conference, flew back to Washington to provide testimony at a hastily arranged House hearing, telling of his dramatic escape from a burning building and fighting "surging mobs armed with clubs and machetes." "This is war as truly as if we were opposed by armed might and a physical enemy," he said, to the standing ovation of his congressional colleagues.[19]

Rather than disrupt the conference, the *Bogotazo* forced a closing of ranks and a heightened urgency among the delegates, who set aside their disappointment regarding Washington's economic proposals to adopt the charter that would create the Organization of American States. Following the conference, the conservative backlash against postwar social democracy that had begun a year earlier gained force throughout the region. Center-left governments were overthrown in Peru in October and Venezuela in November. Costa Rica outlawed its Communist Party in July; Chile did so in September (Neruda, already in exile, was officially removed from his Senate seat). By 1948, most Latin American countries were ruled by dictatorships.

Gaitán's popularity, along with the explosive reaction to his killing, allows for a transnational expansion of Denning's argument that the popular front's power and resonance through the Cold War was not its strategic and fitful alliance between Communists and Liberals but its successful promotion of a broader, organic social-democratic political culture. In Colombia, the leadership of the Liberal and Communist parties was often in conflict, for reasons more to do with local politics than with the Comintern's doctrinal twists. Yet historians have documented that the rank and file of both parties was practically indistinguishable and formed *gaitanismo*'s social base. Gaitán himself—his agrarian radicalism, emphasis on human dignity, and attacks on the oligarchy—represented a sharp break with the urban-focused legalism of the Communist Party. It was not just what Gaitán said but how he said it, with a populist intimacy that shattered the speech-making conventions favored by Liberal and Conservative elites; he was, according to the *New York Times,* "famous as an orator in a country where orators abound and oratory ranks with poetry as an art."[20]

This rupture in both content and form had an unexpected influence on the writer who best represents the Latin American New Left, the man who turned dependency theory into a literary genre. Gabriel García Márquez, a young, obscure law student living in a downtown Bogotá pensión, witnessed the fearsome violence that followed Gaitan's execution. He fled the riots, yet the uprising was the turning point in the development of his method. His memoir *Living to Tell the Tale* recounts how Gaitán's aborted campaign led him to an appreciation of *gaitanismo* as an expression of a distinctly Latin American vernacular, one that by focusing on his country's worsening political repression and rural poverty opened a "breach" in the arid discourse of liberalism, conservatism, and even Communism. García Márquez credits Gaitán with pushing him toward a new narrative voice, which when fully realized in *One Hundred Years of Solitude* would transcend folklorism and florid, overly symbolic *modernismo* to situate Latin America's underdevelopment and seemingly chronic violence within a history of neocolonial dependency.[21]

Associated with the traditional university Left, García Márquez recalls trying to ignore Gaitán. Yet he became captivated after accidentally coming upon the politician making a speech in Bogotá's thin, high nighttime air; his voice, García Márquez thought, was like "lashes of a whip over the astonished city." Hearing Gaitán for the first time in person, he "understood all at once that he had gone beyond the Spanish country and was inventing a lingua franca for everyone":

Not so much because of what his words said as for the passion and shrewdness in his voice. In his epic speeches he himself would advise his listeners in a guileful paternal tone to return in peace their houses, and they would translate that in the correct fashion as a coded order to express their repudiation of everything that represented social inequalities and the power of a brutal government.... The subject of that night's speech was an unadorned recounting of the devastation caused by official violence.... After a terrifying enumeration of murders and assaults, Gaitán began to raise his voice, to take delight word by word, sentence by sentence, in a marvel of sensationalist, well-aimed rhetoric. The tension in the audience increased to the rhythm of his voice, until a final outburst exploded within the confines of the city and reverberated on the radio into the most remote corners of the country. The inflamed crowd poured into the streets in a bloodless pitched battle.... I reached the *pension* dazed by the turmoil of the night and found my roommate reading Ortega y Gasset in the peace of his bed.

"I'm a new man, Dr. Vega," I said.[22]

Needless to say, Washington understood the kind of power here narrated by García Márquez as a threat. The word "populist" would not be coined until a few decades later to describe the politics and rhetoric associated with Gaitán (State Department officials at the time tended to use the phrase "social revolution").[23] Yet for U.S. policymakers, *gaitanismo*—along with *peronismo* in Argentina, *vargismo* in Brazil, *cardenismo* in Mexico, and other forms of mobilized nationalism—were political forces that needed to be contained for three reasons. First, economically, they represented an obstacle to putting into place the kind of open hemisphere policy outlined by Marshall. Second, they were a threat not just to foreign corporations but to the guaranteed flow of oil, tin, and other resources needed for the United States' expanding postwar economy. Third, politically, even if they weren't conscious allies of Soviet Communism these movements were deemed to create the conditions in which Communism thrives, either by raising unobtainable expectations and generating class anger or by provoking a backlash and spurring further radicalization.

On a more intangible, ideational level, movements like *gaitanismo* represented a challenge but also something like a sharpening stone, on which ideas could be honed about what comprises proper, temperate, and responsible politics—particularly important with the postwar reconstitution of U.S. liberalism. This reconstitution was complex and multifaceted, entailing a move away from the assumptions of the economic democrats who comprised the left wing of the New Deal and a return to a more conventional notion that, as Marshall lectured Latin Americans a week before Gaitán's execution, democracy comprised not just political freedom but economic liberty as well. Regulation, welfare, and government intervention in the economy would continue to be tolerated, and the gradual extension of political rights promoted. In Latin America, Washington would continue to abide—for a time and to a certain limit—the developmentalist economics advocated by Prebisch and the UN Economic Commission for Latin America and the Caribbean (ECLAC), including nationalization and land reform. Yet the firewall separating the political sphere (the proper place of representative politics) and the social (where civil society operates and property rights are protected) that was breeched in the 1930s was gradually being rebuilt.

In both economic and political terms—in its unreconstructed push to extend the ideals of equality into the social sphere and willingness to rouse a crowd to do so—populism in Latin America represented the mirror opposite of U.S. Cold War liberalism, with events like the *Bogotazo* dramatically serving to conflate the foreign and domestic threat, a graphic illustration of what lay ahead if liberalism was not contained. Hence the equation—made by the first director of the CIA, Admiral Roscoe Hillenkoetter, at the same congressional hearings where Representative Jackson described his escape from the Latin American mob—of Gaitán with Henry Wallace, fresh from his break with the Democratic Party and in the middle of his bid for the presidency. Gaitán, Hillenkoetter said, was just like "Henry Wallace in our country," a politician who allied with the "extreme left and communists." To drive the point home, he warned that conditions in Colombia are like "those in the United States, except they are advanced by a couple of years." In the weeks that followed, the press continued the comparison. One report even suggested Wallace was more reckless than Gaitán, for while Wallace had broken with the Democrats, Gaitán at least continued to work within the Liberal Party. A letter to the *Chicago Daily Tribune* noted that Henry Wallace's name in Spanish is pronounced Enrique Vayase, which means in English: "Get Lost, Henry." "I have spent many months" in South America, the writer said, "and between the Roosevelt Doctrine and the mouthings of Mr. Vayase, they have done a swell job in making it easy for left wing parties and Communists to stir up trouble."[24] Exactly a century earlier, opinion makers, intellectuals, and politicians measured and confirmed the correctness of the moderation of America's revolutionary tradition in contrast to Europe's social revolutions of 1848, attributing acute violence to either European revolutionaries who didn't know where to stop or ancien régime reactionaries who wouldn't yield. Events in Bogotá allowed for the comparison to be brought closer to home.[25] In a lengthy analysis of the riot, the *Christian Science Monitor* blamed the violence on liberals who irresponsibly supported *gaitanismo*, thus raising unrealizable expectations, and the "strong-arm reaction of the upper classes," whose "islands of well-being look like bastilles to the undernourished workers." "Señor Gaitán," like Wallace, "constantly and vehemently told the masses that 16 years of Liberal administrations"—exactly how long the New Deal coalition had been in office—"had not brought them what they could rightfully expect." The newspaper also compared Gaitán to another U.S. populist, Huey Long, but noted that Long's "elimination did not provoke such destruction in Baton Rouge or New Orleans" as was visited on Bogotá.[26]

The scholars Leslie Bethell and Ian Roxborough have argued that to understand the mainspring of Latin American Cold War polarization one needs to consider the region in relation to Western Europe and Japan.[27] In those areas, public reconstruction aid and capital, in the form of the Marshall Plan, provided more space for an independent, non-Soviet-allied Left— mainly in the form of Social Democratic parties and strong trade unionism—since investment was not based on ensuring absolute labor quiescence and political stability. In Latin America, in contrast, despite Truman's talk about development and equity, most of the desperately needed capital was in the form of loans or private investment, as Latin Americans in Bogotá in 1948 were told it would be. So the twinned promises of democracy and development, which in the early 1940s had seemed mutually dependent, were by 1948 known to be mutually exclusive. In order to create a stable investment climate and absent a Marshall Plan, governments, now fortified with the rhetoric of the Cold War, cracked down on labor unrest and persecuted not just Communists—who in many countries were indispensable to democratic advances—but, eventually, all reformers. This was not unforeseen. Latin American "liberals" at the Bogotá conference, in the days preceding Gaitán's killing, worried, according to the *New York Times*, that the obsessive focus on Communism being pushed by U.S. officials—and taken up by Latin American delegates as a way of winning aid—would allow Conservatives to invoke the "collective anti-Communist declaration as a means of waging war on all oppositionists."[28] In the wake of the Cuban Revolution, that's what happened. Forthcoming aid was overwhelmingly directed to the police and military, accelerating the cycle: U.S. officials would continue to talk about the need to work with a "democratic Left" throughout the Cold War (except during the Reagan years), even as that Left was being slaughtered by the officials' own apprentices.

Returning to the question what makes the Latin American Cold War distinct from Latin America's revolutionary century: it wasn't the actions or the influence of the Soviet Union, which were greatly limited in the region, except in Cuba after its revolution. An honest assessment would admit that there was only one superpower involved in the Latin American Cold War: the United States. Though the general contours of hemispheric relations had earlier been set—with, for instance, U.S. meddling in the Mexican Revolution or its occupations and counterinsurgencies in Nicaragua, Haiti, and the Dominican Republic in the 1920s and 1930s—Washington's containment policy during the Cold War became a more constant variable shaping each nation's history, albeit with differential effects. The massive infusion of counterinsurgent aid quickly led to an erosion of the compromise-seeking center—which in pre–Cold War Latin American politics was already narrowly circumscribed and only tenuously able to incorporate the strains of modern politics. The preponderance of influence exercised by the United States over the hemispheric system—and the organization of the region's nations as a caucus in the United Nations united behind Washington's leadership—ensured that the crisis politics of any given country didn't spill over into external war (except in the case of the Argentine junta's attempt to retake the Malvinas in 1982). Yet it did greatly accelerate the pace of domestic polarization.

Politics and conflict didn't end with the defeat of the Sandinistas or the invasion of Panama, but efforts to transcend the past no longer took the form of opposition to the United States. Rather, they became subordinate to what was called the Washington consensus, a broad policy framework designed to help Latin America move beyond what Cold War social science described as the region's Jacobin populist political culture, corporatist mentalité, and dirigist economics.

The containment of Latin America—and of hemispheric liberalism—was complete, at least as it seemed a decade after the fall of the Berlin Wall.

The Containment of the United States

The preceding account could be considered an update of a New Left revisionist argument about containment in Latin America, albeit one that shifts the focus away from the United States to take in the hemispheric inauguration of the Cold War. There is yet another way to think about containment, one that goes beyond both revisionist and postrevisionist terms to turn the concept on its head: it was not Latin America that was being contained—either during the Cold War or previously—but rather the United States, and it has been Latin America's historical role to do the containing.

Elsewhere I've argued that two bedrock principles associated with modern notions of citizenship and diplomacy—the idea of social rights and the idea of sovereignty—were most forcefully elaborated in Latin America.[29] The region is famous for its revolutionaries, but it also practically invented social democracy. The world's first fully conceived social-democratic charter was ratified in Mexico in 1917, codifying a series of rights that had assumed widespread, common-sense status throughout the region: the rights to collective bargaining; to receive health care, education, and some form of social security; to have a job and a decent life. Efforts to institutionalize social rights entailed state intervention in the economy, which often provoked domestic and foreign interests to retaliate. U.S.-executed or -supported coups in Guatemala (1954), Brazil (1964), and Chile (1973) are among the most well-known examples of such retaliation, though there are many other examples; between 1898 and 1994, according to historian John Coatsworth, Washington had "intervened successfully to change governments in Latin America a total of at least 41 times."[30] In turn, nationalists, social democrats, populists, and socialists came to see social rights and sovereignty as mutually constitutive. In the United States, politicians, diplomats and jurists advanced ideals of citizenship and diplomacy that were nearly exactly the opposite of Latin America's "sovereignty-social rights" complex. They defined individual rights, particularly property rights, as inherent and inalienable, and qualified state sovereignty on responsible public administration that could protect those rights, an "expansionist-individual rights" complex that would justify serial interventions in Latin America.

United States–Latin American relations are often narrated as a litany of outrages. But threading through the narrative of territorial and economic expansion is a slow yet steady effort of Latin Americans to socialize U.S. diplomacy, that is, to "contain" the United States' expansionist–individual rights complex, which however dynamic in spurring territorial increase and capital accumulation in the nineteenth century was too volatile a creed to ground the kind of global superpower the United States would become in the second half of the twentieth.

The United States continued to oppose Latin America's emerging sovereignty–social rights complex until almost midcentury. In 1933, with the United States constrained by the Great Depression, Washington, at the seventh Pan-American Conference held in Montevideo, Uruguay, finally acceded to long-standing Latin American demands to give up the right to intervention and recognize the absolute sovereignty, in both domestic and foreign affairs, of Latin American nations. In retrospect, this concession, along with Franklin Delano Roosevelt's subsequent acceptance of Mexico's right to nationalize U.S. oil interests, has to be considered the most unambiguously successful foreign policy initiative the United States has ever undertaken.

Washington's formal renunciation of the right to intervention combined with FDR's acceptance of limits on U.S. property rights, opened the way for a decade of unparalleled hemispheric cooperation. The final withdrawal of U.S. troops from the Caribbean, where through the 1920s they had been bogged down in a series of morally bankrupting counterinsurgencies, gave Roosevelt a better claim to legitimacy as he advocated for an end to colonialism and militarism elsewhere. The goodwill these moves generated allowed for the negotiation of a series of bilateral trade treaties, indispensable for the United States' economic recovery, which in turn allowed the nation to steady itself for the coming fight against fascism. In the United States, these treaties allowed for the consolidation of an export-focused, labor-intensive, high-tech corporate power bloc that became the foundation of the United States' postwar expansion carried out under the auspices of the New Deal governing coalition.[31]

Rather than weakening Washington's power, Latin America's containment of the United States helped create a new framework through which Washington could project its power and authority in more effective ways. It bound the Americas together in a series of political, economic, military, and cultural treaties and led to the creation of an assortment of multilateral institutions, bodies of arbitration, and mechanisms for consultation and joint action in the case of an extra-hemispheric treaty, providing a blueprint for the regional alliance system the United States would put into place elsewhere (the North Atlantic Treaty Organization was modeled on the 1947 mutual defense Rio Pact). The acceptance of the ideal of national sovereignty along with recognition of the legitimacy of social rights, as elaborated in the UN Declaration of Human Rights (largely based on similar rights charters from Latin America), served as a critical moral instrument to fight the Cold War.

The End of Containment

Though Latin America's socialization of U.S. liberalism served Washington extremely well through World War II and the Cold War, U.S. policymakers and intellectuals continued to bristle at the economic constraints, as suggested by Secretary of State Marshall's lecturing of Latin Americans on the virtues of economic liberalismn. There are numerous other instances of this, including those involving George Kennan, the man most closely associated with the traditional policy of containment.

Kennan's exceptionally racist 1950 report on Latin America has been dissected elsewhere; the historian Gaddis Smith identifies the document as the "single most illuminating document" of U.S. policy toward the region in the years to come. "No other," Smith writes, "better expresses the hard assumptions behind the interventions and threats of intervention undertaken in the subsequent decades and justified by the Monroe Doctrine and amoral realism."[32] Less well known is Kennan's diary of his trip to Latin America, on which he based his report, which includes traveling by train in spring 1950 from Washington DC, through the U.S. Midwest, to Mexico City.

The journal reads like a cross between an impressionistic proto-beat novel, a "lonely-crowd" pop sociology common to the alienated 1950s, and a dyspeptic riff on the dark soul of human nature. Only two years since Latin American politicians in Bogotá signed on to the Cold War and since the region's jurists helped create one of the most optimistic documents of modern times—the UN Declaration of Human Rights—Kennan's description of people and places is pure caricature laced with contempt. Mexicans, he writes in a typical passage, are "wiry, swarthy little men—violent in temper, lacking in self-respect and self-confidence, over-compensating by a dramatized romantic abandon and ferocity in personality. . . ." Contemporary politics are referenced only in passing. Instead, Kennan grounded his observations in a deep history determined by geography, climate, race, the Spanish conquest, and the disruptions of technology. He mentions the Mexican Revolution (in Mexico, the "nouveau riche . . . boils up like foam to the surface of a society that calls itself revolutionary"), Juan Perón, Communists in Guatemala, and even the *Bogotazo*. But his most sustained analysis, made during his visit to Caracas, then undergoing a postwar oil-financed building boom, is on what he calls the "weaknesses and delusions of popular nationalism," particularly as it has to do with the idea of territorial sovereignty:

> Here was a tropical country in the subsoil of which reposed great quantities of a liquid essential to the present state of industrialization in the U.S. Americans were extracting this liquid and hauling it away. The local population had not moved a figure to create this wealth. . . . However, for the privilege of being able to enter and extract this liquid, our firms were paying hundreds of millions of dollars annually to the coffers of the Venezuelan government: a sort of ransom to the theory of state sovereignty and the principle of non-intervention which we had consented to adopt. Incidentally, all of nature in Venezuela was a bilious yellow-brown. [33]

In the decades to come, as the United States gained position and then ultimately triumphed in the Cold War, the "theory of state sovereignty and the principle of non-intervention" would be weakened and then dispatched. Just as Latin America played a central role in the consolidation of these ideals, that region—in Grenada, Nicaragua, and Panama—would be where they were first rolled back. The United States, of course, had "intervened" in Latin American affairs throughout the whole of the Cold War, but it did so in a way that didn't undercut the diplomatic principles of multilateralism. The CIA's successful 1954 Guatemalan coup and its botched 1961 Bay of Pigs invasion, for example, were covert and therefore violations of sovereignty.

But they did not entail a direct ideological challenge to the idea of sovereignty. In fact, these interventions confirmed, formally at least, the principle, since Washington sought and received the Organization of American States' sanction to isolate Guatemala and Cuba diplomatically. The OAS likewise endorsed, with some dissent, President Lyndon Baines Johnson's 1965 invasion of the Dominican Republic.

Starting in the 1980s, however, Ronald Reagan's actions in Central America and the Caribbean did rewrite the terms of law and diplomacy. The war against the Sandinistas in Nicaragua, for example, was meant to be covert. But in response to the International Court of Justice's 1986 ruling that the United States pay Nicaragua billions of dollars for mining its harbor and conducting an illegal war of aggression, Washington opted to withdraw from the court's jurisdiction. Legal scholar Eric Posner argues that this was a "watershed moment" in the United States' relationship with the international community—one that President George W. Bush's ambassador to the United Nations, John Bolton, cited as evidence for why the United States should not abide by other multilateral obligations.[34] The 1983 invasion of Grenada was likewise an important step in expanding the scope of unilateralism. Throughout the Cold War, an ability to move back and forth between the Organization of American States and the United Nations gave Washington room to maneuver while still adhering to the principles of multilateralism—a tactic central to the kind of alliance system the United States built after World War II, allowing for a reconciliation of regionalism with universalism. But in 1983, confronted with an increasingly hostile OAS, Jeane Kirkpatrick, the U.S. ambassador to the United Nations, opted for subdivision, citing treaty obligations to the miniscule Organization of Eastern Caribbean States to justify the landing of marines in Grenada.[35]

Then there's the 1991 invasion of Panama, recently described by Thomas Pickering, then the U.S. ambassador to the United Nations, as paving the way for 2003's unilateral war in Iraq.[36] Like most military actions, this one, coming just over a month after the fall of the Berlin Wall, was justified by a hierarchy of rationales. But high on the list, and unique in its prominence, was the goal of installing democracy in Panama. As such, it had a transformative effect on international law, one that was immediately recognized and opposed by all of Latin America, including close U.S. allies, such as Augusto Pinochet's Chile.[37] The OAS, in an emergency session, unanimously—save for the United States—condemned the invasion. In response, Luigi Einaudi, U.S. ambassador to the Organization of American States, gave a speech that invoked events in Eastern Europe to claim explicitly for the United States the right to intervene in the affairs of another country not just defensively but because it deemed the quality of its sovereignty unworthy of recognition: "Today, we are ... living in historic times, a time when a great principle is spreading across the world like wild fire. That principle, as we all know, is the revolutionary idea that people, not governments, are sovereign."[38] Einaudi was right when he admitted the rationale for war was "by no means a new idea," since it was indeed a return to an earlier conception of international law by which Washington defined sovereignty not as a right based on territory nor as effective control over government, but as the moral quality of rule, which it unilaterally claimed the right to judge.

Concurrent with this dilution of the ideal of territorial sovereignty was an attempt to disentwine social and political rights. In the decade prior to the invasion of Panama, Reagan embraced the rhetoric of human rights in order to reinvest U.S. military power with moral authority. Yet this embrace came with an important caveat: "All too often," wrote Richard Allen, Reagan's national security advisor, in 1981, "we assume that everyone means the same thing by human rights." When the United States talked about human rights, Allen stated, it meant strictly the defense of "life, liberty, and property" and not "economic and social rights." The expansion of human rights into the social realm, he went on, constituted a "dilution and distortion of the original and proper meaning of human rights."[39] That same year, Elliott Abrams, Reagan's assistant secretary of state for human rights, drafted an influential memo, often cited as key in Reagan's efforts to define the Cold War as a righteous fight: after announcing that "our struggle is for political liberty" and in defense of "human rights," Abrams nonetheless felt that the latter expression was too tainted by issues related to economic justice. He suggested a rebranding: "We should move away from 'human rights' as a term, and begin to speak of 'political rights' and 'civil liberties.' We can move on a name change at another time."[40]

The containment of the United States had come to an end.

NOTES

1. Greg Grandin, "Living in Revolutionary Time," in *A Century of Revolution: Insurgent and Counterinsurgent Violence during Latin America's Long Cold War,* ed. Greg Grandin and Gilbert Joseph (Durham, NC: Duke University Press, 2010), elaborates the arguments in the first section of this essay,

2. Friedrich Katz, *The Secret War in Mexico* (Chicago: University of Chicago Press, 1984), for Henry Lane Wilson.

3. Kennan's article was published pseudonymously as "X," "The Sources of Soviet Conduct," *Foreign Affairs* 25:4 (July 1947), 566–582; Robert Heilbroner,

"*Counter-Revolutionary America,*" *Commentary* (April 1967), 31–38. See also John Gerassi, *The Great Fear: The Reconquest of Latin America by Latin Americans* (New York: Macmillan, 1963); David Green, *The Containment of Latin America: Myths and Realities of the Good Neighbor Policy* (Chicago: Quadrangle, 1971); Walter LaFeber, *Inevitable Revolutions: The United States in Central America* (New York: Norton, 1983).

4. See Barnard Yack, "Introduction," in *Liberalism without Illusions: Liberal Theory and the Political Vision of Judith N. Shklar,* ed. Barnard Yack (Chicago: University of Chicago Press, 1996), 2.

5. Benjamin O. Fordham argues in *Building the Cold War Consensus: The Political Economy of U.S. National Security, 1949–1951* (Ann Arbor: University of Michigan, 1998), that the Cold War was a grand compromise between nationalists and internationalists: the former got Taft-Hartley and the latter got the Truman Doctrine and NSC 68.

6. Yack, "Introduction," 2; Mark Kleinman, *A World of Hope, a World of Fear: Henry A. Wallace, Reinhold Niebuhr, and American Liberalism* (Columbus: Ohio State University Press, 2000).

7. Cold War social science's Madisonian distrust of populism was overlaid by, in Niebuhr's case, Christian theology, and, in Schlesinger and Hofstadter, by social psychology, and reinforced, ironically, by Marxist analysis: the Frankfurt School's *The Authoritarian Personality* (1950) argued that monopoly capitalism's weakening of the image of the patriarchal father destroyed the venue in which ego formation could take place, leaving the unanchored self vulnerable to the allure of mass, mobilized politics, thus providing a Marxist scaffolding for positions that saw Nazism and Communism as indistinguishable. See Corey Robin, *Fear: The History of a Political Idea* (New York: Oxford University Press, 2004), for Hannah Arendt's contribution to this equation.

8. Reprinted as "The Causes of the Civil War: A Note on Historical Sentimentalism," in *The American Scene: Varieties of American History,* ed. Robert Marcus and David Burner (New York: The Meredith Corporation, 1971), 1:382

9. Arthur Schlesinger, "Niebuhr's Vision of Our Time," *The Nation* 162:35 (June 22, 1946), 753–754 (quotation on 753).

10. Michael Denning, *The Cultural Front: The Laboring of American Culture in the Twentieth Century* (New York: Verso, 1998).

11. Credit here goes to many helpful discussions with Ernesto Semán, who is writing his dissertation on the centrality of populism, both as a movement and as an idea, in hemispheric relations

12. Ian Roxborough, "Mexico," in *Latin America between the Second World War and the Cold War, 1944–1948,* ed. Leslie Bethell and Ian Roxborough (Cambridge: Cambridge University Press, 1992), 208; Lessie Jo Frazier, *Salt in the Sand: Memory, Violence, and the Nation-State in Chile, 1890 to the Present* (Durham, NC: Duke University Press, 2007), for the Chilean strike.

13. "U.S. Aid is Sought in Latin America," *New York Times,* January 3, 1948.

14. "Studies Prepared for Bogotá Talks," *New York Times,* February 2, 1948.

15. "Marshall Urges Latins to Put Need of Our Help After ERP," *New York Times,* April 2, 1948.

16. "Marshall Urges Latins to Put Need of Our Help After ERP," *New York Times,* April 2, 1948.

17. "Marshall's Bogotá Difficulties," *Washington Post,* April 6, 1948. Latin American nations had little choice but to formally accept the terms offered by Marshall, yet Washington still had difficulty putting a comprehensive legal framework protecting corporate property rights immediately into effect. The U.S. delegation did manage to have the delegates sign on to an "Economic Agreement of Bogotá," designed to regulate the treatment of foreign investors, but eight countries entered reservations to a clause stipulating full compensation for nationalized companies, and the Agreement never went into effect. Furthermore, an effort by Washington earlier in 1948 in Havana, Cuba, to create an International Trade Organization likewise failed.

18. "No Big Applause," *New York Times,* April 9, 1948.

19. "Bogotá Warning Relayed by U.S. Agency," *Christian Science Monitor,* April 14, 1948.

20. "Gaitán Renowned as Colombian Jurist," *New York Times,* April 10, 1948.

21. Another New Left icon, Fidel Castro, was also in Bogotá as part of a student delegation; Castro, who like García Márquez considered himself a rebel against form, against, in his case, Cuba's highly stylized tradition of declamation, made even more rigid when performed by Cuban Stalinists, has likewise praised Gaitán's "precise and eloquent use of language," citing it as influencing his own epic oratory style. Gabriel García Márquez *Living to Tell the Tale*, ed. and trans. Edith Grossman (New York: Vintage, 2004), 278.

22. Ibid., 278.

23. *Foreign Relations of the United States 1951,* vol. 2: *The United Nations; The Western Hemisphere* (Washington, DC: Government Printing Office, 1979).

24. "Bogotá Warning Relayed by U.S. Agency," *Christian Science Monitor,* April 14, 1948, "Congress Told Bloody Revolt Could Happen Here," *Los Angeles Times,* April 16, 1948; "New Dealers Planted the Seed," *Chicago Daily Tribune,* June 11, 1948; "What Really Went on at Bogotá," *Christian Science Monitor,* May 3, 1948.

25. Timothy Mason Roberts in *Distant Revolutions: 1848 and the Challenge to American Exceptionalism* (Charlottesville: University of Virginia Press, 2009).

26. "What Really Went on at Bogotá," *Christian Science Monitor,* May 3, 1948

27. Leslie Bethell and Ian Roxborough, eds., *Latin America between the Second World War and the Cold War, 1944–1948* (Cambridge: Cambridge University Press, 1992).

28. "Latin Republics Look for U.S. Aid," *New York Times,* April 4, 1948.

29. For a fuller discussion of the following argument, see Greg Grandin, "The Liberal Traditions in the Americas: Rights, Sovereignty, and the Origins of Liberal Multilateralism," *American Historical Review,* February 2012.

30. "United States Interventions," *ReVista* (Spring/Summer 2005): 6–9.

31. Lloyd Gardner, *Economic Aspects of New Deal Diplomacy* (Madison: University of Wisconsin Press, 1964); Thomas Ferguson, "Industrial Conflict and the Coming of the New Deal: The Triumph of Multinational Liberalism in America," in *The Rise and Fall of the New Deal Order, 1930–1980*, ed. Steve Fraser and Gary Gerstle (Princeton, NJ: Princeton University Press, 1989).

32. Gaddis Smith, *The Last Years of the Monroe Doctrine, 1945–1993* (New York: Macmillan, 1995), 72. For the report, see Roger Trask, "George F. Kennan's Report on Latin America (1950)," *Diplomatic History* 2:3 (June 1978), 307–312.

33. George F. Kennan Papers, "Diary Notes of Trip to South America," box 299, folder 37, Mudd Library, Princeton University.

34. Eric Posner, "All Justice, Two, is Local," *New York Times,* December 30, 2004; George W. Bush's ambassador to the United Nations, John Bolton, cited this withdrawal as evidence for why the U.S. should not support the new International Criminal Court. See Bolton, "Courting Danger," *National Interest* (Winter 1998–1999); see also Anthony Amato, "Modifying U.S. Acceptance of the Compulsory Jurisdiction of the World Court," *American Journal of International Law* 79 (1985), 385, and Anthony D'Amato, "Trashing Customary International Law," *American Journal of International Law* 81:1 (1987), 101–105.

35. Stuart Malawer, "Reagan's Law and Foreign Policy, 1981–1987: The Reagan Corollary of International Law," *Harvard International Law Journal,* 29:1 (1988), 85–109.

36. Pickering said Operation Just Cause paved the way for unilateral action in Iraq: "having used force in Panama, and in Grenada in 1983, there was a propensity in Washington to think that force could provide a result more rapidly, more effectively, more surgically than diplomacy;" the invasion's success meant "the notion that the international community had to be engaged...was ignored." *Foreign Policy* (December 18, 2009).

37. "U.S. Denounced by Nations Touchy About Intervention," *The New York Times,* December 21, 1989.

38. Luigi Einaudi, "Remarks to Organization of American States" (December 22, 1989) reprinted in U.S. Department of State, *Panama: A Just Cause,* Current Policy Document 1240 (1990), 3.

39. Richard Allen, "For the Record," *Washington Post*, June 4, 1981.

40. In U.S. Congress, House of Representatives, *Review of the 37th Session and Upcoming 38th Session of the U.N. Commission on Human Rights: Hearing before the Subcommittee on Human Rights and International Organizations of the Committee on Foreign Affairs*, 97th Cong., 1st sess., November 16, 1981 (Washington, DC: Government Printing Office, 1982), 12–14. For Abrams' authorship, see Aryeh Neier, *Taking Liberties: Four Decades in the Struggle for Human Rights* (New York: Public Affairs, 2003), 185–186.

3

SOUTHEAST ASIA IN THE COLD WAR

BRADLEY R. SIMPSON

As he welcomed delegates from twenty-nine newly independent states to the Afro-Asian conference in Bandung, Indonesia, in April 1955, Indonesia's president Sukarno warned:

> I beg of you do not think of colonialism only in the classic form which we of Indonesia, and our brothers in different parts of Asia and Africa, knew. Colonialism has also its modern dress, in the form of economic control, intellectual control, actual physical control by a small but alien community within a nation. It is a skillful and determined enemy, and it appears in many guises.[1]

Sukarno's admonition offers a reminder that for many countries the process of decolonization was inseparable from the imperatives of economic and political development and the shadow cast by U.S.-Soviet competition. Nowhere was this more true than in Southeast Asia, where between 1945 and 1975 decolonization and Cold War conflict unfolded with dizzying speed and sometimes unimaginable violence, reshaping the daily lives of citizens, the social and political structures of their states, and the regional and global contexts in which they interacted.

Scholars writing about Southeast Asia and the Cold War continue to wrestle with basic questions of periodization, perspective, and method. When and how did the Cold War "come" to Southeast Asia, transforming myriad local anticolonial and nationalist struggles into geopolitical contests? Why and how did the United States, Soviet Union, China, and the European powers come to view their interests in the region in Cold War terms? What is the most useful analytical framework for apprehending the imbrication of local political struggles with superpower conflict? And how did Cold War dynamics intersect with other processes—demographic, environmental, developmental, and cultural—that preceded, transcended, or don't fit comfortably within a Cold War framework? This chapter briefly examines some of the broad themes animating recent scholarship on Southeast Asia and the Cold War, surveying both the dimensions of superpower competition and intervention in the region and some of the ways that local forces drew upon the ideological and material resources of Cold War conflict to advance their own goals. It argues that the Cold War in Southeast Asia was not simply a geopolitical competition between the United States, Soviet Union, and China, but also an ideological contest rooted in divergent visions of modernity and social change, in which the direction of decolonization, development, and state building served as a key terrain of conflict.

War, Decolonization, and the Eruption of Cold War in Southeast Asia

Decolonization preceded the superpower conflict with which it later became so entwined, but its rapid collapse obscures both the relative stability of empire until 1941 and its continuity with the postwar period.[2] In 1940 only Thailand claimed independence, while the rest of the region remained firmly under American, French, British, Dutch, and Portuguese rule. Although the United States made plans for the eventual independence of the Philippines, its European allies envisioned colonial rule continuing far into the future. Charles de Gaulle's colonial commissioner famously declared in 1944 that "the aims of France in her civilizing work in the colonies exclude any idea of self-government, any possibility of development outside the French Empire."[3]

Japan's wartime conquest of the region, however, exposed the fragility of European and American empire, while revealing deep divisions within anticolonial movements. Some nationalist leaders—such as Aung San of Burma, Thai prime minister Phibun Songkram, and Sukarno of Indonesia—sought through accommodation with Japanese authorities to advance or preserve national independence, while Communist parties generally chose the path of armed resistance and faced harsh repression. Japan's brutal occupations, meanwhile, eroded any initial enthusiasm that its displacement of European overlords created, while inflicting enormous suffering and casualties on the region's inhabitants. The war's destruction also accelerated prewar patterns of anticolonial resistance and visions of eventual independence. Japanese authorities, recognizing by 1943 that defeat was likely, sought to encourage such hopes and, if possible, to galvanize military resistance to reconquering allied forces by granting nominal independence to Burma and the Philippines in 1943 and encouraging Vietnam and Indonesia to declare independence in August 1945.[4]

As the war wound down, both colonizer and colonized maneuvered to legitimize their claims for the reestablishment of colonial control, independence, or social transformation. Colonial powers returning to Burma, Indonesia, Vietnam, and Malaya met nascent armies trained by Japanese occupation authorities, popular militias, and anti-Japanese guerilla movements, often led by local communist parties. Only the Philippines enjoyed immediate independence, granted by United States in 1946 to elites who assured close political continuity with the colonial era. While Britain grudgingly sought to accommodate or moderate the demands of anticolonial activists, giving independence to Burma by 1948 and self-rule for Malaya, both the Netherlands and France sought to reimpose imperial rule, sparking violent resistance.

Forces on all sides of the colonial divide recognized that U.S. power would help to determine the outcome of independence struggles. Although they initially considered the region a British and French responsibility, U.S. officials watched events in Southeast Asia with growing concern, linked to their now global conception of the nation's interests and responsibilities. They hoped to reconstruct a shattered international political and economic order on the basis of collective security, an open world economy, and self-determination—priorities that underpinned their support, in principle, for a gradual transition in Southeast Asia toward self-government. Many officials believed that attempts to restore colonial rule would only strengthen more radical forces, except in places such as Malaya, where victory by Communist insurgents appeared to be the immediate alternative.[5] They also considered Southeast Asian resources as vital to the economic revival and reconstruction of Europe and Japan. U.S. and British bases in the Philippines and Singapore, meanwhile, figured prominently in postwar strategic planning premised upon the projection of U.S. air power and protection of vital shipping lanes. But American anticolonialism often clashed with a deeply held European cultural chauvinism that judged the inhabitants of many Asian colonies unfit for immediate independence or in need of authoritarian rulers.[6]

Though the imbrication of decolonization with superpower conflict was always probable, it was not inevitable. British ambassador to Moscow Frank Roberts reported to Foreign Minister Ernest Bevin in 1946 that Stalin's attention was firmly fixed on the postwar settlement in Europe and that Southeast Asia was "outside the immediate scope of Russian expansionism," with local Communist parties receiving little aid.[7] Two years later, however, a changed international Communist line, emphasizing immutable conflict between the capitalist and socialist "camps"; Communist-led revolts in Indonesia, Burma, the Philippines, and Malaya; and intensified fighting in Indochina raised concerns of a Soviet offensive, though Soviet sources suggest that the initiative lay with local forces.[8] The Philippine and British governments responded by launching broad-based counterinsurgency campaigns, while Indonesia's republican government crushed the so-called Madiun revolt, convincing the Truman administration to finally pressure the Netherlands to grant independence in 1949.

The 1949 Chinese Revolution and the internationalization of the Korean civil war in June 1950 marked a turning point in the Southeast Asian Cold War. In their wake, hawkish officials in London and Paris finally convinced Washington that the French attempt to reconquer Vietnam was a defense of Western interests from global Communist aggression. The Korean War also disrupted U.S. plans to reintegrate Japan's former East Asian colonies with Tokyo's industrial base, heightening Southeast Asia's perceived strategic importance to Japanese recovery in the process.[9] In response, the Truman administration approved the recommendation of NSC-68 to dramatically increase military spending, and threw its support behind the French military effort in Indochina and the Philippine government's anti-Huk campaign. The Soviet Union and China recognized the Democratic Republic of Vietnam (DRV); in January 1950 China began providing substantial military, technical, and financial assistance to Viet Minh forces.[10]

A combination of counterinsurgency tactics and modest political reforms enabled Philippine president Ramon Magsaysay to defeat the politically divided Hukbalahap movement by 1953. The Viet Minh, however, continued to gain strength and the following year inflicted a decisive defeat on the French. Eager to reduce conflict with the United States, Soviet and Chinese officials pressed Malaya's Communist Party and the Viet Minh to negotiate an end to their respective conflicts. Zhou Enlai helped convince Ho Chi Minh to accept a political settlement in May 1954, which temporarily divided Vietnam, with Viet Minh forces occupying the northern half of the country pending national elections.[11] The Geneva Accords convinced many DRV leaders that Moscow and Beijing would prioritize geopolitical and domestic interests over Communist internationalism. The Eisenhower administration quickly rejected the notion of unifying Vietnam under Communist rule. It moved instead to create a new state in the southern half of the country, led by the Catholic anti-communist Ngo Dinh Diem, while seeking to contain the "advance" of Communism throughout the region with the formation of the Southeast Asia Treaty Organization (SEATO).[12] The Southeast Asian Cold War was fully joined.

Superpower Intervention and the Wars for Indochina

Neither superpower wanted to internationalize Vietnam's war for independence—nor did many imagine such an outcome in 1945, as the Viet Minh asserted Vietnam's independence from France following Japan's withdrawal. But after 1954 a wider war became more likely as a succession of American presidents staked their own and the nation's credibility on preserving an "independent," non-Communist South Vietnam, Cambodia, and Laos. U.S. foreign policy elites believed that Vietnamese unification under Communist leadership, backed by China and the Soviet Union, would gravely damage U.S. global interests.[13] Soviet and Chinese officials mostly agreed, viewing the Vietnamese Revolution's success as a barometer for Communist parties everywhere and as validation of their own, oft competing models of socialist transformation.[14] Only by acknowledging the ideological nature of these commitments can the otherwise baffling U.S. and Soviet intervention in landlocked Laos' three-sided civil war be explained. Laos provoked a superpower crisis before cooler heads prevailed and negotiated a settlement between royalist, Pathet Lao, and neutralist forces in 1962.[15]

Northern Vietnam's Communist leadership, while confident of ultimate victory, hoped to buy time while building socialism in the north, agitating peacefully for unification and avoiding conflict with the United States. But Ngo Dinh Diem's fierce repression of former Viet Minh activists forced their hand, and in 1960—again over Soviet and Chinese objections—they authorized the resumption of armed struggle in the south and the formation of the National Liberation Front (NLF). The NLF's military success over the next three years and Diem's inability to garner widespread public support also forced the hand of the Kennedy administration, which acquiesced to a coup against the South Vietnamese president in November 1963, hoping that a new government might turn the tide. These hopes, the Johnson administration soon realized, were ephemeral. Despite European opposition and Johnson's own deep pessimism that a U.S. takeover of the war could prevent defeat, in late 1964 he authorized the bombing of North Vietnam and the introduction of large numbers of U.S. ground forces.[16] By the end of

1965, over 175,000 U.S. troops were fighting in South Vietnam, a number that would triple within two years.

The U.S. escalation of the war unfolded amidst the widening conflict between China and the Soviet Union for self-proclaimed leadership of the international Communist movement.[17] For Southeast Asian Communist Parties the Sino-Soviet split both created opportunities for seeking increased assistance and exacerbated domestic tensions as Moscow and Beijing sought local allies. Mao dramatically deepened Chinese support for North Vietnam in step with the U.S. escalation, sending more than 300,000 troops along with heavy weapons and technical assistance, but he derided Moscow's decision to do the same. "The Soviets are now assisting you," Mao told Pham Van Dong in 1965, "but their help is not sincere. [Vietnam] will be better [off] without the Soviet aid." Though many North Vietnamese officials sided with China on questions of ideology, they grew increasingly dependent upon Soviet assistance, especially after the 1968 Tet Offensive devastated NLF cadres in the south and forced a shift to more conventional combat involving People's Army of Vietnam (PAVN) units.[18] The U.S. "opening" to China further deepened Hanoi's strained relationship with Beijing, which veered into open hostility, and by 1979 into military conflict.

The Sino-Soviet split had an equally dramatic effect in Indonesia, where in 1964 the Partai Komunis Indonesia (PKI) began tilting openly toward China and the increasingly radical Sukarno began identifying Indonesia as part of a "Jakarta-Phnom Penh-Hanoi-Peiping-Pyongyang axis," deepening the already bitter conflict among the PKI, the army, and Muslim forces. Chinese officials threw their weight behind Sukarno's campaign of *Konfrontasi* against the formation of Malaysia and prodded the PKI to launch a campaign of "unilateral action" in favor of land reform, moves which convinced many Western officials that the country was on the road to Communist domination. In response both Britain and the United States intensified covert operations in the hopes of sparking a violent clash between the PKI and the army and resolving the country's seemingly intractable economic and political crises. When disaffected military officers and top PKI leaders attempted a purge of the army high command in late 1965, anti-Communist officers led by Suharto used the failed putsch at a "pretext for mass murder," annihilating the largest nonbloc Communist Party in the world, to the delight of U.S., Thai, Malaysian, and even Soviet officials, who were glad to see a pro-Chinese party removed from the scene.[19] A few months later Sukarno was ousted and relations with China were severed, and Suharto began constructing the Western-backed, anti-Communist "new order" that would keep him in power for the next thirty-two years.

Cold War historians now rightfully place the Vietnam War in an international frame—made possible by the partial opening of Chinese, Russian, and Vietnamese archives—stressing the ways it bound the region together through cross-border flows of resources, solidarities, men, machines, and killing. The PKI's destruction prompted both China and the Soviet Union to redouble their commitment to Vietnam, illustrating the linked fortunes of the Southeast Asian Left. The 1968 Tet Offensive in South Vietnam, though a military defeat and strategic setback for North Vietnam, nevertheless signaled a growing confidence that helped to inspire renewed Communist insurgencies in Thailand, Malaysia, and the Philippines. As during the Korean War, U.S. military spending increased revenues for countries like the Philippines and Malaysia that produced strategic commodities or became sites of war-related subcontracting, but Thailand witnessed perhaps the most dramatic transformation. Tens of thousands of American troops served out their tours on U.S.-constructed air bases that dispatched bombers over North Vietnam, while the fiercely anti-Communist Royal Thai Government contributed a division of combat troops, covertly helped to prop up the non-Communist Royal Lao Government, and organized Hmong tribesmen to fight the Pathet Lao. The U.S. presence profoundly affected Thai society, fueling a massive temporary service economy geared to meeting the economic and sexual needs of American troops, as well as an explosion in the regional trafficking of drugs and women's bodies that long outlasted the war.[20]

New sources and methods for approaching the Vietnam War, however, should not obscure analysis of its central consequences for the people of the region—destruction, death, and displacement on an almost unimaginable scale.[21] American bombing and fighting on both sides killed at least two million Vietnamese, while the U.S. spraying of chemical defoliants in the south destroyed more than thirty million acres of farmland and forest. Laos and Cambodia bore the brunt of the war's expansion, as the Nixon administration in 1969 began secretly bombing both nations in an effort to cut off the Ho Chi Minh trail and destroy the DRV-backed Pathet Lao and Khmer Rouge insurgencies, dropping nearly five million tons of munitions through 1973. Bombardment of such magnitude and invasions by U.S. and Vietnamese troops in 1969 and 1970 shattered both societies, killing hundreds of thousands, uprooting millions, and making Laos the most bombed country in history. The U.S. intervention, moreover, strengthened both insurgencies, forcing a shotgun marriage in Cambodia between the popular Prince Sihanouk and the then marginal Khmer Rouge and dramatically increased the chances that their brutalized, and increasingly brutal, remnants would ascend to power once American troops withdrew.

The withdrawal of U.S. troops begun in 1969 by newly elected president Richard Nixon and the opening to China two years later prompted anxious reappraisals among the nonsocialist states of Southeast Asia "about the uncertainties that had arisen concerning U.S. support," as Thai deputy prime minister General Praphat Charusathien warned the U.S. ambassador.[22] One response was an increasing commitment to regionalism. In 1967 Malaysia, Singapore, Thailand, the Philippines, and Indonesia formed the Association of Southeast Asian Nations (ASEAN) as a vehicle for facilitating greater economic and political cooperation, speaking to the growing desire for "Asian solutions to Asian problems." By 1971 Malaysia was floating proposals to make Southeast Asia a "zone of peace, freedom and neutrality" and proclaiming "that this region of ours is no longer to be regarded as an area to be divided into spheres of influence of the big powers." All Southeast Asian states began looking, however warily, beyond Vietnam and toward a reduced U.S. commitment.[23] Efforts to secure increased economic and military assistance as a hedge against the accelerating U.S. drawdown thus marched hand in hand with initiatives to improve relations with North Vietnam, the Soviet Union, and especially China. Malaysian prime minister Tun Razak described his country's 1974 establishment of diplomatic relations with Beijing as "a psychological breakthrough for Southeast Asia." Other countries soon followed suit.[24]

Just as the politics of the Sino-Soviet split helped to shape the war's escalation, so too did Washington's desire to pursue détente with China and the Soviet Union as a means of extracting itself from Vietnam shape its end. As peace negotiations gathered momentum over the course of 1972, all three countries pressured their ostensible local allies to accept an ambiguous agreement that would leave many of the war's core issues unresolved. North Vietnam's Communist leaders and South Vietnamese president Nguyen Van Thieu both recognized that the decades-long conflict was entering its decisive stage. Both sought to improve their position on the ground and extract maximum aid from their superpower patrons before signing a formal agreement in January 1973.[25] But even possession—on paper—of one of the world's largest and best equipped armies could not resolve the underlying structural weaknesses of the South Vietnamese regime or its cohorts in Laos and Cambodia, or mask the U.S. Congress' unwillingness to continue funding a senseless, destructive war whose outcome was no longer in doubt.[26] A probing operation by North Vietnamese forces in late 1974 quickly turned into a rout of the disintegrating South Vietnamese army, and four months later, on April 30, 1975, PAVN and NLF forces entered Saigon, just two weeks after Khmer Rouge guerrillas took Phnom Penh. By the end of the year, the coalition government established in Vientiane by the Paris Peace Accords also collapsed, and the Pathet Lao established the Lao Democratic Republic. Soon after occupying the Cambodian capital, Pol Pot began emptying it, turning the country's calendar back to Year Zero and setting in motion a genocidal program of revolutionary reconstruction that would take an estimated 1.7 million lives.[27] The wars for Indochina were over. Cambodia's agony was just beginning.

The Dilemmas of Development

The newly independent and decolonizing states of Southeast Asia not only had to navigate the shoals of superpower conflict, but also had to create viable states, pursue economic development, and construct postcolonial national identities. Most achieved only partial success and found themselves yoked to former imperial metropoles by restrictive trade agreements or military bases, dominated by foreign capital, and/or crippled by debt and the demands of postwar reconstruction. All faced "extreme dependence on world markets for primary products," as well as severe shortages of indigenous capital, technology, skilled personnel, and industrial production for local use.[28] Few Southeast Asian governments, moreover, could meet rapidly rising expectations for economic growth and social justice, as foreign investment failed to materialize and terms of trade in raw materials vis-à-vis industrialized nations declined over time, increasing both the appeal of various statist industrialization schemes and the need for foreign assistance.[29]

The United States, Soviet Union, and China viewed Southeast Asia's development challenges as a terrain of opportunity for demonstrating the validity of their own comprehensive visions of social change. Each conceived of development in both economic and ideological terms not only as a bundle of practices, institutions, and growth targets, but also as an expression of national identity linked to their own histories. Many U.S. officials and academics embraced variants of modernization theory, which purported to describe a linear, universal process of development toward a common liberal-capitalist modernity. They believed that comprehensive programs of technical and economic assistance might speed the progress of nations toward self-sustaining growth, while military aid would insure stability amidst the political turbulence that rapid progress unleashed. Soviet officials and intellectuals tended to view development in similar terms, but posited socialist modernity as the endpoint and Communist parties as vanguards. They pointed to the Soviet model of heavy industrialization and authoritarian rule as a more relevant example for newly independent countries seeking to rapidly transform state and society.[30] China's rapid industrialization and land-reform efforts posed challenges to both the United States and the Soviet Union, given the similarities the People's Republic shared with other newly independent Asian nations. Though China was immensely poor and provided little economic and military aid outside of Vietnam, Mao freely proffered advice to Southeast Asian Communist parties, usually pushing for greater militancy on land reform and class struggle. The results were by no means encouraging. The DRV's pursuit after 1954 of a Chinese-inspired program of land reform proved politically disastrous, and the Indonesian Communist Party's intensification of rural class struggle in 1964, partly at the behest of Chinese officials, intensified political conflict with military and Muslim landlords, helping to prepare the ground for political conflagration a year later.

The United States, far and away the world's wealthiest country, between 1945 and 1975 provided tens of billions of dollars in direct and indirect economic, technical, and military assistance to Southeast Asian states, with the lion's share going to Thailand, the Philippines, South Vietnam, and Indonesia. U.S. assistance, joined to a wide range of multilateral institutions such as the UN Economic Commission for Asia and the Far East (ECAFE) and private foundations, aimed to train and equip military and police forces; educate teachers, engineers, agronomists, economists, development planners, and administrators; build roads, dams, factories, and irrigation systems; finance agricultural modernization; and change the eating and reproductive habits of rural dwellers.[31] Though the Soviet Union was initially a minor contributor to regional aid schemes, beginning in the mid-1950s Premier Nikita Khrushchev initiated expansive programs of economic and technical assistance to nonaligned countries such as Burma and Indonesia, the latter of which received more than $750 million in aid between 1956 and 1965.[32]

The United States, Soviet Union, and China all expected that aid would confer influence, and often blamed recipients' culture, race, or general backwardness when it did not. North Vietnamese officials, dependent first on Chinese and then on Soviet military and economic assistance, repeatedly clashed with their purported allies over development plans as well as military and diplomatic strategy. Other Southeast Asian governments played superpower suitors against each other to extract more assistance or increase their internal latitude. Both the United States and the Soviet Union, between 1957 and 1965, plied Indonesia with economic and military assistance, only to watch President Sukarno tilt Indonesia away from both powers and toward Beijing. The Philippines' rapacious President Ferdinand Marcos set the standard, extorting hundreds of millions of dollars in U.S. assistance as a condition of base renegotiations and the dispatch of token forces to Vietnam. But the provision of aid, and the strings with which it was often attached, invariably inflected domestic politics, as local actors often grafted Cold War divisions onto local conflicts. Governments in Indonesia, Burma, Cambodia, and the Philippines each witnessed popular upheavals over the perceived or actual conditions attached to U.S. assistance and the diminution of sovereignty which these implied. Washington's insistence in 1952 that Indonesia sign a mutual security agreement as a condition of economic aid led to the fall of the pro-American Sukiman cabinet. Though utterly dependent on U.S. assistance for their survival, South Vietnamese leaders routinely castigated U.S. administrations to demonstrate their independence and bolster their nationalist credentials against critics both left and right.[33]

Some states were willing to accept aid but unwilling to take sides, and hoped to escape the straightjacket of superpower dependence by pursuing a diplomatic strategy of nonalignment. Sukarno's hosting of the Afro-Asian Conference in Bandung in 1955, and the creation of the Non-Aligned Movement (NAM) in 1961, symbolized postcolonial nations' determination to carve out a space for independent political and economic development. But nonalignment proved difficult in practice, especially for those states bordering China or Vietnam. Prince Norodom Sihanouk desperately attempted to maintain Cambodia's neutrality throughout the 1950s and 1960s as the war in Vietnam expanded, accepting and then rejecting assistance from all sides and even severing relations with the United States. The war ineluctably engulfed his country, however, and he was ousted in a military coup in 1970 by Lon Nol, who promptly aligned Cambodia with the United States for the rest of the war. Only Burma managed to maintain its neutrality throughout the period. After Ne Win came to power in a military coup in 1962, the government declared it would pursue a "Burmese way to socialism," effectively withdrawing from the Cold War system and choosing the path of autarchy, international isolation, and grinding poverty even as it fought multiple ethnic insurgencies.[34]

The daunting challenges of pursuing economic growth and political stability strained the capacities of civilian governments throughout the region. In late 1957 dissident Indonesian military officers rebelled against the central government and its alleged economic neglect of the outer islands, igniting a brief but fierce civil war. In response, Sukarno proclaimed martial law and, with support from much of the armed forces, brought an end to Indonesia's system of parliamentary democracy.[35] Military coups soon toppled civilian governments in Thailand and Burma, suggesting a regional trend toward authoritarian rule. These events, along with the Soviet military and economic "aid offensive" in the developing world, helped nudge President John F. Kennedy toward a counterinsurgency approach to foreign assistance, effectively encouraging postcolonial states to wage war on their own populations in the name of development. South Vietnam served as a laboratory for this militarized approach, which included the forced relocation of peasants into fortified "strategic hamlets," but it was hardly alone. "With subversion, there is no development," Philippine foreign secretary Carlos P. Romulo quipped to U.S. secretary of state Henry Kissinger in 1974, aptly summarizing the logic of "military modernization." The U.S. shift in favor of military-led governments as anti-Communist shepherds of development paralleled the emerging views of armed-forces establishments throughout Southeast Asia, which over the next decade overthrew civilian governments or backed the imposition of authoritarian rule in Indonesia (1966), Thailand (1971 and 1976), and the Philippines (1972).[36]

It is difficult to make broad generalizations about the impact of the Cold War (and especially the Vietnam War) on Southeast Asian development, to disentangle the effects of war, foreign aid, and indigenous agency, or to imagine what might have been. But a few observations can be hazarded. U.S. and Soviet military aid in the region generally strengthened states, armies, and their repressive capacities at the expense of more democratic forces, usually diverting to bloated military establishments resources that might otherwise have been used to foster economic growth, and retarding progress on human rights and political democratization. As historian Nick Cullather suggests, all sides effectively viewed peasants—with their bundles of atavisms—as the enemy, to be forcefully drafted into the modern world by myriad revolutions imposed from above. Both the capitalist and Communist camps justified illiberal rule in Southeast Asia as an expedient to economic and social modernization, but even on their own terms the results were mixed. The region's reasonably steady growth after World War II was fueled in part by a long boom in commodities prices—aided by two Asian wars—that raised national incomes in Thailand, Malaysia, Indonesia, and the Philippines. This outcome may have dovetailed with U.S. hopes "to make continued high-level raw material output consistent with the economic development of the producing countries," as MIT economist Max Millikan put it.[37] But it clashed with the goals of a generation of postcolonial leaders who aimed to alter historically unequal trading relations, tackle rural inequality, create new employment at higher wages, diversify national economies, and fashion new identities. Moreover, many of the policies that nationalist regimes advocated to achieve these goals—import substitution industrialization (ISI), economic indigenization, land and labor reform—raised Cold War concerns insofar as they benefited the Left, strengthened states over markets, threatened the existing social structure in rural areas, and challenged the power of conservative local elites on whom the United States often relied for support.

Twenty years after the end of World War II, the structural position of Southeast Asian states in the nonsocialist world economy remained basically the same. In the mid-1960s, however, the fortunes of the region's countries began to diverge, along lines almost literally etched in the earth by U.S. B-52 bombers. Scholars from various disciplines continue to debate the causes and consequences of rapid economic growth in Southeast Asia, and whether—as Singapore prime minister Lee Kuan Yew wrote to U.S. national security advisor Walt Rostow in 1968—"The United States bought time for the rest of Southeast Asia by her intervention in Vietnam."[38] Rising demand in the United States, Europe, and Japan, partly war-induced, for both food and commodities produced in the region helped to fuel increased exports and both foreign and domestic investment, especially in extractive industries, textiles, and light manufacturing, while domestic demand and savings rates also witnessed a steady rise, at least in ASEAN member states. These trends accelerated after the end of the war, outpacing growth rates in many other regions of the world.

The question is, why? Some scholars, emphasizing macroeconomic indicators and echoing a landmark 1993 World Bank report on the "Asian miracle," suggest that these countries "got the basics right" by following neoliberal policy prescriptions (such as abandoning import-substitution industrialization in favor of export-oriented industrialization) that led to high growth rates.[39] Critics of the "miracle thesis," while not disputing the fact of rapid growth, question whether macroeconomic success outweighs its attendant social, political, and environmental consequences. The Philippines and Indonesia, for example, witnessed steady growth as defined by the World Bank and donor governments, which viewed the latter especially as a Cold War success story despite world-historical levels of corruption. But their comparative advantage in cheap, repressed labor and extractive industries constituted debatable long-term development strategies, though they would prove vastly profitable for foreign investors and local elites. Other scholars note that those states that achieved the highest growth rates after the late 1960s—Malaysia, Thailand, and Singapore—profited from the Cold War system but looked to develop out of it by utilizing various forms of state intervention. They took inspiration not from the United States but from Japan, which emerged as a leading investor, source of foreign assistance, and model "developmental state" seeking state-led, export-oriented growth, and competition in world rather than regional markets.[40]

Vietnam, Cambodia, and Laos moved from tragedy to horror, the developmental hopes of generations wiped out by decades of conflict and a crucial window of opportunity shuttered (the latter two remain among the poorest countries on earth). Following independence, their pursuit of autarkic strategies that cut them off from the larger streams of capital, markets, technology, and expertise available in the West compounded the near-insuperable challenges of recovering from war and, in Vietnam's case, a cruel and punitive U.S. embargo. Hanoi's adoption of the Soviet model of heavy industrialization after 1975 proved particularly ill-timed, positioning Vietnam as an inefficient node in a socialist world system already beginning to disintegrate, riding a product cycle two generations removed from the leading edge of technology.[41]

The Post-Vietnam Landscape and the End of the Cold War

In the end the dominoes did not fall. Neither U.S. nor Soviet nor Chinese ideologues were correct in anticipating that the success of revolutionary movements in the former Indochinese colonies would spread. With embarrassing speed the United States began signaling that Southeast Asia was no longer a geopolitical pivot point and that more mundane concerns such as U.S.-ASEAN trade relations would occupy Washington's attention, rendering the catastrophe to which Laos, Cambodia, and Vietnam were subjected all the more senseless. Singapore's president Lee Kuan Yew joined other Southeast Asian leaders in openly questioning Washington's credibility and commitment to the region, a sentiment Indonesia's President Suharto exploited to gain Washington's support for its invasion of the former Portuguese colony of East Timor in December 1975.[42] But anti-Communism no longer drove regional politics, even if authoritarian regimes continued to trot it out against demonstrating students, striking workers, or intellectuals overly concerned with democracy or civil liberties.

Instead, intra-Communist rivalries, overlaid with older ethno-nationalist and regional tensions between the Chinese-backed Khmer Rouge regime and the Soviet-backed government in Hanoi, emerged soon after the fall of Phnom Penh and Saigon. By now dependent upon Moscow for economic and military assistance, the DRV, struggling to consolidate its revolution after decades of constant warfare, but convinced of its leadership role in the region, developed increasingly bitter relations with China and Cambodia. "Not only does Vietnam want to annex Cambodia and Laos," Pol Pot warned Chinese premier Hua Guofeng in late 1977, "it also wants to occupy the whole of Southeast Asia."[43] In December 1978 Vietnam invaded and occupied Cambodia, quickly overthrowing the Khmer Rouge and installing the pro-Vietnamese Hun Sen regime. China responded two months later with a brief, pointless and costly invasion of northern Vietnam that accomplished nothing but cheering those anxious at the regional implications of Hanoi's actions.

The so-called Third Indochina War heaped dirt on the graves of several Cold War shibboleths, most importantly the notion that Communist internationalism trumped various local solidarities. But it strengthened ASEAN, whose divided member states nevertheless worked for the next decade to resolve the conflict and eventually incorporated the socialist states into its membership.[44] In the end both Cold War and post–Cold War forces led Vietnam to withdraw from Cambodia in 1989 and accept an ASEAN and UN-brokered settlement: the severing of the Soviet Union's $3 billion annual subsidy and Hanoi's desire to end its international isolation and follow the Chinese down the un-Communist road of enmeshment with the world economy. That fall *Fortune* magazine offered an appropriate coda to the end of the Cold War in Southeast Asia. It rhapsodically described the region's growing economic integration, fueled by a "huge supply of cheap and relatively well-educated workers" disciplined by strong states, abundant "oil, natural gas, minerals, and productive farmland," and the migration of declining Japanese and South Korean industries such as textiles, electronics, food processing, and light manufacturing. Labor activists only half-joked that the global shoe giant Nike, which set up shop in the DRV in 1990—subcontracting shoe production to South Korean factory owners employing teenage girls—was the true winner of the Vietnam War. They were half right. In the end the relentless pressures and seductions of the market would prove a far more effective vehicle for regional integration than decades of destructive superpower intervention.[45]

NOTES

1. Ministry of Foreign Affairs, Republic of Indonesia, ed., *Asia-Africa Speak from Bandung* (Jakarta, 1955), 19–29.

2. See Mark Bradley, *Imagining Vietnam and America: The Making of Postcolonial Vietnam, 1919–1950* (Chapel Hill: University of North Carolina Press, 2000).

3. Paul H. Kratoska, "Dimensions of Decolonization," in *The Transformation of Southeast Asia: International Perspectives on Decolonization,* ed. Marc Frey, Ronald W. Pruessen, and Tan Tai Yong (Armonk, NY: M. E. Sharpe, 2003), 11.

4. Ken'Ichi Goto and Paul H. Kratoska, eds., *Tensions of Empire: Japan and Southeast Asia in the Colonial and Postcolonial World* (Athens: Ohio University Press, 2003).

5. Odd Arne Westad, *The Global Cold War: Third World Interventions and the Making of Our Times* (Cambridge: Cambridge University Press, 2005), 115.

6. Seth Jacobs, *America's Miracle Man in Asia: Ngo Dinh Diem, Religion, Race, and U.S. Intervention in Southeast Asia* (Durham, NC: Duke University Press, 2005), 88–126.

7. Geoff Wade, "The Beginnings of a 'Cold War' in Southeast Asia: British and Australian Perceptions," *Journal of Southeast Asian Studies* 40:3 (October 2009), 543–565; Ilya Gaiduk, "Soviet Cold War Strategy and Prospects for Revolution in Southeast Asia," in *Connecting Histories: Decolonization and the Cold War in Southeast Asia, 1945–1962,* ed. Christian Ostermann and Christopher Goscha (Stanford, CA: Stanford University Press, 2009), 123–137.

8. Philip Deery, "Malaysia 1948: Britain's Cold War?" *Journal of Cold War Studies* 9:1 (Winter 2007), 29–54.

9. Mark Atwood Lawrence, *Assuming the Burden: Europe and the American Commitment to War in Vietnam* (Berkeley: University of California Press, 2005), 283–287; Bruce Cumings, "The Asian Crisis, Democracy, and the End of 'Late' Development," in *The Politics of the Asian Economic Crisis,* ed. T. J. Pempel (Ithaca, NY: Cornell University Press, 1999), 20.

10. Yang Kuisong, "Mao Zedong and the Indochina Wars," in *Behind the Bamboo Curtain: China, Vietnam and the World Beyond Asia,* ed. Priscilla Roberts (Stanford, CA: Stanford University Press, 2006), 57.

11. Mark Bradley, *Vietnam at War* (Oxford: Oxford University Press, 2009), 67; Shu Guang Zhang, "Constructing 'Peaceful Coexistence': China's Diplomacy toward the Geneva and Bandung Conferences, 1954–55," *Cold War History* 7:4 (2007), 509–528.

12. James *Carter, Inventing Vietnam: The United States and State Building, 1954–1968* (Cambridge: Cambridge University Press, 2008).

13. On Vietnam War historiography see Gareth Porter, "Explaining the Vietnam War: Dominant and Contending Paradigms," in *Making Sense of the Vietnam Wars: Local, National and Transnational Perspectives,* ed. Mark Bradley and Marilyn B. Young (Oxford: Oxford University Press, 2008); Gary Hess, "The Unending Debate: Historians and the Vietnam War," in *America in the World: The Historiography of US Foreign Relations since 1941,* ed. Michael Hogan, (Cambridge: Cambridge University Press, 1996), 358–394.

14. Qiang Zhai, *China and the Vietnam Wars, 1950–1975* (Chapel Hill: University of North Carolina Press, 2000); Ilya Gaiduk, *Confronting Vietnam: Soviet Policy Towards the Indochina Conflict, 1954–1963* (Stanford, CA: Stanford University Press, 2003).

15. Seth Jacobs, "'No Place to Fight a War': Laos and the Evolution of U.S. Policy toward Vietnam, 1954–1963," in *Making Sense of the Vietnam Wars: Local, National, and Transnational Perspectives*, ed. Mark Philip Bradley and Marilyn B. Young (Oxford: Oxford University Press, 2007), 45–66.

16. Fredrik Logevall, *Choosing War: The Lost Chance for Peace and the Escalation of War in Vietnam* (Berkeley: University of California Press, 1999).

17. Lorenz Lüthi, *The Sino-Soviet Split: Cold War in the Communist World* (Princeton, NJ: Princeton University Press, 2008).

18. Shu Guang Zhang, "Beijing's Aid to Hanoi and United States-China Confrontations, 1964–1968," in *Behind the Bamboo Curtain: China, Vietnam, and the World beyond Asia*, ed. Priscilla Roberts (Stanford, CA: Stanford University Press, 2006), 259–319; conversation between Zhou Enlai and Pham Van Dong, Beijing, October 9, 1965, in "77 Conversations between Chinese and Foreign Leaders on the Wars in Indochina, 1964–1977," CWIHP Working Paper 22 (Washington, DC: Wilson Center, 1998), 85.

19. John Roosa, *Pretext for Mass Murder: The September 30th Movement and Suharto's Coup d'Etat in Indonesia* (Madison: University of Wisconsin Press, 2006); Brad Simpson, *Economists with Guns: Authoritarian Development and US-Indonesian relations, 1960–1968* (Stanford, CA: Stanford University Press, 2008).

20. Sutayut Osornprasop, "Amidst the Heat of the Cold War in Asia: Thailand and the American Secret War in Indochina (1960–74)," *Cold War History* 7:3 (2007), 349–371; Saundra Pollack Sturdevant and Brenda Stoltzfus, *Let the Good Times Roll: Prostitution and the U.S. Military in Asia* (New York: New Press, 1993).

21. See the indispensible Christian G. Appy, *Patriots: The Vietnam War Remembered from All Sides* (New York: Viking, 2003).

22. Telegram 4528 from the embassy in Thailand to the U.S. Department of State, April 4, 1971, *Foreign Relations of the United States, 1969–1976*, vol. 20: *Southeast Asia, 1969–1972* (Washington, DC: Government Printing Office, 2006), 284–286.

23. Shafiah Muhibat, "Third World States in the Midst of the Cold War: A Study of ASEAN's Decision to Establish the Zone of Peace, Freedom and Neutrality Proposal, 1971–1972," Center for Strategic and International Studies (Jakarta, 2004), 13.

24. Chandran Jeshrun, *Malaysia: Fifty Years of Diplomacy, 1957–2007* (Kuala Lumpur: The Other Press, 2007), 132

25. Essential is Lien-Hang T. Nguyen, *Hanoi's War: An International History of the War for Peace in Vietnam* (Chapel Hill: University of North Carolina Press, 2012); Pierre Asselin, *A Bitter Peace: Washington, Hanoi, and the Making of the Paris Agreement*, 1st ed. (Chapel Hill: University of North Carolina Press, 2002).

26. Marc Jason Gilbert, ed., *Why the North Won the Vietnam War* (New York: Palgrave, 2002).

27. Ben Kiernan, *The Pol Pot Regime: Race, Power, and Genocide in Cambodia under the Khmer Rouge, 1975–1979* (New Haven, CT: Yale University Press, 2002).

28. J. Thomas Lindblad, "The Economic Impact of Decolonization in Southeast Asia: Economic Nationalism and Foreign Direct Investment, 1945–1965," in *The Transformation of Southeast Asia: International Perspectives on Decolonization*, ed. Marc Frey, Ronald W. Pruessen, and Tan Tai Yong (London: M. E. Sharpe, 2003), 35–51.

29. Marc Frey, "Control, Legitimacy, and the Securing of Interests: European Development Policy in South-East Asia from the Late Colonial Period to the Early 1960s," *Contemporary European History* 12:4 (2003), 395–412.

30. Marc T. Berger, "Decolonization, Modernisation and Nation-Building: Political Development Theory and the Appeal of Communism in Southeast Asia, 1945–1975," *Journal of Southeast Asian Studies* 34:3 (2003), 426, 429; Michael Adas, *Dominance by Design. Technological Imperatives and America's Civilizing Mission* (Cambridge: Cambridge University Press, 2006), 247, 256.

31. Nick Cullather, "Miracles of Modernization: The Green Revolution and the Apotheosis of Technology," *Diplomatic History* 28:2 (April 2004), 227–254; Matthew Connelly, *Fatal Misconception: The Struggle to Control World Population* (Cambridge, MA: Harvard University Press, 2008).

32. Ragna Boden, "Cold War Economics: Soviet Aid to Indonesia," *Journal of Cold War Studies* 10:3 (Summer 2008), 110–128.

33. Richard Mason, "Containment and the Challenge of Non-Alignment: The Cold War and US Policy Toward Indonesia, 1950–1952," in *Connecting Histories: Decolonization and the Cold War in Southeast Asia, 1945–1962*, ed. Christian Ostermann and Christopher Goscha (Stanford, CA: Stanford University Press, 2009), 39–67.

34. Matthew Foley, *The Cold War and National Assertion in Southeast Asia: Britain, the United States and Burma, 1948–1962* (London: Routledge, 2010).

35. Audrey McTurnan Kahin and George McTurnan Kahin, *Subversion: The Secret Eisenhower and Dulles Debacle in Indonesia* (New York: New Press, 2005).

36. Ang Cheng Guan, *Southeast Asia and the Vietnam War* (London: Routledge, 2010), 99; Jeremy Kuzmarov, "Modernizing Repression: Police Training, Political Violence, and Nation-Building in the 'American Century,'" *Diplomatic History* 33:2 (April 2009), 191–221.

37. Proposal for a Research Program in Economic Development and Political Stability, CENIS (n.d.), reel 115, grant 152–152, Ford Foundation Archives, New York.

38. Guan, *Southeast Asia and the Vietnam War*, 100; Robert McMahon, "What Difference Did It Make? Assessing the Vietnam War's Impact on Southeast Asia," in *International Perspectives on Vietnam*, ed. Lloyd Gardner and Ted Gittinger (College Station: Texas A & M University Press, 2000), chap. 10.

39. Anne Booth, "Initial Conditions and Miraculous Growth: Why Is Southeast Asia So Different from Taiwan and South Korea," in *Southeast Asia's Industrial-*

ization: Industrial Policy, Capabilities and Sustainability, ed. K. S. Jomo (Hound-mills, UK: Palgrave, 2001), 30–58; World Bank, *The East Asian Miracle: Economic Growth and Public Policy* (New York: Oxford University Press, 1993); More gener-ally see Jonathan Rigg, *Southeast Asia: The Human Landscape of Modernization and Development,* 2nd ed. (London: Routledge, 2003), 3–43.

40. K. S. Jomo, ed., *Southeast Asian Paper Tigers? From Miracle to Debacle and Beyond* (London: Routledge, 2003); Peter Dauvergne, *Shadows in the Forest: Japan and the Politics of Timber in Southeast Asia* (Cambridge: Cambridge University Press, 1997).

41. Ronald Bruce St. John, *Revolution, Reform, and Regionalism in Southeast Asia: Cambodia, Laos and Vietnam* (London: Routledge, 2006).

42. Robert McMahon, *The Limits of Empire: The United States and Southeast Asia since World War II* (New York: Columbia University Press, 1999), 182–186; Brad Simpson, "'Illegally and Beautifully': The United States, the Indonesian Inva-sion of East Timor, and the International Community," *Cold War History* 5:3 (2005), 281–315.

43. Conversation between Pol Pot and Hua Guofeng, September 29, 1977, in "77 Conversations between Chinese and Foreign Leaders on the Wars in Indochina, 1964–1977," CWIHP Working Paper 22 (Washington, DC: Wilson Center, 1998), 285.

44. Alice Ba, *(Re)Negotiating East and Southeast Asia: Region, Regionalism, and the Association of Southeast Asian Nations* (Stanford, CA: Stanford University Press, 2009).

45. Louis Kraar, "Asia's Rising Export Powers," *Fortune,* November 13, 1989, 43–50.

4

SOUTH ASIA AND THE COLD WAR

DAVID C. ENGERMAN

C. D. Jackson, President Dwight Eisenhower's irrepressible psychological warfare advisor, reacted with typical bluntness to news in 1955 that the Soviet Union had begun to woo leaders of the newly independent nations of the Third World. The occasion was a top-secret National Intelligence Estimate about the "world situation," highlighting the "grave danger" that Soviet approaches to the Third World "will create an even more serious threat to the Free World than did Stalin's aggressive postwar policies." Jackson wrote to Nelson Rockefeller that the "moment of decision is upon us in a great big way on world economic policy. So long as the Soviets had a monopoly on covert subversion and threats of military aggression, and we had a monopoly on Santa Claus, some kind of seesaw game could be played." But recent Soviet overtures to Third World leaders suggested that the Soviet Union was "muscling in on Santa Claus."[1]

Only days after Jackson's yuletide warnings, Nikita Khrushchev led a Soviet delegation on an extensive tour of South Asia that made abundantly clear that Soviet aims in the Third World had no geographic limit. Even without armed superpower conflict, South Asia became a key spot for American-Soviet competition in the 1950s. Superpower policies in South Asia were at once a microcosm and a precursor of the Cold War in the Third World; the contours of the global Cold War were designed and drawn in South Asia as the countries with interests in the region navigated the rapidly changing geopolitical environment of the 1950s. As a result, South Asia's Cold War was not just a "sideshow to the main drama of the Cold War," as one historian recently put it; South Asia set the pattern for Cold War economic competition in the Third World.[2]

South Asia's Cold War in the 1950s revealed three tendencies that would recur with distressing frequency in the ensuing decades. First, South Asia marked the major entry point for Soviet efforts to win friends and influence policies in the Third World. To symbolize the new Soviet approach to the Third World, Khrushchev organized a five-week tour of South Asia, including India, Afghanistan, and Burma. Second, South Asia showed in especially vivid terms superpower competition over the means and mechanisms of economic development. Aid competition between the superpowers first took shape in South Asia and quickly extended around the globe. Finally, South Asia was a key flashpoint in the Sino-Soviet split, which would reverberate around the world—not just the Third World—in the 1960s and beyond. The Cold War in South Asia, in short, foreshadowed and indeed set the pattern for the Cold War in the Third World, a pattern that, as historian Odd Arne Westad wisely reminds us, devastated nations around the world.[3] This chapter will proceed chronologically from the demise of Britain's empire in South Asia in 1947 through the Sino-Indian border war of 1962, showing how these three trends emerged; a very brief description of how these patterns played out in the 1960s and 1970s will follow. While the primary focus will be upon India, whose founding prime minister, Jawaharlal Nehru, sought (with some success) to make his nation a key player in international politics, it will also include Afghanistan, Burma, Ceylon / Sri Lanka, and Pakistan.

The Neglect of South Asia, 1947–1953

The collapse of the European overseas empires that created the Third World began in South Asia. In a poignant ceremony on August 14, 1947, British viceroy Lord Mountbatten lowered the British flag in Delhi. As of midnight, British India, the star of the British imperial crown, was no more. In its stead were two rival states, India and Pakistan. The bloody partition that year and beyond left millions dead—and introduced the unfortunate phrase "communal violence" to the world. The independence of Ceylon and Burma followed the next year. While other colonies had gained their independence before India and Pakistan, August 1947 augured the eventual demise of the European empires that had organized so much of the world for centuries. This process would be shaped—and indeed would shape—American-Soviet tensions as they expanded into a global Cold War.[4]

In August 1947, officials in Moscow and Washington were consumed by other events, treating the birth of India and Pakistan as a relatively minor event compared with those closer to home: the Marshall Plan (announced two months prior), the upcoming elections in Italy, and American aid in the Greek Civil War. No one felt more confident about the prospects for India and Pakistan than their respective leaders, the violence of the partition notwithstanding. Founding governor-general Muhammed Ali Jinnah garnered wide attention for a speech proclaiming Pakistan a secular republic comprised of diverse religions and ethnic groups. Nehru, meanwhile, declared India's "Tryst with Destiny" and celebrated his country's pursuit of democratic development along what his Congress Party called "the socialist pattern of society."

Representatives of India embarked on a fruitless campaign to win Soviet favor and to obtain an invitation for Nehru to visit Moscow.[5] Stalin's USSR, in its darkest and most doctrinaire days, made little of the transfer of power; its diplomatic organs denounced independent India as having a "repressive" government (in large part because of its efforts against the Indian Communist Party) that was a lackey of British imperialism in a new guise.[6] While the USSR quickly extended diplomatic recognition to India, it conducted its primary foreign policy with that country through the weak and factional Communist Party of India.[7]

American officials were more welcoming, at least by the low standard set by the USSR. Nehru visited the United States in 1949, though the visit did little to improve relations. Accomplishing little of substance, the visit succeeded only in stoking personal animosities. Nehru behaved as if he considered President Harry S. Truman a "mediocre man"—a judgment that reached Truman thanks to a CIA informant in Nehru's retinue. For his part Secretary of State Dean Acheson—whom Nehru apparently considered "equally mediocre"—called Nehru "one of the most difficult men with whom I have ever had to deal."[8] As the State Department official responsible for organizing the state visit concluded, Nehru "succeeded in making himself so unpopular with Americans generally" that it hindered Indian interests.[9] This hardly laid the groundwork for close cooperation between the world's two most populous democracies.

American officials' wariness of Nehru was about more than just personal clashes; the Indian leader's proclamations of nonalignment and his insistence upon India's place as a major diplomatic power rankled Americans. Both of these traits were evident as India arrogated for itself a role in mediating the Korean War between 1950 and 1952. Yet this hardly made the country as important as Nehru believed, at least in the eyes of Truman and Stalin. Stalin continued his policy of malign neglect toward South Asia (and the Third World in general) until his death in March 1953. By that time, an energetic American ambassador, Chester Bowles, had arrived in New Delhi. The liberal Bowles was determined to win over Americans to the Indian cause—and vice versa. He was joined by Paul Hoffman, who moved from his post leading the Marshall Plan in Europe to run the newly founded and well-endowed Ford Foundation. One of Hoffman's first acts at Ford was to approach India; according to one colleague, he believed that world peace "might well be determined by what happened in India."[10] Yet Bowles and others battled against official apathy that began at the top; when Bowles told Truman that he hoped to serve in India, the president replied, "Why in the world would you want to go to India?" The president, as Bowles recalled it, "did not realize that anybody thought [India] was important."[11] The superpowers' underwhelming response to India's arrival on the world stage was due in part to superpower priorities, but also to Nehru's very public professions of nonalignment. This stance implied a rejection of Cold War polarities, a negation of the very ideologies through which Soviet and American officials understood the world. The fact that Nehru was in conflict with India's own Communist Party hardly swayed American officials at the same time that it complicated Soviet-Indian relations. The emergence of the People's Republic of China in 1949 raised the global stakes for India's future, but did not alter India's challenge to the emerging bipolar conflict.

Pakistan had an easier time in Washington in the late 1940s. Pakistan's prime minister, Liaquat Ali Khan, was in worse economic and political straits than Nehru, and he more readily accepted a patron-client relationship with the United States. From the perspective of American policymakers, Pakistan's Muslim majority and its proximity to Iran—already a focus of grave American concern for its oil resources and politically unreliable leadership—made it a focus of lavish attention, eventually backed with economic and military largesse.[12] America's ambassadors to South Asian nations concluded, at a February 1951 meeting, that the "most effective military defense" for American interests in the region required siding with Pakistan rather than India; the latter seemed unlikely to align with the West or meet Western requests for diplomatic and military alignment.[13]

By contrast, Pakistani leaders were willing to work closely with the West. Khan's reasons had little to do with the Cold War; neither Soviet military might nor Communist insurgency at home presented a serious threat. But increasing tensions with India in the wake of the partition, most notably the conflict over Kashmir, led the Pakistani leadership to pursue military aid and alliances of just the sort that the Americans and British were willing to proffer. As Assistant Secretary of State George McGhee summarized, Khan was "a man you could do business with." He and other Pakistani leaders "understood how much help they needed if their new state was to survive.... They openly sought aid on our terms, promising support in our efforts to build a defense against the Communist threat. Compared with the wishy-washy neutralist Indians they were a breath of fresh air."[14] Indian officials, not surprisingly, reacted sharply against the American-Pakistan alliance; rather than leap into the Soviet embrace, though, Nehru proclaimed nonalignment all the more loudly. But American-Pakistani ties undoubtedly offered opportunities for the Soviet Union.

Opening Salvos in the Battle for the Hearts
and Minds of South Asia, 1953–1956

Early 1953 saw changes in the leadership of both superpowers: the inauguration of war hero Dwight D. Eisenhower as American president in January and the death of Soviet dictator Joseph Stalin in early March. The impact of these changes on South Asia's Cold War was not immediately apparent. While Eisenhower campaigned against Truman's foreign policy, and especially against his conduct of the Korean War, the two agreed on the nature of the Cold War and of the Soviet enemy. Both presidents, furthermore, saw little in the Third World beyond opportunities for American businesses on the one hand and dangers of Communist subversion on the other.[15]

Eisenhower expanded Truman's efforts to develop politico-military alliances that covered the world. By 1955, Pakistan was a member of two key regional alliances organized by the U.S. government, the Central Treaty Organization (CENTO) and the Southeast Asia Treaty Organization (SEATO), despite the inconvenient fact that Pakistan was located in neither the Middle East (the basis for CENTO) nor in Southeast Asia. Pakistan's place in these alliances suggests both the framework through which American officials saw Pakistan—as part of its Middle Eastern and its Asian strategies—as well as Pakistani willingness to accede to American requests. These formal affiliations were underwritten by large and long-term American commitments to Pakistan totaling over $170 million in military aid plus economic aid of about two-thirds that amount.[16] A National Intelligence Estimate at the time noted that this expanded U.S.-Pakistan military relationship might "tend to increase Soviet military interest in the subcontinent"—a prophecy fulfilled in subsequent years.[17]

Stalin's death in 1953 was more momentous than Eisenhower's inauguration, setting in motion dramatic changes in Soviet policies at home and abroad. While lines to pay homage at Stalin's tomb still snaked around

Red Square, remaining Politburo members fashioned a leading troika that augured at least some change. While the three (Nikita Khrushchev, Georgii Malenkov, and the Stalinist Viacheslav Molotov) disagreed about much, they all agreed to depose Stalin's executioner, secret police chief Lavrentii Beriia, who was himself soon executed. Aside from initiating the post-Stalinist "thaw" of Soviet society, the three tangled over new directions in Soviet foreign policy. Molotov was the least interested in innovation, insisting the Soviet policy stay on a "class basis," by pursuing revolution around the world through local Communist parties. Malenkov and Khrushchev, in contrast, viewed the Third World as an opportunity. Only months after Stalin's death, Malenkov praised India for its diplomatic efforts to end the Korean War and called for the expansion of cultural, economic, and diplomatic ties between the USSR and India; this was a far cry from the Stalinist position (only two years earlier) that India was heeding the "requirements of the U.S.-British bloc" and would do so until the Indian Communist Party gained power.[18] That same summer of 1953, the Soviets announced that they would contribute a relatively small sum to the United Nations' Expanded Program of Technical Assistance, marking the country's first public support of economic development in the non-Communist world. Around that time, the USSR also signed a trade agreement with India.[19]

By 1955, Khrushchev had redirected Soviet foreign policy to take a more welcoming and flexible attitude toward the former colonies. He was willing to work with leaders who rejected the principles of Communism and the practicalities of Soviet leadership by offering substantial economic and military aid to states of the new Third World. Much as the U.S. National Intelligence Estimate had predicted, the initial Soviet foray would be in South Asia, though not, initially, in the military sphere.

The very first recipient of Soviet economic aid would be neighboring Afghanistan, which had received a small loan in January 1954.[20] Much larger Soviet aid programs in India starting in 1955 were the first substantial ones outside the Communist world. While the timing of these programs owed much to the Americans' decision to favor Pakistan over India, the content and aims of the programs were of longstanding interest to Nehru and Indian policymakers. From the first days of independence, Nehru had pointed to industrialization as the key to India's economic future: its path out of poverty and dependence into prosperity and freedom. And key to industrialization, Nehru and his planning advisor Prasanta Chandra Mahalanobis insisted, was steel.[21] Nehru and his economic staff sought to increase dramatically Indian steel production; toward that end, they took out a World Bank loan to expand private-sector capacity in 1952. But the bulk of the new production,

Nehru argued (following his Congress Party's notion of creating a "socialistic pattern of society"), must take place in the public sector. After seeking engineering and financial advice from Western nations, the Indian government contracted with British and German firms but had little success in the United States. Soviet aid for an Indian steel plant was announced in February 1955; the Soviets would provide credit on relatively easy terms as well as technical expertise to build the steel plant in Bhilai, and would train Indian engineers to run the plant afterwards.[22] Though Bhilai failed to live up to either Soviet or Indian expectations, it would remain a central symbol of Soviet-Indian economic cooperation for decades. Only three months later, Khrushchev hosted Nehru in Moscow—a visit all the more significant given Nehru's high profile at that April's meeting of "Afro-Asian nations" in Bandung, Indonesia.

By fall 1955, Soviet aid programs to India were well underway and rumors were afoot about Soviet aid to build the Aswan High Dam in Egypt. Then came the Soviet announcement that Khrushchev would lead a Soviet delegation to India; side trips to Afghanistan and Burma were announced later. U.S. State Department experts predicted that India was about to join the Soviet camp despite Nehru's constant professions to the contrary.[23] This conjunction of news was responsible for the fearful tone of the American intelligence estimate about the "world situation" as well as C. D. Jackson's musings about Santa Claus—and led policymakers to a broad reassessment about the nature of the Soviet threat.[24]

The Soviet delegation's tour of three South Asian countries over six weeks was more about symbolism than substance. As a symbol of Soviet aspirations in the non-Communist Third World, though, it was a brilliant success. The American press gave extensive coverage to the Soviets' public events. *Time* magazine fretted about the Soviets' "lunge to the south"—referring not so much to a compass direction, but to the "vast, uncommitted softness" that stretched across Asia and the Middle East. *Newsweek* matched this concern and raised it, writing a cover story on the "red blueprint for conquest" and fretting about the Soviet Union's "month-long invasion of Asia."[25]

These concerns were greatly exaggerated. The Soviets engaged in tourism, gave enthusiastic but contentless speeches at dozens of venues, and praised themselves and their Soviet system with mind-numbing frequency. Some of the symbolism amounted to substance, but in a way that belied American concerns; for instance, Khrushchev and his delegation met with government officials but not with the members of Communist parties. Indeed, Khrushchev criticized the Indian Communist Party's publications as "boring" and its activities as "crude." Khrushchev found Bombay, the center of Indian commerce and capitalism, to be "difficult ... from a sanitary point of view"—but, tellingly, not from a political one. This trip also provided the occasion for a larger aid agreement with Afghanistan, which Khrushchev negotiated with his Politburo colleagues by telegram; notes of the Politburo discussions make clear that the Soviets were concerned about establishing appropriate precedents for aid. Khrushchev's deputy Anastas Mikoian argued successfully that the USSR would need to provide aid if it intended to "wage serious competition" with the United States; "from the point of view of state interests"—not international class warfare—"we need to go [ahead] with aid." By the end of the trip, Khrushchev had presented medals to his delegation's pilots (who flew over 22,000 km) as well as his secret police detail. Even old-school (i.e., Stalinist) Politburo members like Molotov and Lazar Kaganovich offered praise and congratulations.[26]

Competitive Coexistence, 1956–1962

Khrushchev's jaunt through South Asia may have had few tangible results—Aeroflot, after all, didn't give frequent flier awards—but it did announce with striking effectiveness that the Soviet Union intended to compete with American aid programs in the noncommitted Third World. It was in response to this "Soviet economic offensive" (as described by observers calmer than the newsweeklies' editors) that American efforts in Third World development accelerated. The battle for the "hearts and minds" of the Third World had been joined. With that phrase came a new phase of superpower competition that Westerners often called "competitive coexistence"; Khrushchev himself preferred earthier language, comparing American and Soviet programs in the Third World to a horse race.[27]

   This battle was welcomed by a contingent of Americans who had been eagerly promoting American aid programs for the Third World—and for India in particular—since the early 1950s. By the end of 1955, they found a far more receptive hearing in the executive branch, aided immeasurably by the threat posed by Khrushchev's trip. Once and future ambassador to India Chester Bowles joined liberal economists like Max Millikan and Walt Rostow at MIT, all trying to convince their friends in the highest reaches of government that India would be the most important test case for American development programs. They made their case, much as Mikoian did in the Soviet Politburo, in terms of Cold War geopolitics.

Their exhortations to reorient American policy toward the Third World finally had the desired effect. As Nelson Rockefeller put it to President Eisenhower, the Soviet visit to India "could mark a turning point for India"— and therefore for the world. The situation in the Third World, Rockefeller warned, "may be as critical for the Free World today as that which Europe faced in 1948"—a dramatic comparison given Soviet activities in Europe that year, including the blockade of western Berlin.[28] Slowly but surely, the Eisenhower administration shifted its economic policies toward the Third World; in the felicitous phrase of historian Burton Kaufman, the administration shifted from "trade not aid" to "trade and aid."[29]

India was the primary focus for American efforts thanks to its size, its policy of nonalignment, and its economic aspirations. India's willingness to accept aid and advice from the USSR, the United States, and their respective allies made it the key site for Cold War economic competition in the Third World. A large and confusing array of advisors and aid officials swarmed through the halls of government offices in New Delhi and throughout the Indian countryside. The American embassy teemed with economists and diplomats eager to share their advice with any Indian who would listen. The Soviet embassy tried just as hard, albeit with less success. Nor were diplomats the only officials in town. Douglas Ensminger, head of the Ford Foundation's India office, with contacts across the Indian bureaucracy and more funds at his disposal than any embassy, fashioned himself the most powerful foreigner in New Delhi and had a fair claim to the honor.[30] Ford spent millions on community development, agricultural technology, and economic advising (to India's Planning Commission). The Rockefeller Foundation, too, had a substantial presence in India, focused on agricultural development and population control.[31] Aside from New Delhi, many foreign economists gathered at the Indian Statistical Institute in Calcutta, which saw itself (in the image of its director, Mahalanobis) as the central node of Indian economic policymaking. Western European and American economists joined Soviet planners and statisticians as visitors; as a result, economist and future American ambassador to India John Kenneth Galbraith recalled, the institute was "a place of easy and intense exchange between peoples of the socialist and the nonsocialist worlds and of the rich countries and the poor."[32] Such exchange was easier for some than for others. Conservative American economist Milton Friedman recalled his revulsion at the general propensity for central planning shared not just by East bloc and liberal Western economists, but even by American organizations like the Ford and Rockefeller foundations. Rostow, similarly, was convinced that Mahalanobis's influence on Indian policy "had not been benign"—but disturbed less by the propensity for central planning than by the emphasis on industrialization.[33]

India may have been a key site for Cold War economic competition, but its economy was hardly the better for it. In spite of all of the advice proffered by foreign experts, the second Indian Five-Year Plan—and the first to implement Nehru and Mahalanobis's strategy of rapid industrialization—quickly faltered. Poor harvests, insufficient exports, and shortages of industrial goods led to a foreign exchange crisis in 1957–1958 that caught the attention of political leaders around the world. A young and ambitious American senator, John F. Kennedy, on the advice of his constituents/advisors at MIT, promoted a newly created Development Loan Fund by highlighting the geopolitical importance of India's economic growth. These efforts culminated in a large American aid package from the newly created Development Loan Fund plus exchange credits from the Export-Import Bank to help ease India's foreign-exchange crisis. It was supplemented by continuing food aid under the PL-480 program, originally designed to reduce American surpluses of food grains. Finally, American officials led a World Bank consortium attempting to resolve some of India's problems in international finance.[34] Yet even these efforts were hardly sufficient to let America's "India lobby" rest easy. A contemporary economist agreed in surprisingly heated prose for an academic journal: "1957 is for our development policy what 1947 was for our European relationships. Unless the U.S. takes a bold stand now—and Indian developments offer a perfect opportunity—there may not be another chance."[35] Two years later, MIT economist Max Millikan still worried: "I cannot escape the conclusion that the shape which development planning in India takes over the next few months may be as crucial a determinant of world history over the next decade as any other single factor."[36]

Political leaders joined experts on pilgrimages to India in the heyday of competitive coexistence. Eisenhower hosted Nehru's return to the United States in 1956 and went to India (as well as Pakistan, Afghanistan, Tunisia, Turkey, Iran, Morocco, Greece, Italy, and France) in December 1959. Khrushchev returned to India three months after Eisenhower left, celebrating the recent opening of the Soviet steel plant with the toast: "Let the friendship between our countries be as strong as metal from the Bhilai metallurgical complex!"[37] He then went on to Burma, Indonesia, and Afghanistan.

As the itineraries of Eisenhower and Khrushchev suggest, India was hardly the only site of Cold War economic competition. Afghanistan—the first recipient of Khrushchev's aid—hosted a number of Soviet development programs in its north (that is, near the Soviet border) totaling over

$100 million. Official American aid programs dominated in the southern parts of the country, closest to Pakistan. Afghanistan encompassed, within the borders of a single country, the superpower competition over economic development—what one American magazine called "a strange kind of Cold War." Or, in the words of a correspondent from the *Atlantic Monthly*, Afghanistan was a "show window for competitive coexistence."[38] Over the ensuing decades, up until its army came to the fraternal assistance of a failing ruler in 1979, the Soviet Union organized some 270 major projects, mostly industry and infrastructure, across northern Afghanistan. Tens of thousands of Afghan technicians and educators were trained by Soviet teachers both at home and in the USSR.[39] Neither Western nor Soviet aid proved sufficient to underwrite major economic improvement for the bulk of the population, and the geographic distribution did little to build a sense of national unity.

Pakistan sat on the sidelines—on the American sideline, to be precise—in competitive coexistence. It received plenty of economic aid, to be sure, but in the context of its close military and diplomatic ties to the West. Its armed forces continued to grow, thanks to American munificence to the tune of $1.5 billion in the decade after 1954.[40] Economic aid was significantly smaller and less effective—though in Pakistan as in India, American experts worked closely with central-planning organs and also provided practical economic aid.[41] In return for this aid, the American government got not just a "team player" willing to join American-sponsored alliances, but also a valuable air base for U-2 overflights of the Soviet Union. Soviet officials visited Karachi in a bid to convince the Pakistan government to close the American air base, but American emoluments were too tempting to give up.[42]

American aid programs were notable for their combination of ideological investment and ideological flexibility. American officials justified American aid to India in ideologically laden terms: expanding the free world, balancing Chinese power in Asia, and challenging the Chinese model of rapid and costly economic development that was, by the late 1950s, responsible for the disaster of the Great Leap Forward. At the same time, though, many American officials exhibited a surprising degree of ideological flexibility; government and foundation programs alike worked closely with India's Planning Commission (much to Milton Friedman's chagrin), and diplomats and experts alike were willing to continue its military and economic aid programs in spite of parallel Indian arrangements with the USSR. By 1961, a leading American aid official said that Soviet aid to India was "all to the good"; Undersecretary of State George Ball concurred, confident that India was "quite capable of absorbing resources from the Soviet Union" with no ill effects.[43]

Soviet aid programs demonstrated a similar combination of ideological investment and ideological flexibility. In South Asia and elsewhere, the USSR continued to support local Communist parties and divide the world into "people's republics" and the "capitalist world." At the same time, though, Soviet officials rarely offered more than token complaints when Nehru acted against Indian Communists. On other matters, too, the Soviets were surprisingly flexible in their relationships with Third World leaders, willing to come to their aid in spite of their refusal to toe the Soviet line. Indeed, Khrushchev boasted about his flexibility when he met President John F. Kennedy in Vienna in 1961: "In India, the Communist Party does not have Nehru's support, but nevertheless we provide aid to India." And Nehru was far from the worst in this regard. Khrushchev complained to Kennedy that Egypt's Gamel Abdel Nasser "puts all Communists in prison" even while receiving substantial Soviet aid.[44]

American-Soviet competition in South Asia grew increasingly complex in the early 1960s, in a way that both reflected and predicted changes around the world. After Soviet pilots shot down a U-2 spy airplane in Soviet airspace, Pakistan's role as the base for the U-2 program became public knowledge. This led Pakistan's prime minister, Muhammed Ayub Khan, to seek ways to reduce tensions with the USSR; by 1961, Pakistan hosted its first Soviet development project.[45] But the largest factor in transforming South Asian diplomacy was China, whose changing relations with the USSR, India, and Pakistan increasingly shaped South Asian diplomacy. A series of domestic and bilateral issues appeared with bewildering complexity; the end result would significantly alter South Asia. By the late 1950s, the first signs of the Sino-Soviet split were apparent. As joint military efforts dissolved in mutual recriminations in 1958, Chinese Communist publications began to deride Soviet complacency in the international sphere.[46]

China's Mao Zedong was not hypocritical. Driven by his belief that the People's Republic of China had supplanted the Soviet Union as the carrier of the Communist banner worldwide, he embarked on increasingly assertive policies at home and abroad. When a secessionist movement brought Tibet to the brink of rebellion in 1959—thanks in part to covert American and Indian aid operations—the Chinese army cracked down. Chinese leaders felt insufficiently supported in this effort by the Soviet Union, which was trying to stay neutral in this dispute as part of its continuing efforts to woo India. Meanwhile skirmishes escalated along the contested China-India border—a border drawn under very different circumstances in 1914. Chinese border patrols notched their first casualty in 1959. Publicly, the USSR maintained neutrality—thus angering Chinese officials—but privately its diplomats scolded their Chinese comrades, whom they blamed for the incident.[47]

Sino-Indian tensions escalated in 1961, as Nehru sought to force the border issue by moving Indian soldiers into the disputed area—an act of boldness that revealed extraordinary misconceptions about Chinese capabilities and intentions.[48] Over the next year, Khrushchev sought to calm tensions between the two countries, both important to the USSR's Asian interests. He pleaded with Mao to reject a "class approach" when dealing with India, a sore point given increasingly vehement Chinese criticisms, in public and private, about the waning of Soviet revolutionary energy. But *Pravda* also rejected the Indian position in the border conflict.[49]

The ensuing Sino-Indian War in October 1962 was a brief and devastating defeat for the Indian army—and for Nehru as well. Khrushchev sought to stand aside from the armed conflict between two allies. How could he choose between his Chinese brothers and his Indian friends? But metaphorical blood proved thicker, and the Soviet Politburo offered strong support for its socialist brethren in China even after complaining that China's position was "difficult to agree with." The Politburo also registered their dissatisfaction with Nehru, suspending a shipment of MiG fighters already promised to the Indian air force.[50]

South Asia after 1962: Regional and
Geopolitical Conflicts Collide

The crushing failure of the Indian armed forces to defend its own territory led to a major shift in international relations in the whole region. South Asia would again demonstrate a Cold War pattern, in this case the deadly consequences of regional conflicts intersecting with geopolitical ones.

American officials had to suppress public expression of their enthusiasm about the turn of events in fall 1962. Even though the Sino-Indian War took place while official Washington (indeed much of the world) was focused on the American-Soviet confrontation over missiles in Cuba, one White House advisor celebrated the Himalayan conflict as one of the most crucial events of the decade. Emergency American military aid to India would at last (by this logic) bring neutralist India firmly within the American orbit.[51] American arms shipments to and military cooperation with India soon followed. This turn of events, predictably, angered India's regional rival, Pakistan, which could be placated only by substantial increases in American aid; arms transfers to Pakistan nearly quadrupled between 1960 and 1963.[52]

The South Asian arms race was speeding up. Regional rivals Pakistan and India were arming themselves against the other, injecting increasing numbers of ever more lethal weapons into a conflict that had already seen substantial violence over the previous fifteen years. While American officials hoped that military aid would bring with it increased loyalty, the opposite happened. Pakistan sought closer relations with India's newest adversary, China, as well as China's northern ally, the USSR. Indian leaders after Nehru (who died in 1964) were similarly uninterested in conforming to American expectations, and they hardly abandoned the pursuit of economic or military aid from the USSR. American officials were spending more on both economic and military aid in the region without advancing either regional stability or American leverage.

China, whose assertiveness had sparked the early-1960s crises, reaped the whirlwind. Soviet influence in the region was reduced by India's turn to American military aid. The Communist Party of India sprouted a Maoist faction that fulminated as much against the Soviet-oriented party as against Congress Party rule. And Mao's rival Khrushchev was deposed in 1964, in a palace coup that accused Khrushchev, among other things, of adventurism and irrationality in the Third World.

The flood of weapons flowing to Pakistan and India made the rivals' ongoing disputes over Kashmir and other contested borders all the more dangerous. By 1965, the two American-supplied armies engaged in a series of fatal skirmishes that soon erupted into a month-long war. The prevalence of American weapons in that conflict led each side to diversify its dependence, with Indian leaders seeking Soviet arms and Pakistani officials firming up their alliance with India's mortal foe, China. And the arms race escalated: Indian generals also reached the conclusion that they should begin serious efforts to build nuclear weapons—a project that culminated with India's "peaceful nuclear explosion" in 1974 and in turn spurred Pakistani's nuclear program. As superpower aid to South Asia expanded to incorporate not just economic but also military components, Cold War competition profoundly exacerbated local conflicts, making them more likely—and more dangerous.[53]

Cold War aid competition in South Asia had set a pattern that would apply not just throughout South Asia's Cold War, but across the whole Third World. South Asia had been the entry point for serious Soviet-American competition in the Third World, leading to the era of "competitive coexistence" that began in the 1950s—a competition that included both economic and military assistance. By the early 1960s, China joined the race, which was again a process that began in South Asia. Events in South Asia had helped precipitate the Sino-Soviet split—a long-running ideological battle that was first clarified by differences over Tibet and India. What began with the Soviet Union's "muscling in on Santa Claus" soon spread conflict around the Third World. But the arrival of superpowers (Santa Claus or his Russian counterpart, Grandfather Frost) spread neither good cheer nor Christmas gifts. Indeed, it was their attention to South Asia and the Third World that made the so-called Cold War a hot one around the globe.

NOTES

1. National Intelligence Estimate (NIE) 100-7-55, "World Situation and Trends," *Foreign Relations of the United States* [hereafter *FRUS*], *1955–57* (Washington, DC: Government Printing Office, 1987), 19:141; Jackson to Rockefeller, November 10, 1955, White House Central Files, Confidential File, Subject Files, box 61, Dwight D. Eisenhower Presidential Library (Abilene, KS).

2. Vojtech Mastny, "The Soviet Union's Partnership with India," *Journal of Cold War Studies* 12:3 (Summer 2010), 88.

3. Odd Arne Westad, *The Global Cold War: Third World Interventions and the Making of Our Times* (Cambridge: Cambridge University Press, 2005).

4. Memo to Molotov, June 29, 1951, Parallel History Project on NATO and the Warsaw Pact, ETH Zurich [hereafter Parallel History Project], http://www.php.isn. ethz.ch/collections/colltopic.cfm?lng=en&id=56285&navinfo=56154.

5. Memo to Molotov, 29 June 1951, Parallel History Project.

6. Surendra K. Gupta, *Stalin's Policy towards India, 1946–1953* (New Delhi: South Asian Publishers, 1988), 78.

7. See the useful overview in Andreas Hilger, "The Soviet Union and India: The Years of Late Stalinism" (September 2008), Parallel History Project.

8. Hillenkoetter memorandum (for Nehru's views), December 20, 1949, quoted in H. W. Brands, *India and the United States: The Cold Peace* (Boston: Twayne, 1990), 50; Dean Acheson, *Present at the Creation: My Years at the State Department* (New York: Norton, 1969), 336.

9. George C. McGhee, *Envoy to the Middle World: Adventures in Diplomacy* (New York: Harper and Row, 1983), 47.

10. Douglas Ensminger, quoted in Eugene S. Staples, *Forty Years, A Learning Curve: The Ford Foundation Programs in India, 1952–1992* (New Delhi: Ford Foundation, 1992), 6.

11. Chester Bowles, *Promises to Keep: My Years in Public Life, 1941–1969* (New York: Harper and Row, 1971), 247; Howard B. Schaffer, *Chester Bowles: New Dealer in the Cold War* (Cambridge, MA: Harvard University Press, 1993), 37.

12. For a cultural explanation of this decision, see Andrew J. Rotter, *Comrades at Odds: The United States and India, 1947–1964* (Ithaca, NY: Cornell University Press, 2000).

13. Robert J. McMahon, *The Cold War on the Periphery: The United States, India, and Pakistan* (New York: Columbia University Press, 1994), 132.

14. McGhee, *Envoy to the Middle World*, 93, 97.

15. For a useful overview, see Robert J. McMahon, "U.S. National Security Policy from Eisenhower to Kennedy," in *Cambridge History of the Cold War*, 3 vols., ed. Melvyn P. Leffler and Odd Arne Westad (Cambridge: Cambridge University Press, 2010), 1:14.

16. Herbert Hoover, Jr., memorandum, October 22, 1954, *FRUS, 1952–54*, 11:1869–1871.

17. NIE 79, "Probable Developments in South Asia" (June 30, 1953), *FRUS, 1952–54*, 11:1087.

18. Malenkov speech, August 8, 1953, and A. Alexyev article, October 31, 1951—both in *Soviet-South Asian Relations, 1947–1978*, ed. R. K. Jain (Atlantic Highlands, NJ: Humanities Press, 1979), 1:203–206.

19. Gilles Boquérat, *No Strings Attached: India's Policies and Foreign Aid, 1947–1966* (New Delhi: Manohar/Centre de Sciences Humaines, 2003), 183–184.

20. For an overview of Soviet aid to Afghanistan, emphasizing academic discussions of development there, see Paul Robinson and Jay Dixon, "Soviet Development Theory and Economic and Technical Assistance to Afghanistan, 1954–1991," *The Historian* 72:3 (Fall 2010), 599–623.

21. Mahalanobis, "Approach to Planning in India" (September, 11 1955), in *Talks on Planning* (New York: Asia Publishing House, 1961), 48.

22. Boquérat, *No Strings Attached*, 185–186; details of agreement (signed February 2, 1955), in *Soviet-South Asian Relations, 1947–1978*, ed. R. K. Jain (Atlantic Highlands, NJ: Humanities Press, 1979), 1:209–223.

23. Walter Robertson, memorandum of conversation, November 18, 1955, *FRUS, 1955–57*, 8:296–298.

24. Robert J. McMahon, "Illusion of Vulnerability: American Reassessments of the Soviet Threat, 1955–1956," *International History Review* 18:3 (August 1996), 591–619.

25. "Communists: Lunge to the South," *Time* 66 (December 19, 1955), 24; "Route of Conquest: Communists Go by Way of Asia—Africa Next," *Newsweek* 46 (November 28, 1955), 47–48ff.

26. On the visit, see *Missiia druzhby: Prebyvanie N.A. Bulganina i N.S. Khrushcheva v Indii, Birme, Afganistane*, 2 vols. (Moscow: Pravda, 1956). On the Politburo debate (December 16, 1955), see *Prezidium TsK KPSS 1954–1964* (hereafter *Prezidium 1954–1964*), ed. A. A. Fursenko, 3 vols. (Moscow: Rosspen, 2003), 1:71–75.

27. Washington's National Planning Association sponsored a series on "Competitive Coexistence" that included seven short monographs in 1959–1960; Khrushchev, "Rech' na torzhestvennom grazhdanskom prieme v Deli (12 February 1960)," in N. S. Khrushchev, *O vneshnei politike Sovetskogo Soiuza, 1960 god*, 2 vols. (Moscow: Gospolizdat, 1961), 1:88.

28. Rockefeller to Eisenhower, November 7, 1955, Declassified Document Retrieval System (DDRS), CK3100180695.

29. Burton I. Kaufman, *Trade and Aid: Eisenhower's Foreign Economic Policy, 1953–1961* (Baltimore: Johns Hopkins University Press, 1982), 95.

30. See the opening sections of Ensminger Oral History, Douglas Ensminger Papers, MS 1315, box 1, Yale University Library, New Haven, CT.

31. Dennis Merrill, *Bread and the Ballot: The United States and India's Economic Development, 1947–1963* (Chapel Hill: University of North Carolina Press, 1990).

32. John Kenneth Galbraith, *A Life in Our Times: Memoirs* (Boston: Houghton Mifflin, 1981), 346–347.

33. Milton Friedman and Rose D. Friedman, *Two Lucky People: Memoirs* (Chicago: University of Chicago Press, 1998), 257; Walt W. Rostow, *Eisenhower, Kennedy, and Foreign Aid* (Austin: University of Texas Press, 1985), 51.

34. Merrill, *Bread and the Ballot*, 144–147. Amit Das Gupta, "Development by Consortia: International Donors and the Development of India, Pakistan, Indonesia, and Turkey in the 1960s," *Comparativ* 19:4 (2009), 96–111.

35. Wilfred Malenbaum, "Some Political Aspects of Economic Development in India," *World Politics* 10:3 (April 1958), 385.

36. Millikan to Trevor Swan, March 5, 1959, in Center for International Studies Records, AC236, box 9, folder 10, MIT Archives.

37. Khrushchev speech to Indian Parliament, February 11, 1960, *O vneshnei politike Sovetskogo Soiuza,* 1:73–74.

38. Quoted in Nick Cullather, "Damming Afghanistan: Modernization in a Buffer State," *Journal of American History* 89:2 (September 2002), 529–530.

39. Robinson and Dixon, "Soviet Development Theory," 600.

40. Amit Das Gupta, "Südasien und der Wettbewerb der Supermächte, 1954–1972," in *Heiße Kriege im Kalten Krieg,* ed. Bernd Greiner et al. (Hamburg: Hamburger Edition, 2006), 242.

41. George Rosen, *Western Economists and Eastern Societies: Agents of Change in South Asia, 1950–1970* (Baltimore: Johns Hopkins University Press, 1985), chaps. 3, 6–7.

42. See brief discussion in *Prezidium 1954–1964,* 1:932n12.

43. Quoted in Boquérat, *No Strings Attached,* 289.

44. Transcript of Khrushchev-Kennedy conversation, June 3, 1961, in *Prezidium 1954–1964,* 3:189.

45. McMahon, *Cold War on the Periphery,* 269.

46. Lorenz M. Lüthi, *The Sino-Soviet Split: Cold War in the Communist World* (Princeton, NJ: Princeton University Press, 2008), chaps. 3–4.

47. Chen Jian, "The Tibetan Rebellion of 1959 and China's Changing Relations with India and the Soviet Union," *Journal of Cold War Studies* 8:3 (Summer 2006), 91–93; Gordon Gray, memorandum of conversation, February 4, 1960, in Office of the Special Assistant for National Security Affairs Records, Special Assistant File, Presidential Subfile, box 5, Dwight D. Eisenhower Presidential Library (Abilene, KS).

48. Srinath Raghavan, *War and Peace in Modern India: A Strategic History of the Nehru Years* (Delhi: Permanent Black, 2010), chaps. 7–8.

49. Mikhail Yu. Prozumenshchikov, "The Sino-Indian Conflict, the Cuban Missile Crisis, and the Sino-Soviet Split, October 1962," *CWIHP Bulletin* 8–9 (1996–1997), 251–257.

50. Politburo documents from October, 11, 14, and 17, 1962, in *Prezidium 1954–1964*, 1:596, 1:616–617, 3:336–339.

51. Robert Komer to Carl Kaysen, November 16, 1962, in National Security Files—NSC Histories, box 24, LBJ Presidential Library (Austin, TX).

52. Stockholm International Peace Research Institute (SIPRI) data from www.sipri.org.

53. This brief summary builds on, among other sources, J. N. Dixit, *India-Pakistan in War and Peace* (London: Routledge, 2002), chaps. 4–5; McMahon, *Cold War on the Periphery*, chaps. 8–9; and Bouquérat, *No Strings Attached*, chaps. 14–15.

5

CHINA, THE THIRD WORLD,
AND THE COLD WAR

CHEN JIAN

On February 22, 1974, Mao Zedong introduced his "Three Worlds" thesis at a meeting with Zambian president Kenneth Kaunda. "The U.S. and the Soviet Union belong to the First World," stated the Chinese chairman. "The middle elements, such as Japan, Europe, Australia and Canada, belong to the Second World." The Third World was composed of "all Asian countries, except Japan, and all of Africa and also Latin America."[1] Three days later, Mao told Algerian leader Houari Boumediene that "China belongs to the Third World, as politically and economically China is not in the same group of the rich and powerful, and thus can only be with those countries that are relatively poor."[2] On April 10, China's vice premier Deng Xiaoping stated at the United Nations that it was the oppressed, exploited, and economically backward Third World that "has represented the major force in promoting progress in the world."[3]

The Maoist Three Worlds thesis had two outstanding features that seemed incompatible with the Cold War's basic framework. First, it took differences in levels of economic development, rather than contests and confrontations between different ideologies and political and social systems, as the basic criteria in defining Three Worlds. Second, it highlighted backwardness as a force of critical importance in bringing about history's progress. While the particular terminology of "Three Worlds" was a new addition to Beijing's official discourse, these two features had long existed in the Maoist representation of the changing world structure. Since the late 1940s, the Chinese Communists had used such concepts as the "Intermediate Zone" and the "Two Intermediate Zones" in defining and illustrating the divided Cold War world. In retrospect, both terms, as the conceptual forbearing of the Maoist Three Worlds thesis of the 1970s, already embodied these two features.

Beijing's adoption of the Three Worlds thesis, which nullified the boundaries between Communism and capitalism, had an enormous impact on the ongoing Cold War. In particular, it further reduced the influence and power of the profoundly divided international Communist movement, creating another important condition for the Cold War to end with the collapse of the Soviet camp.

Why did Mao introduce his Three Worlds thesis in the early 1970s? How did the ideas contained in it come into being? What were the ideological, political, and strategic implications of the Chinese journey toward identifying the Cold War world and China's position in it in ways that finally led to the making of its own Three Worlds notion? In order to answer these questions, it is essential to review Beijing's changing perceptions of and policies toward the Cold War in general and toward the Intermediate Zone/Third World in particular.

In a historical perspective, Mao's unique Three Worlds notion originated and evolved in the Chinese Communist revolution's long course of development. Since its early years, the Chinese Communist Party (CCP) embraced such concepts as "world revolution" and "proletarian internationalism." In the meantime, it also characterized the Chinese revolution as a "national revolution" that stood as an integral component of the oppressed peoples' worldwide cause for national liberation. In the late 1920s, Mao and his comrades began to develop a rural-oriented pattern of Communist revolution. Challenging the orthodox Marxist notion that a Communist revolution would have to be carried out by urban proletarians, Mao contended that China's backwardness made it possible and necessary for a revolution carried out by the peasants—the most oppressed and, therefore, the most revolutionary group in society—to occur. During China's war of resistance against Japan, the Chinese Communists presented their ideology and political strategies in the language of revolutionary nationalism, creating a powerful public image that—no matter to what extent they were loyal to Communism—they were nationalistic in their essence.

When the Chinese Civil War erupted in the context of the rising Cold War in 1946–1947, Mao and the CCP introduced a series of new ideas about the postwar world order, which the party would later name as Mao's Intermediate Zone thesis. Mao and his comrades argued that between the United States and the Soviet Union there existed a vast Intermediate Zone in Asia, Africa, and Europe, and that the U.S. imperialists could not directly attack the Soviet Union until they had controlled the zone. Although the postwar world order was characterized by U.S.-Soviet confrontations, they contended, the principal contradiction in the world rested with the struggles between peoples in the Intermediate Zone and the reactionary U.S. ruling class, as well as between China and the United States.[4]

Mao's Intermediate Zone notion revealed the CCP's determination to challenge the United States as a dominant imperialist power and to stand on the side of the Soviet Union. In the meantime, though, it also exposed a powerful tendency toward Chinese ethnocentrism in the CCP leaders' definition of the Cold War and China's position in it. Indeed, the Intermediate Zone notion, by highlighting the central role that China was to play in bridging the world revolution and decolonization, presaged that the Cold War would have to become a phenomenon more complicated than if there had not been China's input.

In 1949, the People's Republic of China (PRC) was established. Mao announced that the "new China" would "lean to one side," the side of the Soviet Union and the Communist bloc.[5] In February 1950, the PRC signed a treaty of strategic alliance with the Soviet Union. Beijing and Moscow also worked out a "division of labor" agreement—while the Soviet Union would continuously serve as the leader of the world revolution and take the main responsibility in promoting revolutions in the West, the CCP would play a major role in promoting revolutions in the East.[6] Consequently, the PRC's entry into the Cold War not only changed the balance of power between the two contending camps but also enhanced the consciousness on the part of Communists throughout the world that history indeed was on their side.

Yet behind all of this was the reality that Mao and his comrades already perceived the Cold War in ways beyond the bipolar structure. In elaborating the Chinese Revolution's worldwide significance, Mao and his comrades emphasized that the path toward the proletarian revolution's global victory was best opened in the vast Intermediate Zone with the Chinese Revolution as the model. In a widely circulated speech, Liu Shaoqi, the CCP's second in command, pointed out that the CCP's victory served as a successful model for the national liberation movements in all colonial and semicolonial countries to follow. He reasoned that as the Western powers had based their reactionary reigns at home on the exploitation of peoples in other parts of the world, the liberation of the colonies and semicolonies would not only result in the collapse of the worldwide domination of Western imperialism but also lead to the emancipation of peoples throughout the world.[7] In retrospect, this was an approach that contained potential challenges to the international Communist movement's unified structure with Moscow as the undisputed center.

In the first five years of its history, the PRC acted as a radical "revolutionary country" on the international scene, challenging the legitimacy of the existing international system controlled by the United States and other Western powers. In October 1950, Mao and the CCP leadership sent Chinese troops to Korea to support Kim Il-sung's North Korean Communist regime, engaging in a direct military confrontation with the United States that would last until July 1953. Beijing also provided military and other support to the Vietnamese Communists in a war against the French colonialists. PRC policies toward such non-Western countries as Malaya, Burma, Thailand, Indonesia, the Philippines, and, on occasion, India were a mixture of harsh criticism (labeling them as "lackeys of Western imperialism") and attempts to neutralize them in the Cold War environment.[8]

China's revolutionary foreign policies—and its intervention in Korea in particular—bolstered Mao's plans for continuing the revolution at home. During the Korean War years, the Communist regime found itself in a powerful position to penetrate into almost every area of Chinese society through intensive mass mobilization under the banner of revolutionary nationalism. When the war ended in July 1953, China's society and political landscape had been altered: organized resistance to the new regime had been destroyed; land in the countryside had been redistributed and the landlord class eliminated; the bourgeoisie class was under the tight control of the Communist state; and the "petit-bourgeoisie" intellectuals had experienced the first round of Communist reeducation. Consequently, the CCP effectively deepened its organizational control of Chinese society and dramatically promoted its authority and legitimacy in the minds of the Chinese people.

China's revolutionary policies also changed East Asia into a main battlefield of the Cold War. Although the Cold War's logical emphasis should have been Europe and although America's primary enemy was the Soviet Union, policymakers in Washington widely believed that compared with Moscow, Beijing was a more daring and, therefore, more dangerous enemy. This perception justified America's continuous military intervention in East Asia after the Korean War, eventually leading to its involvement in the Vietnam War.

In the meantime, though, the active role that China played also changed East Asia into a strange "buffer" between Washington and Moscow. With China and East Asia standing in the middle, it was less likely that the two superpowers would become involved in direct military confrontation. In this sense, China's revolutionary policies played a role in keeping the Cold War "cold."

A major turning point came in 1954–1955. At the Geneva Conference of 1954, the PRC delegation led by Premier Zhou Enlai took the initiative to meet with delegates from several non-Communist countries. In late June, Zhou visited India and Burma and, together with Indian prime minister Jawaharlal Nehru and Burmese prime minister U Nu, introduced the "Five Principles of Peaceful Coexistence" (also known as Panchasila).[9] In April 1955, Zhou attended the Bandung Conference of leaders from twenty-nine countries in Asia and Africa. He made extensive efforts to have dialogues with leaders from other countries, emphasizing the common historical experience between China and those countries.[10]

Beijing's participation in the Geneva and Bandung conferences was particularly important for Mao and the CCP for both international reasons and domestic considerations. Since the early days of the People's Republic, the announcement that Mao made at the PRC's formation—"We the Chinese people have stood up."—had played a central role in legitimizing the revolutionary programs Mao tried to carry out in China. In 1954 and 1955, when Mao and his comrades were eager to "construct the foundation of a socialist society" in China, they fully understood that if they were able to present a strong case of advancement in the PRC's international status to China's ordinary people—who, informed by their own unique "victim mentality," had been so prone to the revival of China's central position in the world—they would occupy a more powerful position to promote the party's mass mobilization plans at home.

Beijing's presence at Geneva and Bandung and its endorsement of the Five Principles revealed the PRC's continuous challenge to the Western powers and, potentially, also to the Soviet Union by introducing a whole set of new norms and codes of behavior in international affairs. In doing so, Mao again went beyond the Cold War's bipolar framework and used the Intermediate Zone concept to illuminate and define the international structure.[11] In the meantime, Mao and his comrades repeatedly emphasized that China and such former colonies as India and Burma belonged to "Eastern countries," and they shared similar cultural and historical traditions as well as the modern experience of humiliation at the hands of Western powers.[12]

Indeed, the Chinese experience at Geneva and Bandung reflected Beijing's strong desire to play a more central role in international affairs. The Maoist Intermediate Zone thesis of the late 1940s still carried a tendency toward "leaning to one side"; Beijing was then still perceived as Moscow's "younger brother." In the mid-1950s, within the context of the emerging leadership vacuum in the international Communist movement after Stalin's death, Mao increasingly believed that it was Beijing's overall capacity of revolutionizing the worldwide process of decolonization—a capacity that was not possessed by Moscow—that had enabled Beijing's centrality in the world revolution.

In the wake of Bandung, the PRC significantly increased its efforts to develop relations with other Asian and African countries while, at the same time, engaging more actively in international affairs involving the non-Western world. In the second half of the 1950s, the PRC established diplomatic relations with Afghanistan, Cambodia, Ceylon, Egypt, Guinea, Iraq, Morocco, Syria, Sudan, and Yemen. Beijing's attitudes toward the newly emerging nonalignment trend among Asian and African countries were very positive. When the Suez Crisis erupted in 1956, Beijing adopted a high-profile approach to support Nasser's decision to nationalize the Suez Canal.

Beijing and Washington began ambassadorial talks after Bandung, yet the PRC persisted in its confrontational policies against the United States. Mao made it clear that the "peaceful coexistence" principle should not be applied to Beijing's relations with Washington, but, rather, should be used to isolate the U.S. imperialists.[13] In the meantime, Beijing strongly opposed Moscow's attempt to use the Five Principles in dealing with Washington. During Mao's visit to Moscow in November 1957, he deliberately challenged the Soviet leader Nikita Khrushchev's emphasis on "peaceful coexistence" with Western imperialist countries.[14] When the relationship between Moscow and Beijing was in trouble, the bipolar structure of the Cold War was further shaken.

In 1958, the PRC's foreign policy turned more radical when the "Great Leap Forward" swept across China's cities and countryside. The trigger that Beijing used to justify the extraordinary mass mobilization during the Great Leap was the U.S.-British intervention in response to the coup in Iraq led by Abdel Karim Kassim. Under the banner of "supporting the Arabic people's anti-imperialist struggle," Mao ordered the People's Liberation Army to shell the Nationalists-controlled Jinmen Islands. When U.S. president Dwight Eisenhower ordered U.S. naval units in East Asia to help the Nationalists protect Jinmen's supply lines, a serious crisis emerged between Beijing and Washington. As Mao did not inform Moscow in advance of his decision to shell Jinmen, the Chinese-Soviet alliance was further troubled.[15]

The PRC's position and image in the non-Western world hit a major hurdle in 1959, when a series of conflicts erupted between China and India. In March 1959, Beijing used force to suppress an anti–Chinese Communist revolt in Tibet, and the Dalai Lama, Tibet's religious and political leader, took refuge in India, which led to serious tensions in Sino-Indian relations.[16]

In fall 1959, two border clashes occurred between Chinese and Indian garrisons, further shattering any remaining trust between Chinese and Indian leaders. Underlying the deterioration of Chinese-Indian relations, though, was the potential conflict between Beijing and New Delhi concerning which country—China or India—should claim the leadership role in the larger non-Western world in the postcolonial age.

The early 1960s witnessed a temporary relaxation of China's domestic and international policies following the Great Leap's disastrous failure. With Mao retreating to the backstage after 1960–1961, his colleagues, such as Liu Shaoqi and Deng Xiaoping, adopted a series of more flexible domestic policies to pursue economic recovery and social stability. Along with this came the softening of China's international policies as well. Yet this period did not last long. When the Chinese economy showed signs of recovery from the dark shadow of the Great Leap, Mao quickly pushed China toward another period of "revolutionary high tide." In order to legitimate the radicalization of China's domestic political and social life, Mao repeatedly stressed that China was facing an international environment full of crises, arguing that the international reactionary forces headed by the U.S. imperialists were preparing to wage a war against China.[17] Mao also openly criticized the Kremlin's strategy of "peaceful coexistence," claiming that it obscured the fundamental distinction between revolution and counterrevolution.

Against this backdrop, Mao put forward his "Two Intermediate Zones" thesis. He argued that between the United States and the Soviet Union "there exist two intermediate zones." The first was composed of "the vast economically backward countries in Asia, Africa and Latin America," and the second included "imperialist and advanced capitalist countries in Europe."[18] After 1962–1963, Beijing's international discourse increasingly highlighted the central role that China had played in promoting revolutionary movements in the First Intermediate Zone. Beijing also publicly alleged that the center of the world revolution had moved from Moscow to Beijing. Applying China's experience of "encircling the cities by first liberating the countryside" to the entire world, Beijing viewed Asia, Africa, and Latin America as the "world's countryside." By virtue of its revolutionary past, Beijing's leaders believed, China was entitled to play a leading role in promoting revolutionary struggles against the "world cities."[19]

Thus Beijing carried out a series of radical international policies aimed at challenging both the United States and the Soviet Union in the intermediate zones. At the center of Beijing's international policy design was Southeast Asia, as Mao and his comrades believed that there conditions for revolutions were most mature. In summer 1963, Beijing hosted a "strategic planning" meeting attended by leaders of the Communist parties from Vietnam, Laos, and Indonesia, for preparing and waging revolutions in Southeast Asia. In July 1964, Beijing called another meeting of Chinese, Vietnamese, and Laotian Communist leaders. In his keynote speech, Zhou Enlai emphasized that Southeast Asia had been the focus of confrontations between international revolutionary and reactionary forces. Communists in this region should mobilize the masses to carry out revolutionary armed struggles in the countryside. He promised that China would serve as the "great rear" of "Southeast Asian revolutions" with all kinds of support.[20]

In the wake of the Gulf of Tonkin incident of August 1964, Beijing extended comprehensive security commitments to North Vietnam. Along with the escalation of the Vietnam War, China dispatched large numbers of engineering and antiaircraft-artillery troops to North Vietnam, as well as provided Hanoi with substantive military equipment and other materials.[21] When Indonesian president Sukarno, with the support of the Indonesian Communists, launched the New Emerging Force movement that aimed to bring together all "anti-imperialist and anti-colonial forces" in the non-Western world, Beijing endorsed it enthusiastically.

Beijing also endeavored to expand China's influences in Africa. In late 1963–early 1964, Zhou Enlai spent three months visiting ten African countries. During the trip, the Chinese premier repeatedly emphasized that China was a true friend and natural ally of newly independent African countries. In order to prove this point, China began to provide economic, technological, and medical support to the African countries that were most friendly to China, including Congo-Brazzaville, Guinea, Mali, Somalia, Tanzania, and Zambia. Largely because of the endorsement by newly independent African countries, the PRC claimed a major diplomatic victory in 1965, when the UN General Assembly for the first time voted in a draw on recognizing the PRC as China's sole legal representative at the United Nations.

Beijing's attempt to pursue the exclusive leadership role in the non-Western world was fully revealed through its attitudes toward the second conference by leaders of Asian-Afro countries, which was scheduled to be convened in Algeria in June 1965, in commemoration of the tenth anniversary of the Bandung Conference. From the beginning, Beijing firmly opposed allowing the Soviet Union to participate in the conference, even in the capacity as an "observer."[22] Beijing also argued that India, as a "lackey" of Western imperialists, should not be allowed to play a major role at the conference. In the end, the conference was called off after Algerian leader Ben Bella was overthrown in a coup against him in June 1965.[23]

Finally, the PRC's aggressive foreign policies backfired. The "Beijing-Djakarta axis" collapsed after the September 30, 1965, incident in Indonesia, which resulted in the destruction of the Indonesian Communist Party and the downfall of Sukarno. Fidel Castro's Cuba was the first country in Latin America to establish diplomatic relations with the PRC. Yet the relations between Beijing and Havana deteriorated rapidly after 1965 primarily because they differed in their attitudes toward "Soviet revisionism," and they also competed to become models for revolutions in Latin America. Right-wing coups in several African countries that were close to Beijing reversed the trend of the PRC's diplomatic advance in Africa. In 1966, the motion to place the PRC in China's UN seat was defeated by a larger margin.

Beginning in summer 1966, the "Great Proletarian Cultural Revolution" swept across China's cities and countryside. Instead of adjusting its foreign policy, Beijing was more eager to claim "Chinese centrality" in the world revolution and carried out a series of more radical policies in international affairs. China's confrontations with the United States and conflicts with the Soviet Union escalated continuously, and its relations with several neighboring countries, such as Burma and Cambodia, deteriorated. In Chinese–North Vietnamese relations, Beijing's leaders repeatedly urged Hanoi not to negotiate with Washington, while, at the same time, rejecting any attempt by Moscow to use the theme of "supporting the Vietnamese people" to carry out any "united action" against the United States within the international Communist movement.[24] Even Beijing's solidarity with North Korea suffered during the Cultural Revolution years as the Red Guards publicly attacked North Korean leader Kim Il-sung as a "revisionist."

By the late 1960s, China had become one of the most isolated countries in the world, facing serious security threats from all directions. America's intervention in Vietnam kept great pressure on China's southern borders. The hostility between China and the Soviet Union culminated in March 1969, when two bloody clashes erupted between Chinese and Soviet garrisons on Zhenbao Island on the Ussuri River bordering the Russian Far East and China's Northeast.[25] China also faced hostile enemies from the east (Taiwan, Japan, and South Korea) and from the West (India).

The grave security situation that China was facing in the late 1960s, combined with the fading status of Mao's enterprise of "continuous revolution" (indeed, following the failure of the "Cultural Revolution," Mao's programs of transforming China's state and society were increasingly losing the "inner support" from China's ordinary people), created the context in which the Sino-American rapprochement occurred. In February 1972, during "the week that changed the world," U.S. president Richard Nixon made the historic trip to China and met with Mao in Beijing.[26]

The impact of the Sino-American rapprochement was far reaching. It ended the total confrontation between the PRC and the United States that had lasted for almost a quarter-century, opening a new chapter in the development of relations between the world's most populous nation and its most powerful country. It also dramatically shifted the balance of power between the two conflicting superpowers in the Cold War. While policymakers in Washington found it possible to concentrate more of America's resources and strategic attention on dealing with the threats posed by the Soviet Union, Moscow's leaders, having to confront the West and China simultaneously, were more likely to overextend the country's strength and power.

In a deeper sense, though, Beijing's cooperation with Washington and confrontation with Moscow had implications for changing the essence of the global Cold War. Since its beginning in the late 1940s, the Cold War had been a fundamental confrontation between two contending ideologies—Communism and liberal capitalism. The Chinese-American rapprochement obscured the distinctions between socialist and capitalist ways toward modernity at the same time that the Sino-Soviet split buried the shared consciousness among Communists in the world.

It was in the wake of the rapprochement, on April 10, 1974, that Deng Xiaoping, head of the Chinese delegation attending the UN General Assembly, publicly presented Mao's "Three Worlds" notion. Deng emphasized that the First World was made up of the two superpowers, the Soviet Union and the United States, "the two largest international oppressors and exploiters" and the "main war origins in the contemporary era." In comparison, the Soviet Union was more aggressive and, therefore, more dangerous than the United States. The Second World was composed of capitalist/developed countries in Europe and Asia (such as Japan), which, while facing the threat from the two superpowers trying to control them, demonstrated in their policies the legacies of their own past as colonial powers. The Third World, formed by the vast majority of developing countries in Asia, Africa and Latin America, favored the "tendency of revolution" and opposed "the tendency of war"; thus it was the "force playing a major role in promoting progress in the world."[27]

There existed striking similarities in perceptions of how the structure of the world should be defined between Mao's Three Worlds notion and his Intermediate Zone/Two Intermediate Zones thesis: they all posed fundamental challenges to the existing world order and envisioned China as a central actor in bringing about global changes. But there were also significant differences. The earlier Intermediate Zone thesis was formulated around the discourse of "international class struggle." In contrast, the primary concern of the Three Worlds notion was the issue of economic development. Central to the notion was "development" as a question of fundamental importance that China and other Third World countries must encounter.

As is well known, Mao had championed transforming China and the world in revolutionary ways. The introduction of the development-oriented Three Worlds theory toward the end of his life is worthy of some discussion. In the final analysis, this was Mao's way of dealing with the worsening legitimacy crisis that his "continuous revolution" had been facing. Ever since Mao proclaimed at the time of the PRC's formation that "we the Chinese people have stood up," he legitimated his "revolution after revolution" by repeatedly emphasizing how his revolutionary programs would change China into a country of "wealth and power." When the Chinese Communist state was encountering an ever-deepening legitimacy crisis as the result of the economic stagnation and political cruelty that Mao's revolutions had conferred on the Chinese people, the Chinese chairman embraced the Three Worlds notion for emphasizing—first and foremost to the Chinese people— that his revolutions continuously played a central role in benefiting China and transforming the world.

The Three Worlds notion made it necessary and possible for Beijing to redefine its international policies. For the first time in the history of the PRC, Beijing began to give some universality to the Five Principles, allowing them to surpass the doctrine of "international class struggle" to become more fundamental guidelines for international affairs. Accordingly, Beijing gradually moved away from the previous practices of supporting revolutions in other countries, especially by significantly reducing its aid to Communist insurgence and guerrilla activities in Southeast Asia. Toward the last stage of the American-Vietnamese talks in Paris ending the Vietnam War, Beijing's leaders urged their comrades in Hanoi to cut a deal with the Americans. After the signing of the Paris Peace Accords, almost immediately Beijing significantly reduced its military and other aid to Hanoi.[28] In April 1975, against the background of impending Communist victories in Indochina, North Korean leader Kim Il-sung visited Beijing to try to gain China's backing for his renewed aspiration for using a "revolutionary war" to unify Korea. Beijing's leaders demonstrated little interest in, let alone support for, Kim's plans.[29] In the meantime, Beijing took substantial steps to develop state-to-state relations with all kinds of Third World countries, including those ruled by conservative or even reactionary regimes. A revealing example was that Beijing, by citing the Five Principles, continuously maintained normal diplomatic, economic, and even political relations with Augusto Pinochet's military regime in Chile after the 1973 coup that brought down Salvador Allende's left-wing, socialist government.

After Mao's death on September 9, 1976, Deng Xiaoping quickly emerged as China's paramount leader. He managed to abandon Mao's class-struggle-centered discourse and revolutionary practice, allowing economics to take precedence over politics, hoping that the improvement of people's living standards would help legitimize the Communist state.

These developments changed the essence of China's position in the world. Ever since its establishment in 1949, the People's Republic constantly challenged the legitimacy of the existing international order, which Mao and his comrades viewed as the result of Western domination and thus inimical to revolutionary China. The logic of the "reform and opening" process meant that China would no longer behave as a "revolutionary country" internationally, and would gradually change from an outsider to an insider in the international system.

In international affairs, Deng and his colleagues decided to dramatically reduce and, finally, end its support to revolutionary/radical nationalist states and movements in other parts of the world. In the meantime, Beijing adopted a new approach in China's external relations by giving up some of its key ideological bias to develop comprehensive relations with Western capitalist powers. China was already departing the global Cold War a decade before its end.

Yet Deng did not abandon the Three Worlds thesis. As soon as he became China's paramount leader, Deng made it clear that China's international policies would continuously follow the Three Worlds framework that Mao had set up in the last years of his life. Deng and the Chinese leadership believed that the Soviet Union was then on the offensive, whereas the United States was on the defensive, thus they identified the Soviet Union as more dangerous among the two superpowers that formed the First World. Such an understanding allowed Deng and the Beijing leadership to justify the new strategic partnership that China was then pursuing with the United States for the purpose of promoting Deng's reform and opening policies. In treating Second World countries (e.g., Western European countries and Japan), Deng and the Chinese leadership gave emphasis to the role that they could play in containing "Soviet expansion," as well as the contributions that they were in a position to make to China's reform and opening projects.

In dealing with Third World countries, Beijing's policies were formed largely around the perceived needs of establishing a broad united front against "Soviet social-imperialism" as the main danger facing both world peace and China's modernization drive. Thus Beijing carried out a punitive war against Vietnam—perceived by Beijing as a Soviet agent in Southeast Asia—in early 1979, and the confrontation between the two former Communist allies continued throughout the 1980s. From the late 1970s to the mid-1980s, Beijing firmly opposed Cuba's intervention in Africa, viewing it as an example of Moscow's ambitious plots to dominate the world. Regarding other Third World countries or different factions within a certain Third World country, Beijing also took their attitudes toward Moscow as the key criteria to define if they were friends or foes. Unsurprisingly, Beijing stood on the side of the Islamist guerillas in their fights against the Soviet-propped Communist government in Kabul; it firmly supported Jonas Savimbi's National Union for the Total Liberation of Angola in the Angolan Civil War simply because its main enemy was the Moscow-backed Popular Movement for the Liberation of Angola; it was hostile toward Mengistu Hail Mariam's Socialist Ethiopia, yet friendly toward Mobutu Sésé Seko's pro-West and reactionary Zaire. One of Beijing's main purposes was to worsen the overextension in the Soviet Union's position in the Cold War.

In December 1979, Soviet troops invaded Afghanistan. For Beijing's leaders, this confirmed what they had worried about in the past decade: The Soviet threat was not just real but also worsening. Immediately after the Soviet invasion of Afghanistan, Beijing's leaders decided to denounce it. China joined a group of others, mostly Western countries, to boycott the 1980 Olympic Games in Moscow. Throughout the 1980s, Beijing provided substantial military and other support to Pakistan and, largely through Pakistan, to the resistance forces in Afghanistan. The PRC's close cooperation with Pakistan, in turn, made it more difficult for Chinese-Indian relations to improve.

In March 1982, Soviet leader Leonid Brezhnev openly stated that Moscow was willing to improve relations with Beijing. Deng welcomed the gesture. In the meantime, Beijing virtually stopped using Mao's Three Worlds thesis in describing the structure of the world. But Deng also raised removal of "three big barriers" as a precondition for the improvement of Sino-Soviet relations: that Moscow should reduce its military forces deployed on Soviet-Chinese and Mongolian-Chinese borders, that Soviet troops should withdraw from Afghanistan, and that Vietnamese troops should withdraw from Cambodia.[30] The inability on the part of Beijing and Moscow to overcome these barriers, especially the ones in Afghanistan and Vietnam, blocked any substantial improvement of Sino-Soviet relations until after the mid-1980s.

In the second half of the 1980s, it became increasingly evident that the Soviet Union actually was the superpower in decline. Beijing's policies toward the Third World, together with its partnership with Washington, effectively altered the balance of power between the two superpowers. Furthermore, Beijing's repudiation of the Soviet model and its adoption of the capitalist-market-oriented reforms discouraged other Third World countries from taking Communism and the Soviet-style command economy as a useful and competitive path toward modernity. By doing so, China had virtually withdrawn from the Cold War. As we now know, the global Cold War was then already approaching its end—which would come in a few short years along with the collapse of the Soviet Union and the demise of the international Communist movement.

NOTES

1. *Mao Zedong on Diplomacy* (Beijing: Foreign Languages Press, 1993), 454.

2. "Mao Zedong's Conversations with Houari Boumediene," February 25, 1974, CCP Central Committee Document, no. 10 (1974), Fujian Provincial Archive, 244-1-106, 4.

3. *Renmin ribao* (People's daily), April 11, 1974, 1.

4. Mao, "Talks with Anna Louis Strong," *Mao Zedong xuanji* (Selected works of Mao Zedong) (Beijing: Renmin, 1965), 4:1191–1192; *Renmin ribao*, January 4, 1947.

5. Mao, "On People's Democratic Dictatorship," June 30, 1949, *Mao Zedong xuanji* (Beijing: Renmin, 1965), 4:1477–1478.

6. Shi Zhe, "Liu Shaoqi in Moscow," *Chinese Historians* 6:1 (Spring 1993), 84–85.

7. *Jianguo yilai Liu Shaoqi wengao* (Liu Shaoqi's manuscripts since the formation of the PRC) (Beijing: Zhongyang wenxian, 2005), 1:161–162.

8. See, for example, Liu Shaoqi to Stalin, "Report on Strategies of National Revolutionary Movements in East Asia," August 14, 1949, *Jianguo yilai Liu Shaoqi wengao*, 1:50–53.

9. The Five Principles, or Panchasila, included (1) mutual respect for sovereignty and territorial integrity, (2) nonaggression, (2) noninterference in other countries' internal affairs, (4) equal and mutual benefit, and (5) peaceful coexistence.

10. Pei Jianzhang et al., *Zhonghua renmin gongheguo waijiao shi, 1949–1956* (A diplomatic history of the People's Republic of China, 1949–1956) (Beijing: Shijie zhishi, 1994), 231–251.

11. See, for example, Mao's speech at a Politburo enlarged meeting, July 7, 1954. The Chinese chairman stated that "the biggest ambition of the United States

at the moment is to castigate the intermediate zone, including the entire area from Japan to Britain, and to make all these countries cry while castigating them." *Mao Zedong wenji* (A collection of Mao Zedong's works) (Beijing: Renmin, 1999), 6:334.

12. See, for example, Mao Zedong's conversation with Jawaharlal Nehru, October 19, 1954, 204-00007-01, PRC Foreign Ministry Archive, Beijing.

13. Mao's speech at a Politburo enlarged meeting, July 7, 1954, *Mao Zedong wenji* (Beijing: Renmin, 1999), 6:332; Mao Zedong's conversation with Harry Pollitt, April 29, 1955, *Mao Zedong on Diplomacy*, 158–159.

14. Mao Zedong, "Speech at the Moscow Conference of Communist and Workers' Parties," *Jianguo yilai Mao Zedong Wengao* (Mao Zedong's manuscripts since the formation of the PRC) (Beijing: Zhongyang wenxian, 1992), 6:635–636.

15. Chen Jian, *Mao's China and the Cold War* (Chapel Hill: University of North Carolina Press, 2001), chap. 7.

16. For a more detailed discussion, see Chen Jian, "The Tibetan Rebellion of 1959 and China's Changing Relations with India and the Soviet Union," *Journal of Cold War History* 8:3 (Summer 2006), 54–101.

17. Zheng Qian, "The Nationwide War Preparations before and after the CCP's Ninth Congress," *Zhonggong dangshi ziliao* (CCP history materials), no. 41 (April 1992), 205.

18. *Mao Zedong on Diplomacy*, 388.

19. Lin Biao, "Long Live People's War," *Renmin ribao,* September 2, 1965.

20. Tong Xiaopeng, *Fengyu sishi nian* (Forty years of storms) (Beijing: Zhongyang wenxian, 1996), 2:219–220, 2:221; "Summary of the Meeting by Chinese, Vietnamese, and Laotian Party Leaders," July 20, 1964, 203-00581-03, PRC Foreign Ministry Archive, Beijing.

21. Chen Jian, *Mao's China and the Cold War*, chap. 8.

22. "The Question of the Soviet Union's Participation of the Second Asian-Afro Conference," June 16, 1965, 107-00933-01, PRC Foreign Ministry Archive, Beijing; "The Question of the Soviet Revisionists and Other Non-Asian-African Countries' Participation of the Asian-Afro Conference as Observers," June 19, 1965, 107-00933-01, PRC Foreign Ministry Archive, Beijing.

23. Xiong Xianghui, "The Cancellation of the Second Asian-Afro Conference and Zhou Enlai's Style of Diplomacy," *Xin zhongguo waijiao fengyun* (The experience of new China's diplomacy) (Beijing: Shijie zhishi, 1996), 2:168–199.

24. Chen Jian, *Mao's China and the Cold War,* 230–232.

25. Yang Kuisong, "The Sino-Soviet Border Clash of 1969," *Cold War History* 1:1 (August 2000), 25–31.

26. Chen Jian, *Mao's China and the Cold War*, chap. 9.

27. *Renmin ribao,* April 11, 1974.

28. Chen Jian, "China, the Vietnam War, and the Sino-American Rapprochement, 1968–1973," in *The Third Indochina War: Conflict between China, Vietnam,*

and Cambodia, 1972–79, ed. Odd Arne Westad and Sophie Quinn-Judge (London: Routledge, 2006), 53–59.

29. Leng Rong and Wang Zuoling et al., *Deng Xiaoping nianpu* (A chronological record of Deng Xiaoping) (Beijing: Zhongyang wenxian, 2004), 1:36–37.

30. Ibid., 291–292.

6

AFRICA'S COLD WAR

JEFFREY JAMES BYRNE

A half-century after the major wave of decolonization, and two decades after the end of the Cold War, the subfield of African international history is flourishing. Perhaps most visibly, numerous scholars have taken advantage of new archival opportunities (in Africa and beyond) to rewrite the histories of key events such as the Algerian War of Independence or the 1975 Angolan Crisis, for example, while others would argue essentially that independent Africa allows unique insights into systemic global changes, such as the promotion of human rights and the universal recognition of state sovereignty.[1] Indeed, the concerns of international historians, imperial historians, and Africanists have converged in certain respects, since the "new" international history's emphasis on "decentralizing" the Cold War and on sociocultural transnational phenomena is quite similar to recent trends in imperial history, and the new international historians' relentless pursuit of novel sources and alternative perspectives can often appear to be a spiritual successor to longstanding efforts to "decolonize" African history (and that of other postcolonial regions).[2] In short, independent Africa has warranted international historians' increased attention not only by dint of its size and the simple passage of time, but also because some of the barriers between these separate lines of intellectual inquiry are disappearing. The continent has become one of the most important areas for understanding the superpowers' modernizing ideologies, the normative bases of international society, the imperial qualities of American power, or even the fundamental nature of the Cold War itself.

Accordingly, this chapter argues that the histories of the Cold War and modern Africa are inextricably connected—African developments affected the evolution of the global contest between the United States and the Soviet

Union, and, probably to greater degree, the Cold War had a profound and lasting impact across that continent. Without dismissing the important continuities between the colonial and postcolonial periods, or suggesting that Africa was simply a blank canvas for outside forces to illustrate as they pleased, a focus on historical *dis*continuities reveals that the relatively brief Cold War era entailed profound consequences because it coincided with the uniquely impressionable years of decolonization. To fully appreciate the significance of the interaction between the Cold War phenomena, it is necessary to overcome the misleading appearance of inevitability that has set in since the collapse of the Soviet Union and the high-profile failures of so many of Africa's postcolonial endeavors. The end of Europe's empires was above all a time of optimism, ambition, and uncertainty, when even the most fundamental questions about the shape of things to come had no clear answer. At the same time, the Cold War's geopolitical, intellectual, and ideological battles were at their peak intensity and offered irresistible opportunities for Africa's new elites to cope with their daunting responsibilities. Indeed, the extent of the Cold War's legacy can be easily overlooked precisely because it was so deeply implanted in decolonizing Africa's unset political foundations.

Three aspects of the Cold War's legacy are considered here, two of which can be considered "constructive" in the sense that they contributed to the creation of the continental postcolonial order, for better or for worse, while the third seems to have been an almost entirely negative phenomenon. The first was the surprisingly rapid implementation of the sovereign-state model of political organization throughout Africa, as opposed to the various notions of pan-African, regional, or semi-imperial integration that had many advocates and good prospects up to at least the late 1950s. Without the context of the pervasive American-Soviet contest, African and European leaders would not have both so quickly embraced this version of decolonization. Second, the Cold War's ideological dimensions greatly influenced the expression of anticolonial sentiment, in organizational as well as ideational terms, and subsequently also the domestic agendas of many African leaders after independence. As the Ghanaian president Kwame Nkrumah told an audience in New York in 1958, "We cannot tell our peoples that material benefits and growth and modern progress are not for them. If we do, they will throw us out and seek other leaders who promise more....Africa has to modernize."[3] In some instances, the initial euphoria of decolonization combined with the rhetoric of revolution, modernization, and social transformation to instill national elites with genuinely utopian ambitions.

Finally, the last legacy of the Cold War, or its parting gift, was the emphatic puncturing of these lofty dreams. The superpowers' proxy wars achieved their maximum destructiveness in the Horn and southern Africa in the 1970s and 1980s, while in the economic sphere those traveling the socialist road ran out of gas just as the Reagan administration's neoliberal "counterrevolution" in development policy effectively eradicated statist and left-wing models throughout the continent. Thus the Cold War played a key role in the disappointments of the postcolonial era, raising expectations as well as dashing them. But if Africa can claim a disproportionate share of that conflict's victims, so too did it boast many of its most ardent combatants, whether they wielded Kalashnikovs or megaphones.

The African State System and the Cold War Order

Although Africa's Cold War immediately conjures images of interminable proxy wars, guerrilla campaigns, revolutions, coups, and countercoups, in hindsight perhaps the most significant consequence of the superpowers' multidimensional rivalry was to encourage the creation of a continent-wide state system solid enough to withstand even the most severe instability surging within it. Rebels crossed borders without redrawing them, and regimes could rise and fall rapidly without changing the basic characteristic of the countries they governed. Indeed, while American and Soviet policymakers frequently sought to alter a state's government or orientation, on the whole they actually demonstrated a rather conservative Westphalian conception of international politics as far as Africa was concerned, since their subversive schemes rarely if ever went so far as to challenge countries' basic legitimacy or territorial integrity. This surprisingly durable state system was the product of an unspoken consensus forged in the late 1950s and early 1960s between the superpowers, the retreating European imperialists, and emergent nationalist elites, who each preferred this version of postcolonial Africa to the other possibilities touted at the time. International society's recognition of state sovereignty helped secure the position of national regimes, and a clientelist paradigm immediately set in throughout the continent as a result of British and French desires to "manage" decolonization and the escalating competition for influence between the outside powers.

It is easy to forget how quickly this transformation occurred. Even in the late 1950s it was not a foregone conclusion that Africa's complex layers of imperial control and diverse visions of the postcolonial order would be completely supplanted by the sovereign-state model. After all, at the beginning of the decade most anticolonialist politicians and activists still spoke in terms of reforming colonialism rather than eliminating it, and there was widespread support at both ends of the imperial relationship for transitioning toward some sort of "interdependency" between metropole and colony.[4] Most African leaders did not seem to believe that the colonial territories, especially the smaller ones, could be economically viable on their own, while imperial interests were determined to preserve as many of their assets there as possible. There was no agreement on the definition of "decolonization," which was in fact not an event but a prolonged process of negotiation. Describing the "imperialism of decolonization," historians Wm. Roger Louis and Ronald Robinson have pointed out that the British Empire had already become a complex set of unequal accommodations between diverse metropolitan interests and local protonationalists, and they used the term "imperialism of decolonization" to describe London's efforts to orchestrate the peaceful "transfer of power" to whichever local candidates would best accommodate Britain's continued economic and political influence.[5] French strategy was initially more cautious and characteristically more systematic, but it is notable that it was the French government led by Prime Minister Guy Mollet—not African anticolonialists—that favored devolving autonomy to the individual territories of French West Africa through the 1956 *loi-cadre*, which devolved certain powers to local colonial administrations and instituted major legal and electoral reforms. The *Rassemblement Démocratique Africain* (RDA) had lobbied instead for West Africa to be treated as a single entity, and Senegal's Léopold Sédar Senghor warned presciently that this "balkanization" suited imperial interests more than African and that it would create elites preoccupied with local concerns and dependent on French patronage.[6]

The evolution of the British and French strategies of decolonization shows that, contrary to post facto nationalist historiographies, the creation of independent states was at least as much the product of imperialist design as anticolonialist aspiration. Pan-Africanism, the RDA's West African federalism, and the spirit of "Maghrib unity" were all prominent examples of the internationalist or transnationalist spirit of anticolonial militancy up to that point, a philosophy that believed in strength in numbers and saw schemes such as the *loi-cadre* as a continuation of the old colonial "divide and rule" strategy. While still immersed in postwar London's cosmopolitan pan-African scene, for example, Kwame Nkrumah had vociferously denounced narrow-minded territorial nationalism.[7] However, on his return to the Gold Coast, he himself became one of the most pointed examples of the trend Senghor had predicted by becoming a committed

Ghanaian nationalist who, after initially confronting colonial authorities, then took power in Accra with London's blessing. Similarly, Paris granted Morocco and Tunisia their independence in 1956 precisely in order to counter the spirit of North African solidarity and isolate the Algerian *Front de Libération Nationale* (FLN).[8] Ghana and North Africa would each become focal points of Cold War tensions, but at this juncture the colonial powers felt only moderate pressure from the Cold War context. Neither superpower showed much direct interest in Africa, and Washington's first instinct tended to be to buttress its allies' imperial positions in the name of "stability." Indeed, in the early 1950s, the French authorities in Cote d'Ivoire and the new apartheid government in Pretoria both used the specter of Communism in a crude fashion to justify suppressing African anticolonialism.[9]

In this respect, the Suez Crisis of 1956 stands out as the major turning point for the Cold War in Africa, for it forced a change in thinking for Britain, France, the United States, Soviet Union, and African anticolonialists alike. First, the spectacle of the two superpowers forcing British and French soldiers out of Egypt showed that the Cold War could be used to gain leverage over the imperialists, and in the longer run validated Gamal Abdel Nasser's use of nonalignment not as passive neutrality, but as an assertive and proactive strategy of exploiting international tensions. The leaders of the Algerian FLN, for example, now concluded that if they were to prevail against the French, then "Algeria must become a pressure point in the bidding war between the two great powers," and accordingly reached out to the Communist bloc for support.[10] Second, and in relation to the previous point, Suez greatly increased Washington's and Moscow's interest in the continent, since it alerted the Soviets to the new diplomatic opportunities there and convinced the Americans that their European friends could not be relied on to manage the situation.[11]

Additionally, Suez accelerated the abandonment of federalist or transnationalist notions of the postcolonial order in favor of state sovereignty and nationalist agendas. Nasser's commitment to pan-Arabism notwithstanding, the crisis had confirmed the nationalization of the vital canal and granted total independence to Egypt after many decades of only nominal sovereignty. The triumph of the occasion thus helped make national independence the new "gold standard" of anticolonial achievement. Yet the imperialists and nationalists agreed on this outcome, for London, Paris, and Brussels subsequently altered course by hastening decolonization even as they agreed to this new, more maximal definition of its endpoint. The British now cooperated closely with the Americans to ensure the smoothest possible transfer of power to the most reliable-seeming local candidates so far as Cold War alignments and Western commercial interests were concerned.[12] In contrast, however, many French policymakers concluded from Suez that they were now actually competing with Washington for influence in francophone Africa, and Charles de Gaulle warned his foreign minister, Maurice Couve de Murville, that they would be very foolish to cede their position in their former colonies to the United States through some misguided sense of Western solidarity. Consequently, his French Community proposal of 1958 implemented a far more complete version of African independence than French officials could countenance even a few years earlier, but it still featured certain curtailments on economic and diplomatic sovereignty in order to prevent the former colonies from slipping naturally into an American orbit, as had already happened with Morocco and Tunisia.[13]

The cases of Guinea, Ghana, and "Belgian" Congo demonstrated the onset of nationalist "balkanization" and Cold War competition by the beginning of the 1960s. Historian Elizabeth Schmidt has recently argued that it was Cold War ideological tensions with the RDA that led to Guinea seceding from the movement and rejecting membership in the French Community in the first place, but certainly after independence Guinea and Ghana served as precedents for decolonization leading quickly to clientelism and authoritarianism.[14] Over the following years, Ahmed Sékou Touré and Nkrumah oscillated between dependency on the two superpowers and their former colonial metropole, searching for the "best deal" in terms of economic and state-building support. Regardless of their orientation at any given moment, the Cold War competition generally seemed to encourage the consolidation of dictatorial regimes. At one point, the KGB assumed responsibility for the personal security of both men, while the CIA plotted either to win them over or to overthrow them, successfully achieving the former with Touré in 1962 and the latter with Nkrumah four years later. In both cases, the country was the geopolitical prize.[15] "Belgian" Congo was a similar case, although Patrice Lumumba offers an example of badly miscalculating the dangerous game of exploiting Cold War tensions. Crucially, for all of the instability in Congo in the early 1960s, in the long run both superpowers backed their clients' efforts to unify the country (at the expense of democracy). In that sense, chaotic Congo paradoxically testifies to the *solidity* of the new African state system.[16]

Finally, it is worth reinforcing the point that intense Cold War competition and clientelism was quite compatible with the era of internationally recognized sovereignty. One political scientist has used the term "quasi-state" to describe those countries, quite numerous in Africa, that were too weak to defend or assert their territorial integrity without the legitimation of a seat in the UN General Assembly, and this phenomenon offered a powerful motivation for anticolonial elites to abandon pan-African dreams or other constructs in favor of the Western state—the universally accepted building block of global politics.[17] Moreover, not only did international norms constrain external powers from explicitly breaking up states or redrawing borders (if they had so desired), in many cases that seat in New York was actually the vital prize being contested. The two Germanies, the two Chinas, and Israel battled one another throughout the Cold War to secure African governments' diplomatic recognition; and in this competition between Bonn and Berlin, Beijing and Taipei, and Tel Aviv and its Arab foes, even the weakest and poorest African country boasted a General Assembly vote equal to anyone else's. In return, inducements of development assistance and military aid served to further strengthen the continent's state structures and regimes.[18]

Africa in the Shadow of Wilson and Lenin

As recent scholarship suggests, the Cold War's ideological dimensions had at least as great an impact on the decolonizing world as geopolitical trends.[19] Africa was no exception, as the continent's new leaders found the United States and Soviet Union offering appealing prepackaged solutions to the daunting social and economic challenges before them, while the optimism that characterized the immediate postcolonial moment encouraged them to think big and act boldly. In other words, not only did the superpowers (and certain lesser powers) materially and financially abet many of independent Africa's misguided development strategies and authoritarian policies, the rhetorically supercharged atmosphere of the Cold War era inspired those policies in the first place. Yet, it is also true that the prevailing ideological currents manifested themselves most often through the widespread adoption of certain political *practices*, as opposed to *ideas*. A common sight throughout Africa in the 1960s and 1970s was the regime that publically distanced itself from either bloc's doctrine by pursuing a supposedly "authentic" or nativist revolution that nevertheless relied on the substance of the Leninist and especially Bolshevik examples in a practical and operational sense. Thus, although only a small minority of African elites (or would-be elites) were conscious converts to Soviet-Chinese Communism or American liberal capitalism, those hegemonic messages helped postcolonial regimes to define their goals—and the methods to achieve them.

First of all, to a significant degree practically all of the continent's pro-tonationalists can be considered products of the Wilsonian-Leninist century. Certainly, numerous intellectuals and political and religious leaders had already been challenging their European conquerors on their own terms for decades, using the language of the Enlightenment, the American civil rights movement, and the Bible, but in 1918 President Woodrow Wilson's Fourteen Points elevated the liberal critique of colonialism to a new level of public awareness and moral authority, and together Wilson and Lenin provided the actual tools for anticolonial forces to dismantle the imperial order.[20] Wilson himself and the League of Nations emphatically declined to support that effort, yet "Wilsonianism" as a strategy of harnessing international opinion still grew in potency alongside the United States' geopolitical ascendency, with President Franklin Delano Roosevelt's Atlantic Charter of 1941 promising to succeed where the league had failed, and obliging the British government and de Gaulle's Free French movement to commit to the liberal agenda in the campaign against fascism. Consequently, a Nigerian serviceman observed in 1945 that "we all overseas soldiers are coming back home with new ideas....We want freedom and nothing but freedom," to which his compatriot and comrade-in-arms Mokwugo Okoye added that "revolutionary ideas were set afloat during the 193945 war."[21] Moreover, the Wilsonian message was not simply a source of inspiration, since in practical terms it also offered Africans a viable international strategy of "playing the American card," which Algerian anticolonialists first attempted during the U.S. army's wartime occupation, and then perfected in the course of the FLN's liberation struggle a decade later.

Meanwhile, on the other side of the ideological divide, Lenin's *Imperialism: The Highest Stage of Capitalism* (1917) was of unquestioned importance in shaping several generations of African elites' conception of the international economy, and their continent's role within it. Though Lenin's slim volume represented almost the entire Soviet literature on the "colonial question" until the early 1960s, his basic description of imperialism as a Western-controlled global system that rapaciously exploited the developing world for raw materials and monopolistic markets had achieved the status of conventional wisdom in Africa's nationalist circles by that point. As early as 1927, the African National Congress (ANC) president, J. T. Gumede, demonstrated the relevance of Marxist analysis to conditions in Africa. "These people on the farms work from four in the morning till seven at night for next to nothing," he said. "Those in the mines—what do they get? They get two shillings a day. They have to go down [into] the bowels of the earth to bring up gold to enrich the capitalist."[22] *Imperialism*'s central thesis correlated well with the African experience of colonialism and capitalism to that point, but vitally also suggested an actionable remedy for underdevelopment: minimizing dependence on the capitalist international trading system through nationalization, industrialization, and self-sufficiency.

Even after some early admirers of the Soviet Union, such as the Trinidadian pan-African activist George Padmore, recoiled from the realities of life there, a great many nationalist figures still desired to implement Communism's programmatic content so long as it could be stripped of undesirable ideological and cultural baggage. Guinea's Touré, for example, espoused Marxism in its "African dress," or "the Marxism which had served to mobilize the African populations, and in particular the working class…amputated of its characteristics which did not correspond to African realities," while Algeria's Ahmed Ben Bella explained that Islam precluded him from sharing the Communists' philosophy, but that he had to "admit the force of their economic reasoning."[23] In fact, the Leninist critique of the existing structures of global trade was so widely accepted that even an avowedly capitalist, Western-oriented country like Kenya still subscribed to its own form of "African socialism." The theory's elegant simplicity increased its transmissibility and adaptability—even to the point of dovetailing nicely with the postcolonial invention of tradition and national myth-making.[24]

Moreover, an important element in socialism's appeal was that it effectively asserted the primacy of politics over economics and facilitated the expansion of state control. Accordingly, it was in the area of political organization and development that the ideas of Karl Marx, Lenin, and later Mao Zedong had their greatest influence. The role of left-wing methods of labor mobilization, popular protest, and underground activism in African anticolonialism from the 1920s onward is well established, but the trend continued after independence as most of the continent's governments quickly set about creating one-party dictatorships with more than a passing resemblance to Joseph Stalin's Soviet Union in terms of the structures of governance, nomenclature, and political culture.[25] Unapologetically despotic heads of state defended authoritarian rule on the basis that it reflected "authentic" African culture—"Can anyone tell me if he has ever known an African village where there were two chiefs?" Mobutu Sese Seko asked—or that independence was still too fragile to resist external centripetal forces and internal subnational tensions with supposedly manipulable and corruptible democratic institutions. However, there was hardly much precolonial precedent for political police forces and pervasive unitary party organizations that disseminated national ideology and monitored the population, while the cults of personality diligently crafted around someone like Mobutu were hardly the resumption of "traditional" sources of legitimacy, despite the symbolism. Not that the Zairean state functioned anywhere near as effectively as the Soviet Union, but the intent of replicating Bolshevism's proven methods of building a state and holding power was clear, and these methods were valid regardless of a regime's actual orientation vis-à-vis the Cold War. Also reflecting the times, the 1961 founding of the Nkrumah Ideological Institute, a center for training Ghana's future administrators and bureaucrats, reflected the widely held belief that a conscious ideology was another vital ingredient of governance.

Of course, numerous liberation movements and revolutionary groups offered the most vivid use of Communist methods of political organization. As the leader of the nationalist movement of Guinea-Bissau and Cape Verde (*Partido Africano da Independência da Guiné e Cabo Verde*, PAIGC), Amilcar Carbral, told a Cuban journalist in 1968, "[A]lready a wealth of experience has been gained in the national liberation armed struggle throughout the world[;] the Chinese people fought[,] the Vietnamese people have been fighting more than 25 years.... [They] have struggled and have made known to the world their experiences."[26] However, in the case of such liberation movements, their reliance on Communist revolutionary practices tended to instill an appreciation for revolutionary ideology in a way that was not necessarily true of nationalist regimes that gained power peacefully. When African rebels traveled to Beijing and Hanoi, their hosts stressed the ideological underpinnings of a successful guerrilla campaign, underlining the necessity of some degree of political education to maintain discipline and a compelling revolutionary agenda to win the peasantry's loyalty.[27] This message was also passed from one generation to another within the transnational network of guerrilla training camps and safe havens in places like Congo-Brazzaville, Egypt, and Tanzania. By the late 1960s, for example, Algerian instructors taught their trainees from Angola, Mozambique, Rhodesia, and elsewhere that "the main enemy is imperialism, and the final objective is to establish democratic and progressive regimes with a program for social revolution.... Consequently, victory depends on an ideological clarification within the movements themselves."[28]

The emergence of a more overtly Marxist-inspired trend in Africa in the late 1960s and early 1970s is therefore partly attributable to the fact that movements such as the PAIGC, the Liberation Front of Mozambique (FRELIMO), and the Popular Movement for the Liberation of Angola (MPLA) had been struggling in this radicalizing transnational underground for nearly a decade already.[29] Additionally, the Cold War's geopolitical sands were shifting in favor of "orthodox" (from Moscow's perspective) Marxist-Leninism as opposed to autonomous socialist experiments. On the one hand, some of the liberation movements' primary sponsors and inspirations, such as Cuba, were themselves hewing more faithfully to Soviet economic advice and development strategies on account of the poor outcomes of their own homegrown efforts. On the other hand, Leonid Brezhnev's Kremlin appraised Third World radicalism conservatively, believing that the ideological flexibility Nikita Khrushchev had shown toward "African socialists" and their ilk had backfired badly.[30] Therefore, Moscow was more receptive to Fidel Castro's strong advocacy on behalf of Cabral's PAIGC and Agostinho Neto's MPLA in the early 1970s because the Cuban leader was himself more deferential to Soviet wisdom than before, and the African nationalists had the same incentive to "say the right things" to win Soviet approval.[31] Similarly, although the left-wing military coups in Somalia in 1969 and Ethiopia in 1974 were products of those countries' internal circumstances, it follows that Muhammad Siad Barre and Mengistu Haile Mariam may have been motivated to use such strikingly orthodox Communist pageantry and rhetoric in order to cement their alliances with a Soviet Union that now assessed revolutionaries by stricter standards.

If it seems that Lenin ultimately cast a longer shadow over Africa than his American contemporary, Wilson, it is because the Bolshevik leader's genius in the art of seizing, holding, and extending state power had no equal, and no postcolonial leader could afford to ignore that example, regardless of ideological preferences. Single-party rule and "democratic centralism" appealed even to solid Western allies like Mobutu or Tunisia's Habib Bourguiba, although of course Stalin's talent for surveillance and self-aggrandizement also earned many admirers. Nonetheless—and somewhat paradoxically— the Wilsonian principles of self-determination and a rules-bound international society continued to dominate the diplomatic behavior even of highly authoritarian states. It was international law, after all, that guaranteed their sovereignty, and numerous despots habitually invoked liberal principles in the context of their relations with the industrialized world, while flouting them daily in the governing of their own people.

Cold War Endgames: A Collaterally Damaged Continent

If the first half of Africa's Cold War can be judged to have had a mix of positive and negative consequences for the people who lived there, in the 1970s and 1980s the superpowers' rivalry inflicted a catalog of destructive forces and tragic events on the continent with scarcely any silver linings to speak of. Most prominently, proxy wars in places like the Horn, Angola, and Mozambique devastated whole societies and reinforced the popular perception (outside the United States and the Soviet Union at least) that American and Soviet policymakers were conscienceless cynics who played lightly with the lives of the "darker nations." Indeed it is morally imperative for any accounting of the Cold War to acknowledge that many of its most direct casualties were African—nearly a million in Mozambique alone. Likewise, the continent would claim a great number of the Cold War's "indirect" victims—that is, those who suffered the consequences of ideological warfare or revolutionary experimentation. In fact, the widespread economic devastation of the 1980s is probably of greater long-term significance for the continent as a whole than even proxy wars such as those in Angola and Mozambique, since it affected every country and emphatically extinguished any remaining embers of postcolonial optimism. While various African governments and leaders believed themselves in the early 1970s to be on the verge of creating a New International Economic Order (NIEO), which would multiply the revenues of commodities-exporting countries and underwrite their ambitious domestic development goals, within a decade the twin excesses of socialism run amok and a neoliberal capitalist "counterrevolution" had ground these dreams into dust.

Recently scholars have been especially prolific on the subject of the superpowers' interference in southern Africa's liberation struggles during this period. In addition to the steady progress of declassification in Western countries, historians have taken advantage of research opportunities in the archives of the former Soviet Union, Eastern Europe, South Africa, and Cuba (among others) to shed new light on the motivations of regional governments, liberation movements, and their foreign allies.[32] The decolonization of southern Africa seems to have been so much more violent than elsewhere—Congo-Zaire being an exceptional case of direct superpower intervention—because of the combination of white intransigence and a narrower space for maneuver between the two superpowers. Both the white minority regimes and their nationalist foes enjoyed only as much freedom of action as their external backers allowed through diplomatic, financial, or material assistance. With China now being a clear enemy of the USSR, Cuban involvement being as intolerable to the Americans as the Soviet kind, and the intransigence of Portugal and apartheid Pretoria not offering the same opportunity for a sort of ambiguously aligned, postcolonial middle ground vis-à-vis the Cold War as many former French and British colonies had enjoyed, local actors effectively had to opt for either Washington or

Moscow to fulfill their aims. Thus, when these outside interests decided to tip the balance, as occurred most vividly with the three Angolan nationalist movements in 1975, they encouraged the escalation of violence as well as simply facilitating it. Consequently, the end of the Cold War's ideological battle resolved the region's main contentions: the ANC accepted capitalism; Pretoria embraced democracy; Mozambique gradually quieted; and though bloodshed continued, in Angola in particular, the fighting was no longer really about anything other than profits and power.[33]

The Soviet and American proxy wars in the Horn of Africa in the late 1970s were similarly devastating for the region and its peoples. When the avowedly Marxist Derg took control in Ethiopia, Moscow switched its attentions to Addis Ababa from Siad Barre's less ideologically gratifying regime next door, and then intervened massively to save its new ally from the Somali invasion in late 1977 and early 1978. As in Angola, Cuban troops played a vital role, but this time the Soviet leadership actually chose to send their own officers, military advisors, tank crews, and fighter pilots, and the entire operation was supported by an impressive "air bridge" that conveyed armaments and supplies directly from the USSR to the front lines. The combined effect of the successful Soviet-Cuban interventions in Angola and Ethiopia outraged U.S. policymakers, with Jimmy Carter's national security advisor, Zbigniew Brzezinski, famously recording in his memoirs that Soviet-American détente lay "buried in the sands" of the Ogaden Desert where most of the fighting took place. For this reason, the Ethiopian-Somali War is perhaps the strongest example of African events directly affecting the ebb and flow of the Cold War, but this achievement brought only lingering horrors for the Horn's inhabitants. Siad Barre's military defeat and his defection from the socialist road started to undermine the integrity of Somalia itself, leading directly to the state's collapse in the late 1980s and its continuing miseries.[34]

Moreover, victorious Ethiopia also consumed itself in the decade following the Derg's ascent, marking a grim denouement to thirty years of Soviet-African cooperation in pursuit of socialist development and modernization.[35] On account of the Derg's claimed devotion to Marxist-Leninism, Soviet officials accepted or even approved of Mengistu's bloody "Red Terror," unleashed on perceived internal enemies and counterrevolutionaries in 1977.[36] Evidence from the Soviet archives shows that the Kremlin was determined to prevent the reemergence in Addis Ababa of "nationalistic moods" that expressed growing skepticism about the economic benefits of relations with the socialist bloc, while the West supposedly lurked with the intent of seducing Moscow's new ally away from it.[37] "It is precisely the economic factor that the Western countries are bearing in mind as they pursue a long-term struggle for Ethiopia," warned an August 1978 report from the Soviet embassy there. "They will push Ethiopia toward economic collaboration with the West...to encourage the Ethiopian leadership, if not to supplant, then to cut back on the influence of the USSR."[38] Therefore, Mengistu continued to enjoy Moscow's support as he instigated a catastrophically reckless campaign to transform Ethiopian society, employing ruinously intensive "socialist" farming practices that resulted in deforestation, soil erosion, and man-made famines in the mid-1980s that cost millions of lives. While the latter, widely reported tragedy tarnished the reputation of Moscow's advice and socialism as a development strategy for poor countries, it also completed Soviet officials' growing disillusionment with Africa and the Third World.

By then, Africa was already feeling the full effects of what some scholars dub the neoliberal "counterrevolution" in economic thought and development theory. The Reagan administration quickly appointed convinced neoliberals to run the International Monetary Fund (IMF), which demanded that developing countries ruthlessly cut state budgets, yield to the logic of comparative advantage in the "rational" global market, and terminate expensive policies intended to promote national self-sufficiency and diversification. Tanzania's Julius Nyerere was not alone in perceiving a Western conspiracy to force poor countries to abandon socialism. "When did the IMF become an international Ministry of Finance? When did nations agree to surrender to it their powers of decision making?" he asked Dar-es-Salaam's diplomatic community on New Year's Day, 1980. "[The IMF] has an ideology of economic and social development which it is trying to impose on poor countries irrespective of our own clearly stated policies."[39] As the pioneer of *ujamaa*, Tanzania's unique bid for socialist self-dependence, Nyerere resisted neoliberal reforms until he stepped down from the presidency several years later, but thereafter the country's officials agreed to fundamentally alter the structure of their economy in accordance with the IMF's wishes.[40] So, too, did other would-be shop windows of African socialism, such as Algeria and Ghana.

However, not even the traditionally Western-oriented countries, like Côte d'Ivoire, were spared the counterrevolution's strictures. At independence, Félix Houphouet-Boigny had famously wagered Nkrumah that Ivoirean capitalism would outperform Ghanaian socialism, and indeed his country had enjoyed the best economic performance in sub-Saharan Africa by staying tied to the French currency system and concentrating on maximizing exports of the two colonial crops (cocoa and coffee). Yet Côte d'Ivoire suffered a serious debt crisis when market prices collapsed in the 1980s, and submitted to repeated IMF-mandated reforms that erased the prosperity gains of the past two decades and saw social indices stagnate.[41] Overall, from 1980 to 1990, income per capita in Sub-Saharan Africa declined by 30 percent relative to the West.[42] The neoliberal counterrevolution thus acted as a great leveling force across a diverse continent: the ideological debates, hopes, experiments, successes, and failures of the 1960s and 1970s were rendered irrelevant by the Washington consensus and its generally immiserating effects, at least in the short-term.[43]

Perhaps because there is blood enough in this tale to soak everyone's hands, passions often run high in the retelling of the late Cold War in Africa. Defenders of the Soviet and Cuban involvement in southern Africa rightly point out that Moscow and Havana were on the side of black liberation, while American policymakers have preferred to gloss over their continued support for Pretoria as a regional bulwark against Communism during the 1980s (including even cooperation with the civilian aspects of South Africa's nuclear program) in order to emphasize instead Washington's successful peace-making efforts throughout the region at the end of the decade and in the early 1990s.[44] Both sides like to evoke Nelson Mandela, provider of the only firm moral ground amid the ruins of bygone realpolitik and ideological imperatives.

Likewise, in the economic realm, socialism and capitalism each emerged from the 1980s with damaged reputations in the African context. The defenders of neoliberal structural adjustment would argue that the long-term benefits outweigh the short-term damage, but it is certainly true that the IMF's agents in particular were focused narrowly on abstract economic theories and measures of success, not social concerns and human consequences, and the same criticism can be leveled at the planners of misguided revolutionary experiments such as Ethiopia's. Notably, whereas transnational liberation movements gravitated towards radicalism in the 1960s and 1970s, by the end of the 1980s at least some exiled ANC activists had abandoned their hopes for rapid socioeconomic transformation in post-apartheid South Africa after witnessing firsthand the failures of such dreams in countries such as Zambia.[45] On the whole, therefore, Africa looks to have suffered severe collateral damage from the superpowers' high-stakes geopolitical and ideological confrontations in the closing stages of the Cold War, greatly contributing to the widespread pessimism gripping the continent.

The coincidence of the totalizing conflict between the United States and the Soviet Union with the vital, impressionable period of decolonization affected Africa in significant and lasting ways. It helped shape the fundamental political structures of the postcolonial era, inspire dreams of a prosperous and modern independence, and enable nationalist elites to take and hold onto power in the deceptively durable countries left among the detritus of empire.

One of the earliest, and perhaps the most profound, consequences of the Cold War order was to help channel anticolonial sentiment into nationalist expression—first because the major powers had established a world of states in 1945, and African politicians had to conform to this paradigm in order to seem "credible," "reasonable," or simply comprehensible before international opinion; and second because the irresistible logic of clientelism encouraged the consolidation of state power and the prioritization of *national* interests above other causes. Yet, while the triumph of nationalism and the creation of dozens of independent African states was undoubtedly a positive change from the unjust colonial order, it did by necessity entail the death of certain alternative visions. By 1966, for example, Julius Nyerere recognized that these new political structures almost certainly precluded the implementation of any concrete form of pan-African unity. "For the truth is that there are now 36 different nationalities in free Africa," he told a crowd of Zambian university students. "Each state is separate from the others: each is a sovereign entity . . . which is responsible to the people of its own area—and only them. . . . Let us be honest and admit that [nationalism and pan-Africanism] have already conflicted."[46] Likewise, independence doomed the long-standing dream of Maghrib unity, since Algeria, Morocco, and Tunisia immediately found themselves locked into antagonistic Cold War client-patron relationships and on opposing sides of the era's main left-wing ideological fault line. Even efforts of federalism between philosophically kindred states foundered on the prerogatives of national interests, as was the case for the attempted union of Ghana and Guinea in late 1950s. In short, the realities of the Cold War international system certainly contributed to shattering the sense of internationalist solidarity that had characterized the anticolonial independence movement.

The Cold War's effect on postcolonial dreams of nation- and state-building is also clear, with the modernizing ideologies of East and West promising fast and effective solutions to the poverty gripping most African societies. Though few postcolonial elites actually embraced Communism or Western capitalism without modification or adaptation, the key programmatic elements of those doctrines were fused with new nationalist mythologies to legitimate the rule of the few over the many. In combination, the hopeful expectancy that independence brought and the convincing futurism of Cold War rhetoric were almost guaranteed to disappoint, but the disillusionment was deeper and came more quickly than most would have thought possible in those early days of bunting and celebration. Whereas nationalist elites cultivated an aura of sacrifice and asceticism at first, especially in the self-avowed "revolutionary" countries, by the late 1980s they had almost universally succumbed to the tempting comforts of villas, limousines, and schooling abroad for their children, while simultaneously cutting back on the modernizing social programs once hailed as the nation's raison d'être. In 1992, an Angolan novelist and former MPLA militant, Artur Carlos Maurício Pestana dos Santos, captured the post–Cold War mood with *A Geração da Utopia* (The generation of utopia). This semifictional chronicle followed a group of young revolutionaries from the enthusiasm and danger of the 1960s and 1970s through to a dispiriting decade of postcolonial corruption, complacency, and rampant globalization—the "most savage capitalism seen on Earth"—that the author believed threatened the very fabric of the Angolan nation.[47]

In the two decades since the collapse of the Soviet Union, the changes in U.S. policy toward Africa have being telling. From the unprecedented decision to send American troops into Somalia in 1993, to the subsequent refusal to be drawn into other major conflicts where no national security interests are at stake—such as Rwanda, Congo, and Sudan—it is clear that Washington feels neither constrained nor compelled by a geopolitical rivalry such as that which existed with the USSR. Interestingly, since the end of the Cold War, American policymakers have openly countenanced the idea of redrawing Africa's borders, either in the troubled Great Lakes region or, most currently, the southern half of Sudan. While sustained violence between subnational ethnic or religious groups has inspired such proposals, conflict of that nature has been a common enough occurrence since the late 1950s, so perhaps the key development is the disappearance of Communist diplomatic and material support for the centralizing, nationalist factions that would accuse the United States of neoimperialist, divide-and-rule tactics. For all the discussion of Beijing's support for the government in Khartoum in the early twenty-first century, China's interests in Africa are emphatically business-minded and nonideological, precluding a new Cold War–like dynamic.[48]

Above all, it should be recognized that the continent was not simply a passive victim of outside interference, since its postcolonial elites exploited geopolitical tensions and fought the Cold War's ideological battles as ardently—and frequently more bloodily—as their peers elsewhere. Not that the degree of local empowerment should be exaggerated either, for the penalty for miscalculation vis-à-vis the great powers was severe, but African states did often benefit significantly from the contest between Washington and Moscow.[49] While superpower competition fueled proxy wars and insurgencies, it also enabled the state-building schemes that at least produced a marked improvement in social indicators such as life expectancy and literacy rates during the 1960s and 1970s.[50] In the final analysis, therefore, it is difficult to say whether the reduction in clientelist opportunities since the 1980s is an unambiguous improvement for Africa. In light of the traumas of that decade and subsequent years, it may even be that the worst aspect of the Cold War was the nature of its ending.

NOTES

1. Odd Arne Westad, "Moscow and the Angolan Crisis: A New Pattern of Intervention," *Cold War International History Project Bulletin* 8–9 (1996/1997), 5–31; Piero Gleijeses, *Conflicting Missions: Havana, Washington, and Africa, 1959–1976* (Chapel Hill: University of North Carolina Press, 2002); Sergey Mazov, *A Distant Front in the Cold War: The USSR in West Africa and the Congo, 1956–1964* (Stanford, CA: Stanford University Press, 2010); Sue Onslow, *Cold War in Southern Africa: White Power, Black Liberation* (London: Routledge, 2009); Anna-Mart Van Wyk, "Apartheid's Atomic Bomb: Cold War Perspectives," *South African Historical Journal* 62:1 (March 2010), 100–120; Ryan M. Irwin, "A Wind of Change? White Redoubt and the Postcolonial Moment, 1960–1963," *Diplomatic History* 33:5 (November 2009), 897–925. For archival reports, see Eric J. Morgan, "Researching in the Beloved County: Archives and Adventure in South Africa," *Passport: The Newsletter of the SHAFR* 38:3 (December 2007), 44–47, and Sue Onslow, "Republic of South Africa Archives," *Cold War History* 5:3 (August 2005), 369–375.

2. Jeremi Suri, "The Cold War, Decolonization, and Global Social Awakenings: Historical Intersections.," *Cold War History* 6:3 (2006), 353–363; Tony Smith, "New Bottles for New Wine: A Pericentric Framework for the Study of the Cold War," *Diplomatic History* 24:4 (Fall 2000), 567–591; James Thompson, "Modern Britain and the New Imperial History," *History Compass* 5:2 (March 2007), 455–462; Paul Tiyambe Zeleza, "The Pasts and Futures of African History: A Generational Inventory," *African Historical Review* 39:1 (January 2007), 1–24.

3. Quoted in Michael E. Latham, "The Cold War in the Third World, 1963–1975," *The Cambridge History of the Cold War* (Cambridge: Cambridge University Press, 2010), 1:480.

4. Frederick Cooper, "Possibility and Constraint: African Independence in Historical Perspective," *The Journal of African History* 49:2 (July 2008), 167–196.

5. Wm. Roger Louis and Ronald Robinson, "The Imperialism of Decolonization," in *Ends of British Imperialism: The Scramble for Empire, Suez, and Decolonization:*

Collected Essays, ed. Wm. Roger Louis (London: I. B. Tauris, 2006). See also Jama Mohamed, "Imperial Policies and Nationalism in the Decolonization of Somaliland, 1954–1960." *English Historical Review* 117:474 (November 2002), 1177; and Paul Kelemen, "The British Labor Party and the Economics of Decolonization: The Debate over Kenya," *Journal of Colonialism and Colonial History* 8:3 (Winter 2007), 6.

6. Frederick Cooper, *Africa since 1940: The Past of the Present* (Cambridge: Cambridge University Press, 2002), 80.

7. Immanuel Geiss, *The Pan-African Movement*, trans. Ann Keep (London: Methuen, 1974), 418.

8. Martin Thomas, "France's North African Crisis, 1945–1955: Cold War and Colonial Imperatives," *History* 92:306 (April 2007), 207–234; Ryo Ikeda, "The Paradox of Independence: The Maintenance of Influence and the French Decision to Transfer Power in Morocco," *Journal of Imperial and Commonwealth History* 35:4 (December 2007), 569–592; El-Mostefa Azzou, "La propaganda des nationalistes marocains aux Etats-Unies (1945–1956)," *Guerres Mondiales et Conflits Contemporains* 58:230 (April 2008), 89–98; Klaas Van Walraven, "Decolonization by Referendum: The Anomoly of Niger and the Fall of Sawaba, 1958–1959," *Journal of African History* 50:2 (July 2009), 269–292.

9. Martin Thomas, "Innocent Abroad? Decolonisation and US Engagement with French West Africa, 1945–56," *Journal of Imperial and Commonwealth History* 36:1 (March 2008), 47–73. See also Abolade Adeniji, "The Cold War and American Aid to Nigeria," *Lagos Historical Review* 3 (2003), 112–131.

10. Letter from Hocine Aït Ahmed to FLN leadership in Tunis, July 29, 1960, dossier 8.26, Archives de la Révolution Algérienne, Conseil National de la Révolution Algérienne (CNRA), Algerian National Archives, Algiers.

11. Salim Yaqub, *Containing Arab Nationalism: The Eisenhower Doctrine and the Middle East* (Chapel Hill: The University of North Carolina Press, 2004); Nigel John Ashton, *Eisenhower, Macmillan, and the Problem of Nasser: Anglo-American Relations and Arab Nationalism, 1955–59* (London: Palgrave Macmillan, 1996).

12. Hakeem Ibikunle Tijani, "Britain and the Foundation of Anti-Communist Policies in Nigeria, 1945–1960," *African and Asian Studies* 8:1/2 (February 2009), 47–66; Ritchie Ovendale, "Macmillan and the Wind of Change in Africa, 1957–1960," *Historical Journal* 38:2 (June 1995), 455–477; Ann Lane, "Third World Neutralism and British Cold War Strategy, 1960–62," *Diplomacy and Statecraft* 14:3 (September 2003), 151–174.

13. Peter J. Schraeder, "Cold War to Cold Peace: Explaining U.S.–French Competition in Francophone Africa," *Political Science Quarterly* 115:3 (Fall 2000), 395; Berny Sebe, "In the Shadow of the Algerian War: The United States and the Common Organisation of Saharan Regions (OCRS), 1957–62," *Journal of Imperial and Commonwealth History* 38:2 (June 2010), 303–322; El-Mostafa Azzou, "La présence militaire américaine au Maroc, 1945–1963" (French), *Guerres Mondiales et Conflits Contemporains* 53:210 (April 2003), 125–132; Irwin M. Wall, *France,*

the United States, and the Algerian War (Berkeley: University of California Press, 2001); Matthew James Connelly, *A Diplomatic Revolution: Algeria's Fight for Independence and the Origins of the Post–Cold War Era* (New York: Oxford University Press, 2002).

14. Elizabeth Schmidt, *Cold War and Decolonization in Guinea, 1946–1958,* (Athens: Ohio University Press, 2007).

15. Thomas J. Noer, "The New Frontier and African Neutralism: Kennedy, Nkrumah, and the Volta River Project," *Diplomatic History* 8:4 (Winter 1984), 61–79; Philip E. Muehlenbeck, "Kennedy and Touré: A Success in Personal Diplomacy," *Diplomacy and Statecraft* 19:1 (2008), 69–95; Sergey Mazov, *A Distant Front in the Cold War: The USSR in West Africa and the Congo, 1956–1964* (Stanford, CA: Stanford University Press, 2010).

16. Madeleine Kalb, *Congo Cables: The Cold War in Africa from Eisenhower to Kennedy* (New York: Macmillan, 1982); Crawford Young and Thomas Turner, *The Rise and Decline of the Zairian State* (Madison: University of Wisconsin Press, 1985); Larry Devlin, *Chief of Station, Congo: Fighting the Cold War in a Hot Zone* (New York: Public Affairs, 2008); Sergie Mazoz, "Soviet Aid to the Gizenga Government in the Former Belgian Congo (1960–61) as Reflected in Russian Archives," *Cold War History* 7:3 (August 2007), 425–437.

17. Robert H. Jackson, *Quasi-States: Sovereignty, International Relations, and the Third World* (Cambridge: Cambridge University Press, 1993); Bertrand Badie, *The Imported State: The Westernization of the Political Order* (Stanford, CA: Stanford University Press, 2000); James R. Brennan, "Lowering the Sultan's Flag: Sovereignty and Decolonization in Coastal Kenya," *Comparative Studies in Society and History* 50:4 (October 2008), 831–861.

18. Sara Lorenzini, "Globalising Ostpolitik," *Cold War History* 9:2 (May 2009), 223–242; Massimiliano Trentin, "Tough Negotiations. The Two Germanys in Syria and Iraq, 1963–74," *Cold War History* 8:3 (August 2008), 353–380; Brigitte Schulz, *Development Policy in the Cold War Era: The Two Germanies and Sub-Saharan Africa, 1960–1985* (Berlin: Lit Verlag, 1995).

19. Odd Arne Westad, *The Global Cold War: Third World Interventions and the Making of Our Times* (Cambridge: Cambridge University Press, 2007); James C. Scott, *Seeing Like a State: How Certain Schemes to Improve the Human Condition Have Failed* (New Haven, CT: Yale University Press, 1999); Forrest D. Colburn, *The Vogue of Revolution in Poor Countries* (Princeton, NJ: Princeton University Press, 1994).

20. Jason C. Parker, "'Made-in-America Revolutions'? The 'Black University' and the American Role in the Decolonization of the Black Atlantic," *Journal of American History* 96:3 (December 2009), 727–750; Erez Manela, *The Wilsonian Moment: Self-Determination and the International Origins of Anticolonial Nationalism* (New York: Oxford University Press, 2009).

21. First quotation from Basil Davidson, *Modern Africa: A Social and Political History* (London: Longman, 1995), 65; excerpt from *Storms on the Niger* by Mok-

wugo Okoye, reproduced in *Ideologies of Liberation in Black Africa, 1856–1970: Documents on Modern African Political Thought from Colonial Times to the Present*, ed. J. Ayodele Langley and Immanuel Wallerstein (London: R. Collings, 1979), 3:405.

22. Speech of J. T. Gumede, president of the African National Congress, at the International Congress against Imperialism, Brussels, February 10–15, 1927, http://www.anc.org.za/show.php?id=4544&t=The%20Early%20Years.

23. Colin Legum, "African Outlooks toward the USSR," in *Communism in Africa*, ed. David E. Albright (Bloomington: Indiana University Press, 1980), 7–25; Ben Bella quoted in Robert Merle, *Ben Bella*, trans. Camilla Sykes (London: Michael Joseph, 1967), 146.

24. Daniel Speich, "The Kenyan Style of 'African Socialism': Developmental Knowledge Claims and the Explanatory Limits of the Cold War," *Diplomatic History* 33:3 (June 2009), 449–466.

25. Frederick Cooper, *Decolonization and African Society: The Labor Question in French and British Africa* (Cambridge: Cambridge University Press, 1996); Tony Chafer, "Education and Political Socialisation of a National-Colonial Political Elite in French West Africa, 1936–47," *Journal of Imperial and Commonwealth History* 35:3 (September 2007), 437–458.

26. Amilcar Cabral, interviewed in *Tricontinental* (Havana) 8 (September-October 1968), reproduced in *African Liberation Reader: The National Liberation Movements*, ed. Aquino de Bragança and Immanuel Wallerstein (London: Zed Press, 1982), 2:163–165.

27. For example, see Yves Loiseau and Pierre-guillaume de Roux, *Portrait d'un révolutionnaire en général: Jonas Savimbi* (Paris: La Table Ronde, 1987), 106–107; Steven Jackson, "China's Third World Foreign Policy: The Case of Angola and Mozambique, 1961–93," *China Quarterly* 142 (1995), 388–422; Alan Hutchinson, *China's African Revolution* (London: Hutchinson, 1975).

28. Undated report by the Africa Desk of the Algerian foreign ministry (probably from 1965), "La Lutte de libération en Afrique australe: Eléments pour une stratégie, document de base," box 93, series 33/2000, Archives of the Ministère des Affaires Etrangères, Algerian National Archives, Algiers.

29. David Priestland, *The Red Flag: A History of Communism* (New York: Grove Press, 2009), 396–398, 469–473.

30. Gleijeses, *Conflicting Missions*, 242; David E. Albright, "Moscow's African Policy of the 1970s," in *Communism in Africa*, ed. David E. Albright (Bloomington: Indiana University Press, 1980), 40–42.

31. Westad, *Global Cold War*, 213–215.

32. See, for example, Westad, *Global Cold War*, 207–249; Piero Gleijeses, "Moscow's Proxy? Cuba and Africa, 1975–1988," *Journal of Cold War Studies* 8:2 (Spring 2006), 98–146; Piero Gleijeses, "Cuba and the Independence of Namibia," *Cold War History* 7:2 (May 2007), 285–303; Sue Onslow, "A Question of Timing: South Africa and Rhodesia's Unilateral Declaration of Independence, 1964–

65," *Cold War History* 5:2 (May 2005), 129–159; and Chris Saunders, "Namibian Solidarity: British Support for Namibian Independence," *Journal of Southern African Studies* 35:2 (June 2009), 437–454.

33. For an excellent overview of the late Cold War in southern Africa, see Chris Saunders and Sue Onslow, "The Cold War and Southern Africa, 1976–1990," *The Cambridge History of the Cold War* (Cambridge: Cambridge University Press, 2010), 3:432–470, as well as the accompanying bibliographic essay on 3:1079–1083.

34. For a detailed history of the Ethiopian-Somalian conflict, see Gebru Tareke, *The Ethiopian Revolution: War in the Horn of Africa* (New Haven, CT: Yale University Press, 2009).

35. Donald L. Donham, *Marxist Modern: An Ethnographic History of the Ethiopian Revolution* (Berkeley: University of California Press, 1999); Andargachew Tiruneh, *The Ethiopian Revolution, 1974–1987: A Transformation from an Aristocratic to a Totalitarian Autocracy* (Cambridge: Cambridge University Press, 2009).

36. Westad, *Global Cold War*, 274

37. See the July 14, 1978 decision by the Central Committee of the Communist Party of the Soviet Union to provide more aid to Ethiopia, and the accompanying July 11, 1978 note from the foreign ministry, *Cold War International History Project* online archive, www.cwihp.org.

38. Soviet Embassy in Ethiopia, background report on "Ethiopia's Relations with Western Countries," August 14, 1978, *Cold War International History Project* online archive, www.cwihp.org.

39. Quoted in James M. Boughton, *Silent Revolution: The International Monetary Fund, 1979–1989* (Washington, DC: IMF, 2001), 598–599.

40. Werner Biermann and Jumanne Wagao, "The Quest for Adjustment: Tanzania and the IMF, 1980–1986," *African Studies Review* 29:4 (December 1986), 89–103.

41. See figures in Cooper, *Africa since 1940*, 93–97.

42. Giovanni Arrighi, *The Long Twentieth Century: Money, Power, and the Origins of Our Times* (London: Verso, 2010); Jeffry Frieden, *Global Capitalism: Its Fall and Rise in the Twentieth Century* (New York: Norton, 2006), 363–391.

43. James M. Boughton, *Silent Revolution: The International Monetary Fund, 1979–1989* (Washington, DC: IMF, 2001), 578–585.

44. Vladimir Shubin, *ANC: A View from Moscow* (Cape Town: Mayibuye Books, 1999), and *The Hot "Cold War": The USSR in Southern Africa* (London: Pluto Press, 2008); Chester Crocker, *High Noon in Southern Africa: Making Peace in a Rough Neighborhood* (New York: Oxford University Press, 1992); Peter W. Rodman, *More Precious than Peace* (New York: Charles Scribner's Sons, 1994). On U.S.–South African nuclear cooperation, see Anna-Mart Van Wyk, "Ally or Critic? The United States' Response to South African Nuclear Development, 1949–1980," *Cold War History* 7:2 (May 2007), 169–225, and the same author's "Sunset over Atomic Apartheid: US–South African Nuclear Relations, 1981–1993," *Cold War History* 10:1 (February 2010), 51–79.

45. Hugh MacMillan, "The African National Congress of South Africa in Zambia: The Culture of Exile and the Changing Relationship with Home, 1964–1990," *Journal of Southern African Studies* 35:2 (June 2009), 303–329.

46. Julius Nyerere, *Freedom and Socialism: A Selection from Writings and Speeches, 1965–1967* (Dar es Salaam: Oxford University Press, 1968), 207–217.

47. Artur Carlos Maurício Pestana dos Santos, *A Geração da Utopia* (Alfragide, Portugal: Pepetela, 1992), quoted in Phyllis Anne Peres, *Transculturation and Resistance in Lusophone African Narrative* (Gainesville: University Press of Florida, 1997), 84–87.

48. For a useful overview, see Jessica Achberger, "The Dragon Has Not Just Arrived: The Historical Study of Africa's Relations with China," *History Compass* 8:5 (May 2010), 368–376.

49. See, for example, Jamie Monson, *Africa's Freedom Railway: How a Chinese Development Project Changed Lives and Livelihoods in Tanzania* (Bloomington: Indiana University Press, 2009).

50. Cooper, *Africa since 1940*, 93–97.

7

DECOLONIZATION, THE COLD WAR, AND THE POST-COLUMBIAN ERA

JASON C. PARKER

Christopher Columbus departed this earth in Spain in 1506. There is, however, another sense in which he died four and a half centuries later, and in many places all at once. Scholars speak of the pre-Columbian era before 1492; the twentieth-century retreat of the overseas European empires logically suggests the start of the post-Columbian era—and the case can be made for a bigger watershed still. Postwar decolonization not only dissolved the European empires; it ended formal, territorial empire itself as a norm and practice. Formal-imperial expansionism had defined "state" actors dating back to ancient Egypt. In the historical blink of an eye after 1945, it was disavowed. The persistence of informal empire suggests it may be too much to say that the "age of empire" has ended. But the disappearance of formal empire surely ended an era. Just as Columbian colonialism had helped to launch the European-dominated era of world history five centuries ago, decolonization brought it to a close.

Decolonization culminated during a Cold War that ended Europe's short twentieth century. Although the superpowers' arsenals produced the threat of apocalyptic war, at ground zero in Europe the conflict yielded the "long peace." This was not the case outside Europe. Because the Cold War was a comprehensive struggle—geographical, ideological, and psychological—there was no dimension of international or domestic society it could not potentially touch. For the superpowers and the retreating empires alike, this meant an inclination to view events through the prism of the Cold War.[1] Actors across the global South often did not reply in kind. As historian Thomas Borstelmann notes, it was colonialism, not Communism, that was most on colonial minds in the 1940s.[2] But colonials could rarely prevent the superpower conflict from seeping into their struggles. When this occurred, and the Cold War took demonic possession of a local transition, the results counted among the bloodiest of postwar episodes.

The overlapping timelines of decolonization and Cold War create a fascinating interrelationship. Decolonization is dizzying in its scale and complex in its definition; it was shared by more people on the planet than virtually any other postwar historical phenomenon.[3] It entailed not just the transfer of juridical sovereignty but also an intellectual process that dethroned European assertions and affirmed nationalist self-rule—and it began, in fits and starts and in many places, well before the Cold War. But the Cold War in many of those places shaped how it would end. In some of these, the incursion produced disaster; in all, it was an unavoidable if not always a decisive presence. Recent scholarship reveals that the relationship of decolonization to the Cold War was as much complicated, chronological, and coincidental as it was straightforward, organic, and hereditary. One phenomenon did not give birth to the other, though the relationship once developed was no less consequential for it.

Decolonization served as the main conduit by which the Cold War reached—and in a sense created—the "Third World."[4] It could do so in a variety of ways, and from either direction. The superpowers could inject t Cold War into anticolonial struggles, sometimes disfiguring them recognition—but local actors had considerable latitude in e their own purposes. The discovery of this Third World agency pally from historians' embrace of "transnational" approaches a and from the integration of area-, empire-, and subaltern-studi literature on postwar global relations. Together, these suggest an scholarly definition of decolonization and its place in international The ultimate dimensions of the process—already underway by the ti the Cold War, which first slowed and then sped it along—make it a la and longer-running twentieth-century story than the superpower conflict.

*   *   *

The Cold War was such a "total" phenomenon in its time that it recast the templates by which world events were understood.[5] But its era incorporated currents, such as anticolonial nationalism, that long predated the superpower conflict. That nationalism, which energized the push for independence, had its origins in day-to-day encounters on the colonial ground, and in transformative experiences in the metropoles. Of the latter, colonials' World War I service in Europe and expatriate life in the interwar metropoles were especially profound.[6] These became the basis for a reimagining of destiny

along various lines, among them national, racial, regional—but always, ultimately, postimperial. This protonationalist activism hit an early peak in the
"Wilsonian moment" of spring 1919.[7] President Woodrow Wilson's validation of "self-determination" at Versailles electrified nationalists the world
over, who saw it as a potential watershed in their countries' fates. Wilson's
endorsement did not intend this anytime soon, and his rhetoric on its own did
not spark their anticolonial visions. But Wilson's stance was welcome evidence that norms were evolving. If the Wilsonian promise proved short-lived,
it still sufficed to harden the nationalists' convictions that the colonial regime
would not prove eternal. That regime was yet hardy, bolstered by the League
of Nations Mandate system. In the 1930s it was buffeted by widespread,
violent colonial unrest, and undercut by diasporan "visionary" movements
that envisioned various racial-cum-national destinies, all of which prompted
nationalists to imagine alternatives to the colonial regime.[8]

Whatever legitimacy the imperial system retained on the eve of World War
II it lost in that cataclysm. Many nationalists recognized that the war tested
the empires' strength in both practical and moral terms. In most incarnations
of that test, the empires failed. The Japanese conquest, culminating in the
February 1942 fall of Singapore, for example, offered a brutal verdict, as the
Asians in whose name the supposedly beneficent empire existed refused to
take up arms in its defense. The Quit India movement—even allowing for
its limited strength and quick demise—warned that a similar situation might
unfold if the Japanese pressed their advance.[9] In the conquered British and
French colonies, local elites sold cheap whatever popular legitimacy they had
by collaborating. That legitimacy, and the mantle of true nationalism—those
who would fight for the "nation" against outsider rule—transferred to figures
like Sukarno and Ho Chi Minh. Such Asian leaders could hear in President
Franklin Delano Roosevelt's rhetoric and in the August 1941 Atlantic Charter
an echo of Wilson's support for self-determination.[10] Nationalists realized
that the imperial reflex did not disappear during the war. They saw, too, to
their disappointment, that at war's end the forces of the imperial status quo
had maneuvered the United Nations into agnosticism on colonial questions.
But most activists believed that momentum was largely on their side and
that, sooner or later, some combination of nationalist pressure, European
bankruptcy, and American acquiescence would crack the colonial edifice for
good. At any rate, neither they, nor most U.S. and European actors, thought
in 1945 that the story was over.

In the strange postwar twilight before the Cold War took definitive
shape, decolonization advanced in certain locales, though it stalled in
most, as nationalist agitation met imperial resolve. If any common theme

guided events at this stage, it was the double helix of European recovery and global stability amid an international environment of uneasy flux. The possible spread of Communism as such was not yet a globalized concern for Washington; it was localized within Europe, except in areas like Indochina where an indigenous voice spoke it. Importantly, the double helix could point in either direction—either toward decolonization or toward reasserted empire. The decision on which direction to go depended heavily on the strength and character of a given nationalist movement. The Netherlands and France, for example, facing strong nationalist leaders in Indonesia and Indochina, pushed to reimpose their rule, seeking to retain the colonial economic output crucial to metropolitan recovery. Britain, by contrast, argued the importance of recovery in advancing decolonization in the subcontinent and the Levant. London envisioned a transfer of power in some colonies but a withdrawal of influence in almost none.[11] Nonetheless, many nationalists thought this "imperialism of decolonization" a lesser concern, to be overcome after independence. The transfer of political-juridical power was the key and the goal.[12] As for the United States, Washington practiced a kind of passive-progressive decolonization in the Philippines in 1946 and otherwise generally deferred to its allies' judgment. The notable exception was Indonesia, which the Truman administration supported against the Dutch once Sukarno showed his willingness to suppress Communists.[13]

In most of these early episodes of "first wave" decolonization—that is, from 1946 to 1949—the Cold War was no more than a secondary or post facto concern. This owed in large measure to the fact that the conflict was itself, as yet, less than fully formed. To the extent the Cold War had begun casting shadows, it did so overwhelmingly in Europe and its near periphery. The tensions that had begun rising at Yalta, Westminster College, the United Nations, and elsewhere had not yet coalesced into a fully global conflict. The closest it had yet come was the March 1947 Truman Doctrine, which declared a conflict of global scope. The doctrine generated another, meaner echo of the "Wilsonian moment," in referring to "free peoples…resisting attempted subjugation by armed minorities or by outside pressures." The point was directed at European "majorities" such as the Greeks or Czechs, but colonial ears could plausibly hear it as indicating the European empires.

The Indian reception of the Truman Doctrine five months before independence illustrates the rank of the Cold War in the calculations of the nationalist leadership. It was a distraction from plans underway and secondarily a threat to the multilateral institutions set up to organize the postwar order.[14] By contrast, for Washington the Communist specter was already hovering—but more above the continued privation in continental Europe than above the prospect of distant swaths of the globe turning red. Moreover, for Washington, that prospect could cut in both policy directions, and did cut toward whichever was the more pressing anti-Communist concern. Hence the United States threw its support to France against Ho, but at the crucial moment to Sukarno against the Netherlands. By contrast, as seen from New Delhi or from the Southeast Asian countryside, the independence struggles engaged Communism instrumentally, as one tool in the local fight. Both Ho and Sukarno, for diametrically different reasons, invoked it. But both were—and were understood by their populaces to be—nationalists above all.

At the crest of the "first wave," India and Pakistan became independent in August 1947. There, too, Communism played little more than a bit part— and a forgettable one compared to the horrific violence that followed. A contemporaneous partition in the Middle East produced Arab-Israeli violence the next year. While Cold War concerns played into American and Soviet—and to a lesser extent, Israeli and Arab—decision making, they were of less importance than the dynamics on the Palestinian ground. The Cold War presented certain fundamentally external factors, even potential threats, to both players in both partitions. But its overarching battles were not their own. In his speech at independence, for example, Nehru acknowledged geopolitical reality—but then avowed a destiny beyond it: "It is a fateful moment...for all Asia and for the world. A new star rises, the star of freedom in the East...a vision long cherished materializes." By the time the first wave ebbed in Indonesia in 1949, the Cold War had begun intruding there, finally leading the United States to take sides with Sukarno as an anti-Communist bulwark. This reflected, at a distance, that the Cold War had by then taken on recognizable form, molded by events in Europe. But by that moment, with the notable exception of Indochina, the first-wave battles were over.

The U.S. stance on this first wave was somewhat confused, ad hoc, and dominated by anti-Communism. In practice, this meant that as decolonization began to take shape, Washington actively—though in the end temporarily—ensured the continuation of Europe's empires. It did so largely unenthusiastically, as officials recognized the contradiction with America's oft-stated anticolonial principle. The Truman and Eisenhower administrations sought to reconcile this contradiction by gently pressing allies to ensure that imperial rule would neither restore the bad old days nor last forever, but would begin winding down in orderly fashion. As early as 1947, the State Department was arguing internally that the "political advancement of dependent peoples is inevitable.''[15] However, in most cases Washington came down on the side of the imperial status quo for fear that change might offer the Communists an opening. Indochina showed how colonial struggles could morph into Cold War battles—and of the time, effort, and machinations required to do so. Tellingly, even at a site where a nationalist of Communist sympathies like Ho was present, the metamorphosis from colonial struggle to Cold War theater depended on Western officials winning bureaucratic battles and shaping U.S. perceptions.[16] Nor was there much evidence of active Soviet interest in most such first-wave extra-European theaters, especially relative to the much greater enthusiasm that would follow Stalin's death. At this early stage, then, an organic connection to Communism on the ground was an essential but not sufficient element to turn a colonial struggle into a Cold War one.

This early Cold War moment of relative fluidity regarding decolonization's first wave, from 1946 to 1949, ended with the outbreak of war in Korea. The war there—technically a decolonizing area—illustrated the dangers of political transition infected by the superpower conflict. It did not wholly freeze anticolonial nationalism, but it slowed metropolitan plans and nationalist hopes. These, in a sense, had been going in opposite directions. London, for example, saw the first wave as being the only wave in the near future, believing the empires had some decades yet to run. The nationalists, by contrast, were finding their voice—and each other. They saw the first wave not as a one-off but as a precedent—though not necessarily as a blueprint, as activists turned to violence in places like Malaya, Kenya, and Algeria.[17] But on the whole, the Korea-hardened Cold War stances of the superpowers outside Europe led most parties to tread carefully. When Eisenhower's U.S. Information Agency made the non-European world a priority, or when Khruschev toured newly independent nations, superpower interest was confirmed—as was the delicacy of engagement. As a result, the first half of the decade saw a notable freeze in the decolonization process.

At that point, a cluster of six events changed the global conversation about imperial and racial relations. Few of these events had more than a second-tier Cold War dimension in their initial stages, though some later acquired one. The forty months between May 1954 and September 1957 altered the dynamics in what were, in retrospect, remarkable ways. Three of the events seemed uniquely American: the May 1954 *Brown v. Board of Education* decision; the December 1955 Montgomery Bus Boycott; and the September 1957 Little Rock school desegregation crisis.[18] Though not directly connected to decolonization, these nonetheless indicated that race relations—both within citizenries and between nations—were in flux.

African-American activists and colonial nationalists watched each others' struggles, finding unexpected connections that gave a world-historical scope to what seemed otherwise local battles.[19] A fourth event, the Bandung Conference of April 1955, provided the clearest instance of this. Bandung brought together twenty-nine emerging nations to declare, among other things, a shared commitment to anticolonialism, antiracism, and "neutralism." Bandung in the end had greater symbolic than consequential importance. Its significance, in the eyes of many in Washington, was its utility in stabilizing the Cold War in Asia. But to others there, as well as to observers such as Richard Wright, it signaled a potentially radical departure. It suggested that even if the actual power and unity of the Afro-Asian world was still limited, the determination to keep up the pressure for decolonization was nonetheless strong.[20] Henceforth, diverse African and Asian voices, as the pan-African magazine *Presence Africaine* put it, would assert "the solidarity of the colonized peoples."[21]

Events later in the decade further altered global norms and advanced the decolonization process—none more so than the Suez Crisis. When Egyptian premier Gamal Abdel Nasser nationalized the Suez Canal in July 1956, he set in motion an international crisis culminating in an Anglo-French-Israeli military intervention, one ultimately ended by Washington's forcing its allies to withdraw. This turn of events repercussed through both East-West and North-South relations, and the U.S. role in the crisis followed both axes. American determination to block the expansion of Soviet influence was not the only motivation. Equally or more powerful was, in Salim Yaqub's phrase, the "containment of Arab nationalism."[22] In a sense, Washington's commitment to a dual Cold War–decolonization imperative led the United States to take actions that helped to invigorate decolonization. Among Suez's consequences were the triumph of Nasser and of "Third World" assertiveness; the end of interventionist European imperialism; and the utter demoralization of the stewards of the British Empire. The debacle, and the ongoing bloodshed in Algeria, showed all parties what could happen if decolonization was done "wrong" by a recalcitrant metropole, an invigorated nationalism, or a violent resistance movement.

A sixth event, mere months later, was the March 6 independence of Ghana. The transfer of power in Accra was the antithesis of Suez: peaceful, cooperative, methodical, and applauded by virtually all parties. The superpowers were lavish in their praise of the new state and restrained in their Cold War overtures to it.[23] This owed in no small part to the accurate calculation that bombast would backfire. By all indications, the Cold War mattered less to new premier Kwame Nkrumah than did African nationalism, pan-Africanism, and the orderly devolution of authority. Careful observers knew that Nkrumah had sought this moment since the 1930s—that is, since before the Cold War—and that he and a transnational cohort of nationalists such as Nigeria's Nnamdi Azikiwe saw the moment as a millenial event in the history of race relations more than as part of the superpower conflict.[24] It was not only that, as Nkrumah put it, "Africans have no intention of becoming part of…this tragic polarization." It was also that, as the December 1958 All-African People's Conference declared, Africans had a positive and more important duty: to overcome the "artificial frontiers drawn by imperialist powers to divide [African] peoples."[25] The final event, chronologically, in this cluster, the Little Rock Crisis, similarly had Cold War overtones— insofar as global-South audiences saw in its newsreels a vivid contradiction of American claims to being the leader of the "free world"—but it had a race-revolution core that, in the freedom of sub-Saharan Africa, contrasted with events in Ghana. It was the racial conflict, thought Nkrumah and his cohort, that must be kept at bay to the degree possible. They saw that the Cold War offered certain opportunities for emerging states. But they were determined to keep their focus on the national, and possibly transnationally racial, destiny that decolonization held out before them.

As sub-Saharan Africa followed Ghana into the "second wave," cautionary tales abounded. The intransigence of the Salazar regime left Portuguese Africa basically untouched by the "winds of change" that British prime minister Harold Macmillan acknowledged in 1960. The agony in Algeria moved France to dismantle its empire elsewhere. De Gaulle's 1958 declaration of a "French community" accompanied independence in all remaining French colonies except Guinea.[26] The abruptness of France's departure was matched by Belgium's, which abandoned the Congo pell-mell in 1960 just as Patrice Lumumba's Congolese National Movement (MNC) gained critical mass. The chaos of the Belgian departure induced a power struggle among Congolese factions and a contest for influence between the superpowers. Lumumba's disillusionment with the West, along with his openness to the East bloc, helped to turn the Congo into a Cold War pawn. His murder in January 1961 at the hands of Katangan enemies abetted by the Belgians and the CIA, and the installation of pro-Western strongman Mobutu, demonstrated the degree to which the Cold War could infiltrate and brutalize a decolonization process. Moreover, the enthusiastic Communist-bloc interest in what Khrushchev called the "world-historical opportunity" of Third World decolonization hinted that this would not be the last such infiltration.[27] If the December 1960 "Decolonization Declaration"—adopted by the UN General Assembly without dissent—reflected the year's tenor, the next month Eisenhower's actions on the Congo and Khrushchev's support for "wars of national liberation" were reminders that the Cold War could leach into any opening that the decolonization process might present.[28]

One striking aspect of the Congo tragedy, however, is less that its decolonization became consumed by the Cold War than that it was relatively alone among contemporaries in doing so. In 1960, the "Year of Africa" in which sixteen other countries won independence, most of their transitions won rhetorical and even material support from the superpowers. But none of them were transformed from colonial struggle to Cold War theater quite so fully as Indochina and the Congo. The exceptionalism of the bloodiest cases became a vivid reminder of what could go wrong, and the pattern across both the first and second waves of decolonization was by now clear. Any transition had the potential to be hijacked by the Cold War. However, most of the cases from Asia in the 1940s to Africa between 1957 and 1963 had the Cold War as background music, not as script. Even in dramatic cases such as Kenya, the violence had only a passing connection to the superpower conflict, and was rooted more deeply in communal struggles for power, imperial repression, or both.

This would prove less true for the frequently bloody "third wave," from the late 1960s to the mid-1970s—partly for a reason coming from outside the decolonizing world. The Cuban Revolution helped to infuse the Cold War into the decolonization of Portuguese Africa. Fidel Castro's triumph inspired the aging Soviet leadership, and his regime became a patron and radical role model to African revolutionaries.[29] Their homelands witnessed some of the most bitter fighting of the decolonization struggle, prolonged by the intrusion of the Cold War and by the obstinance of the Salazar regime. That regime's fall in 1974, in part due to the colonial wars, was a final necessary element in the decolonization of Africa. The role of South Africa in the denouement underlined the now-contradictory dimensions of race: the change in the international dynamics of race relations was palpable, but holdouts in southern Africa suggested that the "millenial" visions of global race-revolution that had helped to drive the independence struggle were not an inevitable destiny. Nonetheless, the independence of Angola and Mozambique in 1975 ended European empire in Africa. The denouement that same spring of Vietnam's thirty years of war make it a convenient, if admittedly imprecise, endpoint for the third wave, during and after which the Soviets believed that "the world was going [their] way" in the global South, acting there enthusiastically and accordingly.[30] During the next decade, bloody epilogues across the Third World affirmed that decolonization was not the only momentous transition of the postwar era. Moreover, these showed that Cold War factors did not require decolonization in order to insert themselves into local political flux, which they had a continuing power to warp even after independence.[31]

*   *   *

As the third decade of the post–Cold War era begins, and as the nation-states born of decolonization pass through middle age, international-history scholarship has begun to treat the interactions between the two epochal phenomena in their fullest scope. Much earlier work on diplomatic history concentrated on strategy and security and on bilateral relations between super- and other powers. Much earlier work on decolonization likewise focused on a particular bilateral relationship and on a basically political-mechanical process. Few treated the subject as a problem much broader than the case at hand. This owed partly to the scale of the archival research required to cover more than one bilateral relationship. But it also owed to the "bounded" nature of the approach. If the transfer of power in, say, India is seen primarily as an extended constitutional negotiation, it misses any number of angles: cultural and intellectual dimensions; the global strategic picture; and the mutual influence of India and its peers at places like Bandung that connected points along a periphery.

Recent works have begun to "unbind" the literature, illuminating the interrelationship between decolonization and the Cold War. This has helped to disentangle the conceptual and more elementally the chronological threads between them. It becomes clear, for example, that some components of the decolonization process date back to the 1930s, and even to the 1910s.[32] Moreover, the fluid onset of the Cold War meant that it arrived in different places at different times, and did not reach many parts of the world until well after it had become entrenched in Europe. The arrival, moreover, took varied forms. It could produce, as in Zaire (the former Congo), a strongman-puppet of a superpower. But the intervention of area-studies scholarship argues against seeing this as wholly a creation of the Cold War.[33] The machinery—such as it was—of the colonial state inherited by the nationalists long predated the Cold War's predations, and in most cases had a larger impact on day-to-day postcolonial life. Furthermore, a case like Zaire had more in common with many of its neighbors based on their shared inheritance of the colonial state than it differed from them based on the Cold War. For all its blood and drama, the Cold War thus perhaps had less to do with decolonization as a global process than one might suppose based on their chronological coincidence—or based on the fact that at certain sites, the former twisted the latter into something awful. For Third World actors, the Cold War was but one (albeit enormous) strategic factor with which to contend. At particular sites, it was overpowering. But at others, it could present opportunities, threats, or even, in the long run, mere background noise.

The transnational consequences of the Cold War–decolonization collision could be large indeed. Chief among these must be counted the genesis of the "Third World" as a geopolitical concept, as its coalescence into the Non-Aligned Movement altered the original design and tenor of the United Nations in ways that body's creators hardly anticipated. But closer to the formerly colonial ground, continuities and inheritances dominated. These underscore the agency of nationalist actors and the salience of factors besides the Cold War in shaping the transition to independence and the transformation of the atlas. As the literature on that transformation continues to combine the best aspects of Cold War historiography with those of imperial and area studies, it forms a fuller map of the modern era—one perhaps as intellectually provocative as the one Columbus brought back to Spain.

NOTES

1. Matthew Connelly, "Taking off the Cold War Lens: Visions of North-South Conflict during the Algerian War for Independence," *American Historical Review* 105:3 (June 2000), 739–769.

2. Thomas Borstelmann, *Apartheid's Reluctant Uncle: The United States and Southern Africa in the Early Cold War* (New York: Oxford University Press, 1993), 195.

3. In John Darwin's phrase, no "other recent historical experience unites so much of the world's population." John Darwin, "Decolonization and End of Empire," in *The Oxford History of the British Empire,* vol. 5: *Historiography,* ed. Robin W. Winks (New York: Oxford University Press, 1999), 556. See also Prasenjit Duara, *Decolonization: Perspectives from Now and Then* (New York: Routledge, 2003), 1; and Frederick Cooper, *Decolonization and African Society: The Labor Question in French and British Africa* (New York: Cambridge University Press, 1996).

4. Though the term *Third World* has fallen into disfavor, Odd Arne Westad argues for its historical importance as a creation of the Cold War. Odd Arne Westad, *The Global Cold War: Third World Interventions and the Making of Our Times* (New York: Cambridge University Press, 2005). See also Arturo Escobar, *Encountering Development: The Making and Unmaking of the Third World* (Princeton, NJ: Princeton University Press, 1995).

5. Kenneth Osgood, *Total Cold War: Eisenhower's Secret Propaganda Battle at Home and Abroad* (Lawrence: University Press of Kansas, 2006), 1–2; Cary Fraser,

"A Requiem for the Cold War: Reviewing the History of International Relations since 1945," in *Rethinking the Cold War*, ed. Allen Hunter (Philadelphia: Temple University Press, 1997), 93–116.

6. On the effect of war and "exile," see Glenford Howe, *Race, War, and Nationalism: A Social History of West Indians in the First World War* (Kingston, Jamaica: Ian Randle Publishers, 2002); Winston James, *Holding Aloft the Banner of Ethiopia: Caribbean Radicalism in America* (New York: Verso Press, 1996); Jason Parker, *Brother's Keeper: The United States, Race, and Empire in the British Caribbean, 1937–1962* (New York: Oxford University Press, 2008); and Gary Wilder, *The French Imperial Nation-State: Negritude and Colonial Humanism between the Two World Wars* (Chicago: University of Chicago Press, 2005).

7. Erez Manela, *The Wilsonian Moment: Self-Determination and the International Origins of Anticolonial Nationalism* (New York: Oxford University Press, 2007).

8. The riots were seen as a harbinger in W. M. Macmillan, *Warning from the West Indies: A Tract for Africa and the Empire* (London: Penguin, 1936). See O. Nigel Bolland, *On the March: Labour Rebellions in the British Caribbean, 1934–1939* (Kingston, Jamaica: James Currey Publishers, 1995); and Robert D. Pearce, *The Turning Point in Africa: British Colonial Policy 1938–48* (London: Routledge, 1982).

9. Christopher Bayly and Tim Harper, *Forgotten Wars: Freedom and Revolution in Southeast Asia* (Cambridge, MA: Belknap Press, 2007); Manzoor Ahmad, *Indian Response to the Second World War* (New Delhi: South Asia Books, 1987).

10. Wm. Roger Louis, *Imperialism at Bay, 1941–45: The United States and the Decolonization of the British Empire* (New York: Oxford University Press, 1977); David Reynolds, *The Creation of the Anglo-American Alliance, 1937–41: A Study in Competitive Cooperation* (Chapel Hill: University of North Carolina Press, 1981); Elizabeth Borgwardt, *A New Deal for the World: America's Vision for Human Rights* (Cambridge, MA: Belknap Press, 2005). Below the diplomatic stratum, reformers recognized the charter's potential in the struggles against racism and colonialism. Penny Von Eschen, *Race against Empire: Black Americans and Anticolonialism, 1937–1957* (Ithaca, NY: Cornell University Press, 1997).

11. Wm. Roger Louis, "The Dissolution of the British Empire," in *The Oxford History of the British Empire*, vol. 4: *The Twentieth Century*, ed. Judith Brown and Wm. Roger Louis (New York: Oxford University Press, 1999), 329–356, and "The Imperialism of Decolonization," *Journal of Imperial and Commonwealth History* 22:3 (September 1994), 462–511.

12. As Kwame Nkrumah would later describe it to Richard Nixon: "[Nkrumah's] main preoccupation, now that Ghana is about to attain political independence, is to assure the country's economic independence." Memorandum of Conversation, Nixon, Nkrumah, et al., March 4, 1957, Accra, doc. no. 129, *Foreign Relations of the United States 1955–1957*, vol. 18: *Africa* (Washington, DC: Government Printing Office, 1989), 375.

13. Robert McMahon, *Colonialism and Cold War: The United States and the Struggle for Indonesian Independence, 1945–49* (Ithaca, NY: Cornell University Press, 1981).

14. The brother-in-law of Pandit Nehru told a U.S. official that "the tombstone of the United Nations [will read] 'Here lies UN, Killed March 12th by Harry Truman.'" U.S. Consulate-Bombay to State, June 18, 1947, Department of State Central Files, Record Group 59, CDF 711.00/6-1847, box 3145, National Archives and Records Administration, College Park, MD. On India, see Kenton Clymer, *Quest for Freedom: The United States and India's Independence* (New York: Columbia University Press, 1995); and Robert McMahon, *The Cold War on the Periphery: The United States, India, and Pakistan* (New York: Columbia University Press, 1994).

15. State Department Committee on Dependent Areas report, "US Policy Regarding Non-Self-Governing Territories," December 15, 1947, Department of State Central Files, Record Group 59, Lot Files, Lot 65D140, box 4, National Archives and Records Administration, College Park, MD.

16. Mark A. Lawrence, *Assuming the Burden: Europe and the American Commitment to War in Vietnam* (Berkeley: University of California Press, 2005).

17. T. N. Harper, *The End of Empire and the Making of Malaya* (New York: Cambridge University Press, 2001); David Anderson, *Histories of the Hanged: The Dirty War in Kenya and the End of Empire* (New York: Norton, 2005); Todd Shepard, *The Invention of Decolonization: The Algerian War and the Remaking of France* (Ithaca, NY: Cornell University Press, 2008); Matthew Connelly, *A Diplomatic Revolution: Algeria's Fight for Independence and the Origins of the Post–Cold War Era* (New York: Oxford University Press, 2002).

18. Thomas Borstelmann, *The Cold War and the Color Line* (Cambridge, MA: Harvard University Press, 2001), 93; Mary Dudziak, *Cold War Civil Rights: Race and the Image of American Democracy* (Princeton, NJ: Princeton University Press, 2000); Cary Fraser, "Crossing the Color Line in Little Rock: The Eisenhower Administration and the Dilemma of Race for U.S. Foreign Policy," *Diplomatic History* 24:2 (Spring 2000), 233–264.

19. James Meriwether, *Proudly We Can Be Africans: Black Americans and Africa, 1935–1961* (Chapel Hill: University of North Carolina Press, 2001); Kevin Gaines, *American Africans in Ghana: Black Expatriates and the Civil Rights Era* (Chapel Hill: University of North Carolina Press, 2007); Von Eschen, *Race against Empire;* Nikhil Pal Singh, *Black Is a Country: Race and the Unfinished Struggle for Democracy* (Cambridge, MA: Harvard University Press, 2005).

20. Cary Fraser, "An American Dilemma: Race and Realpolitik in the American Response to the Bandung Conference, 1955," in *Window on Freedom: Race, Civil Rights, and Foreign Affairs, 1945–1988,* ed. Brenda Gayle Plummer (Chapel Hill: University of North Carolina Press, 2003), 115; Matthew Jones, "A 'Segregated' Asia? Race, the Bandung Conference, and Pan-Asianist Fears in American Thought and Policy, 1954–55," *Diplomatic History* 29:5 (November

2005), 841–868; Paul Gordon Lauren, *Power and Prejudice: The Politics and Diplomacy of Racial Discrimination* (Boulder: Colorado University Press, 1988), 209; Nicholas Tarling, "'Ah-Ah': Britain and the Bandung Conference of 1955," *Journal of Southeast Asian Studies* 23:1 (March 1992), 74–112; Jason Parker, "Cold War II: The Eisenhower Administration, the Bandung Conference, and the Re-periodization of the Postwar Era" *Diplomatic History* 30:5 (November 2006), 867–892; Westad, *Global Cold War*, 99–103; Robert Vitalis, "The Midnight Ride of Kwame Nkrumah and Other Fables of Bandung," unpublished paper, in author's possession.

21. Cited in John Munro, "The Anticolonial Front: Cold War Imperialism and the Struggle against Global White Supremacy, 1945–1960," Ph.D. diss., University of California-Santa Barbara, December 2010, 25.

22. Salim Yaqub, *Containing Arab Nationalism: The Eisenhower Doctrine and the Middle East* (Chapel Hill: University of North Carolina Press, 2006); Wm. Roger Louis and Roger Owen, eds., *Suez 1956: The Crisis and Its Consequences* (New York: Oxford University Press, 1989); Wm. Roger Louis, *Ends of British Imperialism: The Scramble for Empire, Suez, and Decolonization* (New York: I. B.Tauris, 2006); Peter Hahn, *The United States, Great Britain, and Egypt, 1945–1956: Strategy and Diplomacy in the Early Cold War* (Chapel Hill: University of North Carolina Press, 1991).

23. U.S. Embassy-Accra to State, March 19, 1957, Foreign Service Post Files, Records Group 84, Accra, General USIS Records 1951–58, folder "B-Program-1957," box 1, National Archives and Records Administration, College Park, MD.

24. See Meriwether, *Proudly We Can Be Africans*; Brenda Gayle Plummer, ed., *Window on Freedom: Race, Civil Rights, and Foreign Affairs, 1945–1988* (Chapel Hill: University of North Carolina Press, 2003); Borstelmann, *Cold War and the Color Line*; Jason Parker, "'Made-in-America Revolutions'? The 'Black University' and the American Role in the Decolonization of the Black Atlantic," *Journal of American History* 96 (December 2009), 727–750.

25. Nkrumah, *I Speak of Freedom* (Westport, CT: Praeger Publishers, 1961), 101.

26. Elizabeth Schmidt, *Cold War and Decolonization in Guinea, 1946–1958* (Athens: Ohio University Press, 2007).

27. Westad, *Global Cold War*, 136–141, 165–166. Westad observes, however, that Sino-Soviet competition for Third World influence grew in this decade to such proportions that at times it eclipsed the U.S.-Soviet contest there.

28. http://daccess-dds-ny.un.org/doc/RESOLUTION/GEN/NR0/152/88/IMG/NR015288.pdf?OpenElement (accessed January 18, 2010).

29. Aleksandr Fursenko and Timothy Naftali, *"One Hell of a Gamble": Khrushchev, Castro, and Kennedy 1958–1964* (New York: Norton, 1997), 39; Piero Gleijeses, *Conflicting Missions: Havana, Washington, and Africa, 1959–1976* (Chapel Hill: University of North Carolina Press, 2002); Westad, *Global Cold War*, chap. 6; and Jorge Dominguez, *To Make a World Safe for Revolution: Cuba's Foreign Policy* (Cambridge, MA: Harvard University Press, 1989).

30. This imprecision owes in part to the fact that decolonization is not "over"; according to the United Nations, the process is still underway in more than a dozen territories.

31. Christopher Andrews, *The World Was Going Our Way: The KGB and the Battle for the Third World* (New York; Basic Books, 2005). Melvyn Leffler notes that the Brezhnev regime, despite détente, felt a Soviet duty to support the "'forces of national liberation'... according to its revolutionary conscience and communist convictions." Leffler, *For the Soul of Mankind: The United States, the Soviet Union, and the Cold War* (New York: Hill and Wang, 2007), 258–259.

32. For examples of protonationalism, see Rebecca Karl, *Staging the World: Chinese Nationalism at the Turn of the Twentieth Century* (Durham, NC: Duke University Press, 2002); and Joel Beinin and Zachary Lockman, *Workers on the Nile: Nationalism, Communism, Islam, and the Egyptian Working Class, 1882–1954* (Princeton, NJ: Princeton University Press, 1988). For a more systemic analysis see Ronald Hyam, *Britain's Declining Empire: The Road to Decolonisation, 1918–1968* (New York: Cambridge University Press, 2007).

33. See, for example, Crawford Young, *The African Colonial State in Comparative Perspective* (New Haven, CT: Yale University Press, 1994); Daniel Branch, *Defeating Mau Mau, Creating Kenya: Counterinsurgency, Civil War, and Decolonization* (New York: Cambridge University Press, 2009); Yasmin Khan, *The Great Partition: The Making of India and Pakistan* (New Haven, CT: Yale University Press, 2008).

8

THE RISE AND FALL OF NONALIGNMENT

MARK ATWOOD LAWRENCE

The history of the Cold War reverberates with Manichean rhetoric. U.S. president Harry S. Truman set the tone in March 1947, declaring in a speech before Congress that the world had been split in two. "At the present moment in world history," he asserted, "nearly every nation must choose between alternative ways of life."[1] Communist leaders shot back with stark words of their own. Nations around the world had divided themselves into "two diametrically opposed camps," declared the Soviet bloc in September 1947.[2] Across the remainder of the Cold War, both superpowers worked hard to give substance to such words. Through political, military, economic, ideological, propagandistic, and covert means, Washington and Moscow drew country after country into their geostrategic orbits, giving shape to a global order that observers at the time—and scholars ever since—had little difficulty labeling "bipolar."

Yet the Cold War order was hardly so simple as that label suggests. Studies focusing on the 1970s make clear, for instance, that the global order lost much of its bipolar character with the dramatic U.S.-Chinese rapprochement and the less-noted acceleration of global communications and flows of capital and investment.[3] Another body of new scholarship has pointed out that small nations often exercised a surprisingly high degree of autonomy vis-à-vis their alleged superpower masters, calling into question just how tightly knit the two blocs ever really were.[4] But the most striking challenge to the bipolar vision of the Cold War has drawn the interest of scholars for many years: the strenuous efforts by a large and diverse group of developing countries to avoid alignment with either the Soviet Union or the United States and to chart an independent course. For its champions, nonalignment meant nothing less than a "third way" for young nations that had little to gain by siding with the Communist East or the capitalist West and no stake in the East-West military rivalry.

Viewed within the context of the global history of the twentieth century, nonalignment seems an eminently sensible response to Cold War binaries by poor nations that had suffered under colonial domination and sought to enjoy independence free of domination by new foreign masters. The "colonial world" was, in the words of radical philosopher Frantz Fanon, a "Manichean world," pitting colonizer against colonized in a struggle that allowed no middle ground.[5] It is thus hardly surprising that many postcolonial governments rejected membership in Cold War blocs that appeared likely to submerge the independence of weak states within broad geopolitical agendas established in far-away capitals. Far more perplexing are the reasons why nonalignment did not take root and thrive more than it did. To be sure, nonalignment inspired a potent global movement in the 1950s and 1960s and left an imprint on international affairs visible long after the end of the Cold War. Yet nonalignment as both an idea and a movement never achieved the grand ambitions that advocates articulated during its heyday, and it faded into the background of global politics during the 1970s.

The story of nonalignment is, then, largely a story of rising ambitions and disappointing results that played out across the globe over several decades. The scope and complexity of this rise and fall surely helps account for the fact that remarkably few historians have studied the phenomenon in an all-encompassing way.[6] Rather, scholars have mostly examined small slices of the larger arc, isolating either particular moments such as the 1955 Afro-Asian Conference at Bandung, Indonesia, or the experiences of individual countries such as Egypt and India, which played key roles in the Non-Aligned Movement. It is possible, however, to piece this scholarship together and trace the basic trajectory of nonalignment during the Cold War. This chapter attempts to accomplish this goal by answering three questions that loom large in any general history of the nonaligned ideal. First, what basic ideas motivated the champions of nonalignment and fueled the rise of the movement during the 1950s and 1960s? Second, how did the superpowers—the United States and the Soviet Union, but also China—respond to assertions of nonalignment during those same years? Third, why did nonalignment dwindle thereafter as a geopolitical force? The following pages argue above all that nonalignment had considerable appeal as an abstract aspiration but lacked a program capable of bridging the innumerable fault lines that ran through the developing world and withstanding the counterpressure of the superpowers, especially the United States.

The Rise of the Nonaligned Ideal

The intellectual roots of the nonaligned ideal reach back long before 1945. The first three decades of the twentieth century witnessed an explosion of anticolonial agitation and organizing in many parts of the world. Such activities were greatly facilitated by new communications and transport technologies, which enabled individuals in different regions to recognize their common plights and, to a degree, to negate the colonizers' divide-and-rule strategies. But geopolitical developments played the most obvious role in sparking anticolonialism. Just as the colonial powers expanded their control over larger swaths of the earth's surface, European supremacy started to come unraveled with the Japanese military victory over Russia in 1904. Growing consciousness of political and racial oppression—and of the possibility of challenging the dominant system—gave rise to an array of movements and gatherings such as the Universal Races Congress, the Pan-African Congress, the Asian People's Conferences, the League Against Imperialism, and the League of Colored Peoples.[7] These forums promoted solidarity among oppressed populations but also prefigured later nonaligned initiatives by fostering hostility to the political and social norms upheld by the world's most powerful nations and articulating alternative visions of human progress.

Nonalignment per se took shape only after 1945, however, as two momentous developments—the formation of the rival Cold War blocs and the first steps toward the dissolution of the colonial empires—transformed global geopolitics. These events not only generated the bipolar system against which nonaligned leaders would position themselves, but also brought into existence ambitious new governments eager to claim a distinct role in world affairs. Nationalist movements and new nations benefited enormously from two features of the postwar international order as they struggled to carve out independent global roles. The weakening material and moral authority of the European metropoles, a process underway before 1939 but strongly intensified by World War II, created vast new receptivity within colonial societies to fresh ideas about economic and political development. Meanwhile, the new superpowers, though unquestionably armed with ideas of their own about how to promote such development, were constrained in their efforts to impose them by their frequent wartime declarations that they were fighting for the principles of national self-determination and sovereignty of all nations.

The intellectual trendsetter among the new postcolonial regimes was India, which gained its independence from Britain in 1947. Like many governments that ultimately participated in the movement, New Delhi's unwillingness to side with either superpower flowed from both ideological conviction and calculated self-interest. Nonalignment reflected deeply rooted Hindu principles as well as a desire among the new Indian political class to play a major peacemaking role. But it also sprang from a pragmatic assessment of the country's needs as it confronted debilitating poverty and an unpredictable geopolitical environment. By avoiding alignment with either Cold War bloc, Indian leaders hoped to preserve their nation's flexibility, win a leadership role in the nonwhite world, and gain economic aid from as many sources as possible.[8] It was a delicate balancing act, but Indian prime minister Jawaharlal Nehru believed his country was managing it successfully by 1949. "We have friendly relations with both the blocs and yet maintain our freedom," Nehru proudly declared that August. "[T]his is the policy best suited for our country and also...the only one by which we can serve the cause of world peace."[9]

Similar words echoed elsewhere in South and Southeast Asia, where Pakistan, Ceylon, Burma, and Indonesia also gained independence between 1947 and 1949. Indeed, within a few years, the new nations of Asia, loosely organized as the "Colombo powers" in recognition of their founding session in the Ceylonese capital, had begun informally cooperating with one another and had even broached the possibility of organizing an international meeting to discuss the concerns of Asian and African peoples. That idea gained momentum as the Korean War, the climax of the First Indochina War, and the formation of the U.S.-led Southeast Asia Treaty Organization (SEATO) brought the superpower rivalry fully onto the Asian continent, raising fears of new great-power domination hard on the heels of the retreating imperial order. At the end of 1954, the Colombo nations invited governments stretching from East Asia to West Africa to send delegations to Bandung, an ideal symbolic backdrop since the city was only just recovering from destruction suffered during Indonesia's recent independence struggles.

The Bandung Conference of April 1955 had a broad agenda, and the principle of nonalignment did not figure prominently in the proceedings. Indeed, the twenty-nine participating nations hardly indicated a strong commitment to skirt Cold War antagonisms. Participants such as the People's Republic of China and the Democratic Republic of Vietnam had clearly lined up on the Communist side, while others such as Pakistan, Iran, and the Philippines were obviously oriented toward the U.S. camp. Some observers celebrated this diversity as a major breakthrough for solidarity among the world's oppressed populations. "I could sense an important juncture of history in the making," recalled the African-American activist and writer Richard

Wright, who covered the conference as a journalist. "Every religion under the sun, almost every race on earth, every shade of political opinion, and one and a half billion people from 12,606,938 square miles of the earth's surface were represented here," Wright marveled.[10] Yet other observers viewed diversity as an obstacle to the development of a coherent program. For example, Allen Dulles, the director of the U.S. Central Intelligence Agency, dismissed the meeting in advance as a "very odd assortment" of countries that, divided as they were among different ideological camps, shared little of real significance.[11]

Both Wright and Dulles were, in a sense, correct. As innumerable commentators have asserted, the Bandung Conference was a landmark moment in the development of a Third World consciousness—a "feeling of political possibility," in the words of historian Christopher Lee[12]—and established the broad goals that would animate "Third-Worldism" over the decades to come: decolonization, antiracism, global disarmament, economic development, and the protection of local cultures. The conference stopped short, however, of translating these aspirations into a specific policy program setting participating nations apart from the bipolar global alliance system. To be sure, many speakers left no doubt about their hostility to the superpowers. Indonesian leader Sukarno, for example, insisted that the most powerful states showed little regard for the "well-being of mankind" and seemed instead determined on "controlling the world" for selfish purposes, even at the risk of obliterating the world in the process. Sukarno even hinted at the possibility that the Bandung nations might play a proactive role in world affairs, calling vaguely on his colleagues to use the "Moral Violence of nations in favor of peace."[13] Yet such appeals meant little in practice, partly because of the preliminary nature of the Bandung meeting but even more so, as Dulles predicted, because of the impossibility of organizing such a diverse array of nations around a single agenda.

A true nonaligned movement came about only gradually as key nations made difficult decisions about how to build on the foundations laid at Bandung. The central dilemma, clear in retrospect if not at the time, was whether to steer in a radical direction by prioritizing hostility to Western-style colonialism or in a moderate direction by pursuing independence from both the Western and Eastern blocs. The radical approach gained momentum in the immediate aftermath of Bandung with the establishment in 1957 of the Afro-Asian People's Solidarity Organization (AAPSO). That body, spearheaded by Asian Communist parties, pursued a vehemently anti-Western agenda that dominated a series of international meetings in the late 1950s and early 1960s.[14] But the radical approach gradually lost traction as the

Sino-Soviet split transformed AAPSO meetings into shouting matches among Communist factions, as AAPSO's pro-Communist flavor alienated key countries, and as Yugoslav leader Josep Broz Tito took the lead in articulating a different vision of Third World solidarity.

Yugoslavia's history and location made it a natural champion of genuine nonalignment as the core aim of Third World coalition building. Having broken dramatically with the Soviet Union in 1947 but still wary of the West, Tito wished to steer a course separate from both Cold War blocs. As the leader of a European nation, meanwhile, he rejected the notion that such a movement should be limited to Asia and Africa, preferring political rather than geographical or racial criteria for membership. Tito's approach was obviously self-interested, for he desperately needed allies to bolster his defiance of the Soviet bloc. Yet Tito found considerable enthusiasm elsewhere. His commitment to socialist principles while accepting U.S. aid offered an attractive model to many poor nations, and staunch Yugoslav support for anticolonial causes won Tito friends around the globe. Above all, Tito successfully cultivated the partnership of Egyptian leader Gamal Abdel Nasser and India's Nehru. Personal bonds were cemented by rapid escalation of U.S.-Soviet hostility from 1958 to 1961. Finding a third way seemed more urgent than ever.[15]

Nonalignment became the centerpiece of Third World organizing in 1961, when for the first time a coalition of nations committed itself explicitly to the principle. At a meeting in June, key governments laid down basic criteria for membership in the Non-Aligned Movement (NAM): commitment to an independent foreign policy, dedication to the principle of peaceful coexistence, support for movements of national liberation, and refusal to join Cold War military alliances. Four months later, leaders of twenty-five nations gathered in Belgrade, Yugoslavia, to launch the new organization and articulate an agenda of ending both colonialism and the Cold War, which NAM members saw as twin barriers to progress by poor nations. Judged by the number of participants, the Belgrade summit marked a step backward from the Bandung Conference. Yet, as Tito and other leaders hoped, the NAM benefited from greater cohesion. By omitting Communist nations such as China and North Vietnam and U.S. allies such as South Vietnam, Turkey, and Libya, the new organization promised to speak with a bold and independent voice in global affairs.

The high-water mark of the Non-Aligned Movement came in October 1964, when almost twice as many governments gathered for a second summit, this time in Cairo. New members came mostly from Africa, while Fidel Castro's Cuba became the first Latin American participant.

The most remarkable aspect of the Cairo meeting was the unity among participating nations. Delegates focused less attention than they had at Belgrade on the perils of nuclear war, which seemed to have eased as a consequence of the 1963 Limited Nuclear Test Ban Treaty and other conciliatory gestures by Moscow and Washington.[16] Spurred above all by Nasser, they spoke with unprecedented vigor against colonialism as well as a newer problem preoccupying them: interference by the great powers in the affairs of newly independent nations. "Colonialism has many forms and manifestations," asserted the declaration issued at the end of the conference. "Economic pressure and domination, interference, racial discrimination, subversion, intervention and the threat of force are neo-colonialist devices against which the newly independent nations have to defend themselves."[17]

The Great Powers and Nonalignment

Perhaps the best evidence of the momentum that nonalignment had gathered by the early 1960s is the seriousness with which the global powers viewed the phenomenon and worked—mostly unsuccessfully—to influence it. China, the weakest of the Cold War powers, had the most complicated relationship to nonalignment. From the founding of the People's Republic of China in 1949, Beijing saw considerable political and geostrategic advantage in casting itself as part of the Third World and therefore as entitled to a leading role in Third World organizations. Chinese premier Zhou Enlai emphasized the point at Bandung, consistently identifying his nation with the plight of Third World states. "We have to admit that among our Asian and African countries, we do have different ideologies and different social systems," Zhou Enlai told the meeting. "But this does not prevent us from seeking common ground and being united."[18] Such unity proved elusive, however, and China gradually lost its place at the center of the Third World movement. Many governments were wary of China's Communist orientation and feared being drawn into Sino-Soviet squabbling as the rift between Beijing and Moscow widened. For its part, the Chinese government did little to calm such anxieties, insisting on the radical vision embodied in AAPSO. The founding of NAM and China's failure in 1965 to rally support for a "Bandung II" meeting that might have revived the more revolutionary Afro-Asian approach amounted to a stinging defeat for Chinese ambitions. Unquestionably, China continued to seek influence in the developing world. But it did so more in the way of the United States and the Soviet Union—not from within the Third World movement, but as a great power standing apart from the smaller nations.

Both Moscow and Washington viewed the Cold War as a global competition by 1950 and naturally regarded the rise of nonalignment as a threat. On the Soviet side, one outspoken ideologue assailed nonalignment as an "imperialist device, the purpose of which was to slander the USSR by placing it on the same level as American imperialism."[19] For a variety of reasons, however, the Soviet Union regarded nonalignment with less alarm than did Washington, especially after Moscow shifted to a more proactive policy in the Third World in the mid-1950s. Above all, Soviet officials took satisfaction from the fact that most newly independent nations focused their strongest criticism on the Western powers that had once colonized them. Though Third World states had proclaimed "nonparticipation in the blocs as a principle of their foreign policy," they were in fact natural partners of the socialist world in constructing a "vast Zone of Peace" comprising the "majority of the population of our planet" and united by common hostility to Western colonialism, Soviet leader Nikita Khrushchev declared in 1956. The willingness of the Soviet Union to provide development aid with no strings attached would, Khrushchev added, promote partnership and pose "a major stumbling block" to the perpetuation of colonialism.[20] Moscow undoubtedly drew confidence as well from the tendency of new nations to embrace statist economic policies that resembled the Communist world more than the free-market West.

Soviet leaders were, however, consistently disappointed in their efforts to capitalize on ostensible overlaps of interests. Strenuous Soviet efforts to cultivate close relationships with nations such as India, Indonesia, Burma, Syria, and Egypt—all founding members of the Non-Aligned Movement— brought little but frustration. Khrushchev clearly read too much into his friendships with leaders such as Nehru and Nasser, and planned economies proved weak indicators of pro-Soviet attitudes, no matter how much aid Moscow lavished on Third World states.[21] But the biggest error by Soviet leaders was to underestimate the determination among Third World nations to guard their independence. In this regard, Nasser proved the biggest disappointment. After leaning toward the Soviet Union in earlier years, Nasser had jailed many Egyptian Communists by the late 1950s and castigated Khrushchev for failing to back Egypt more strongly during the 1956 Suez Crisis.[22] A few years later, Khrushchev discovered that even an avowed Communist state within the Non-Aligned Movement—Fidel Castro's Cuba—might place its desire for a leading role in the Third World ahead of its loyalty to Moscow. The Havana government showed scant fealty for

Soviet wishes as it vigorously assisted liberation movements in several parts of Africa during the 1960s and 1970s.[23]

U.S. leaders responded to nonalignment in a way roughly parallel to their Soviet rivals, first showing hostility but later attempting—with similarly unimpressive results—to cultivate partnership. The Truman administration set the early pattern in 1947, when Indian policy elicited condemnation from U.S. leaders anxious about Soviet expansion in Asia. Henry F. Grady, the U.S. ambassador to New Delhi, expressed Washington's attitude in no uncertain terms, telling Nehru that the U.S.-Soviet rivalry was "a question that cannot be straddled and that India should get on the democratic side immediately."[24] American antipathy to nonalignment culminated a few years later, when John Foster Dulles, secretary of state in the Eisenhower administration, publicly excoriated neutralism as "an obsolete conception," even an "immoral and short-sighted conception."[25] Such attitudes clearly carried over into policymaking during the 1950s and early 1960s, when the United States attempted to overthrow the governments of Iran, Indonesia, Cuba, and other countries that seemed to teeter in Communist direction.

Yet the quickening pace of decolonization and growing awareness of racial injustices led in the late 1950s to a somewhat more tolerant American attitude toward nonalignment and, more generally, the sensitivities of Third World states. Whereas American leaders had previously dismissed non-alignment as a sign of immaturity among young nations, they showed more understanding by the turn of the 1960s and recognized that simple rejection of nonalignment would be counterproductive. Only during the Kennedy administration, however, did U.S. leaders fully articulate a desire to move beyond the simple binaries of the Cold War. "We wish to see emerge out of the powerful ferment of modernization a community of independent nations," Secretary of State Dean Rusk asserted in 1961. "We wish to see them modernize not in our image but in the image they themselves formulate out of their own unique histories, cultures, and aspirations."[26] The Kennedy administration's logic resembled Khrushchev's a few years earlier. By accepting political diversity and providing economic support, the United States could exploit commonalities of interests with nonaligned countries.

Some historians argue that Kennedy, despite his administration's rhetoric, waged the Cold War in the Third World at least as aggressively as his predecessors.[27] Such scholars point especially to Kennedy's combativeness in Latin America and Vietnam. But with regard to leading nonaligned nations, Kennedy clearly embraced a more flexible policy in practice as well as rhetoric.[28] He undertook initiatives to improve relations with Nehru and Nasser and risked political damage by defending U.S. development aid to nonaligned countries that criticized the United States. Regardless of the extent of Kennedy's departure from earlier patterns, however, there is little question that his experiment in toleration for nonalignment ended during the Johnson presidency. Johnson lacked Kennedy's nuanced understanding of the profound transformation taking place in the Third World. Meanwhile, the Vietnam War made Johnson less willing to run risks anywhere else and contributed to the rapid souring of U.S. policy toward many Third World states. Indeed, Washington shifted toward a foreign policy rooted in strong alliances with Third World nations such as Iran, Israel, Brazil, and Pakistan that would reliably serve U.S. interests.

Like China and the Soviet Union, then, the United States failed to gain influence over nonaligned states by emphasizing common outlooks and cultivating partnerships. Undoubtedly, Washington had moments of success. In the early 1960s, for example, Kennedy earned gratitude in India by supporting that country's war effort against China and briefly developed a working relationship in Egypt with Nasser. Yet none of this produced lasting results. The most dramatic U.S. gain in the nonaligned world came not through cooperation but through overthrow, when Indonesian officers ousted Sukarno in 1965. By the early 1970s, many nonaligned states were focusing their wrath as never before on the United States, using UN and NAM forums to lambaste Washington over the status of Taiwan, Palestinian refugees, economic policy, white rule in southern African, and the Vietnam War. Meanwhile, President Richard Nixon embraced his predecessor's preference for reliable authoritarianism in the Third World and enshrined it as the Nixon Doctrine, under which the new administration promised large amounts of U.S. military and economic aid to loyal U.S. allies.

The Decline of Nonalignment

Nonalignment as both aspiration and organization persisted across the remainder of the Cold War and by some measures gained stature. The Non-Aligned Movement convened summits in Lusaka (1970), Algiers (1973), Lima (1975), Colombo (1976), Havana in (1979), New Delhi (1983), Harare (1986), and Belgrade (1989). Membership increased to seventy-five by the mid-1970s, and new institutional machinery was established to organize meetings. Perhaps most significant of all, the NAM began taking more assertive positions on economic questions. Though central to Third World organizing during the 1960s, those matters lay mostly within the purview of separate bodies such as the Group of 77 and the United Nations Conference on Trade and Development (UNCTAD), both of which were founded in 1964 to promote stabilization of commodity prices, access to markets in the industrialized world, and expanded development aid programs.[29] Greater attention to economic issues within the NAM raised the organization's profile among Third World states by linking its critique of the international political order to structural economic disadvantages that many leaders increasingly considered the core of their problems.

At the same time, however, nonalignment lost much of the momentum that it had gathered during the 1960s, when it had seemed a rapidly rising force in global affairs, perhaps even the makings of a third geopolitical bloc. Across the 1970s, the movement proclaimed its unity and criticized the superpowers as stridently as ever, but such assertions rang increasingly hollow. The superpowers viewed nonalignment as a factor of declining significance in international affairs. But the problem lay as much with the nonaligned states, which failed to cultivate unity in practice as well as rhetoric and ultimately embraced a radical agenda that put them on a collision course with the West. By the time the Cold War intensified again at the end of the 1970s, little remained of the bold nonaligned vision that Nehru, Tito, and others had once articulated. This trend resulted from the confluence of several developments that transformed the prospects for a robust nonaligned force in global politics.

Perhaps most important, the nonaligned states had to cope with an international atmosphere increasingly hostile to their project. While the Vietnam War and the accompanying perception of national crisis made Washington less willing to tolerate diversity—and therefore unpredictability—in the Third World, the intensifying Sino-Soviet split had a similar effect on Moscow. Rivalry with China for leadership of the Communist world gave Soviet leaders incentive to emphasize their commitment to revolutionary change and strong ideologically committed alliances. The U.S. defeat in Vietnam appears to have pushed in the same direction by encouraging Moscow to believe conditions were ripe to achieve bold gains abroad, especially in Africa.[30] The overall effect of these trends was to encourage ideological polarization throughout the Third World. While Washington backed right-wing coups, Moscow worked to establish or buttress pro-Soviet regimes in Angola, Ethiopia, Afghanistan, and elsewhere. Making matters even more challenging for the nonaligned cause, polarization of Cold War rivalries in the Third World was accompanied by détente in other arenas of superpower relations. Nonaligned states thus lost some of their ability to posture as a sensible third way between reckless great powers at just the moment when key states were tipping fully in one direction or the other.

As the broad geopolitical environment underwent these changes, the nonaligned cause was hampered as well by ruptures and shifts within the movement. For one thing, the loss of several of the key architects of non-alignment deprived the movement of the leadership and charisma that it had enjoyed in its formative years. The blow of Nehru's death in 1964 was quickly compounded by Sukarno's overthrow in 1965, Nkrumah's ouster in 1966, and Nasser's death in 1970. Conflicts within the Third World did even more to undermine prospects for a vigorous nonaligned coalition. The potential for damaging ruptures within the movement became clear in 1962, when India and China went to war over territorial disputes along their long common border. As recently as 1954, the two nations had proclaimed their attachment to the "Five Principles of Peaceful Coexistence" (or Panchasila), a key early expression of the nonaligned impulse. The outbreak of war eight years later not only underscored the volatility of relationships within the Third World, but also undercut India's nonaligned credentials by forcing it into uncomfortable dependence on the United States.[31] India's leadership in the Third World was further undercut by its war against Pakistan in 1965, an event that drove a wedge between two of the Colombo powers and heightened their reliance on the superpowers. The 1967 war took a similarly heavy toll on nonalignment in the Middle East by exposing Egyptian weakness and driving the superpowers into larger diplomatic and military roles in the region.

Policy debates deepened the fracture lines in the 1970s. Most strikingly, the NAM experienced a resurgence of the old debate over how radical an agenda to adopt. Yugoslavia remained the principal proponent of a moderate activism predicated on simple nonattachment to either global alliance system. On the other side, Algeria picked up the baton dropped by China several years earlier and led the drive for a more radical program devoted above all to vigorous support of national liberation movements. While Tito insisted that the Non-Aligned Movement had successfully established itself as a "moral and political force" in international politics, Algerian president Houari Boumédienne urged that the movement embrace a more proactive approach that he dubbed "positive content."[32] The difference manifested itself most obviously in clashing positions on Indochina in 1969 and 1970. While the radical states wished to admit the South Vietnamese Provisional Revolutionary Government and a neutralist Cambodian regime to participate in NAM councils, moderate states wished to exclude the Vietnamese revolutionaries and to seat a pro-Western Cambodian government.[33]

The radicals' victory on these and other policy questions marked a significant shift in nonaligned politics that briefly energized the movement but ultimately damaged it by placing it in direct conflict with the United States and its allies—yet another reason for the declining influence of nonalignment across the 1970s. Decisions about membership in the NAM reflected a growing willingness within the movement, spurred by disgust over the Vietnam War, to identify with Communist bloc nations and openly criticize the United States. That drift had already become evident in 1968, when most nonaligned governments, to Tito's chagrin, endorsed the Soviet invasion of Czechoslovakia.[34] It became much clearer at the 1973 nonaligned summit in Algiers, where radical states resoundingly defeated moderates who insisted that the movement oppose both Western and Communist forms of imperialism. "Any attempt to force a collision between the nonaligned countries and the socialist camp is profoundly counter-revolutionary and serves exclusively the interests of imperialism," Castro declared at Algiers.[35] Bangladeshi prime minister Sheikh Mujibur Rahman captured the radicals' logic even more clearly: "The term 'third world' must not allow us to forget basic realities," he stated. "The world is divided into the oppressors and the oppressed."[36] Tito's vision of a movement distinct from the two blocs had collapsed.

The eclipse of political nonalignment was followed by the collapse of the economic program to which nonaligned nations increasingly committed themselves in the early 1970s. At the 1973 Algiers summit, the Non-Aligned Movement insisted on the establishment of a "new international economic order" more favorable to Third World interests. A year later, a large coalition of Third World nations used the slogan for the boldest initiative yet to revamp the global economy. The occasion for the promulgation of the New International Economic Order (NIEO) was a watershed development in the history of the global economy since 1945. During the 1973 Middle East war, Saudi Arabia and other Arab oil-producing nations embargoed oil sales to the United States and other nations, wreaking havoc on the world's leading industrialized nations. For the Arab countries, and indeed for the Third World generally, it was a moment of breathtaking triumph. For the first time, Third World nations used their grip over a raw material to exert strong leverage throughout the international system. Impressed by their achievement and hopeful that it would usher in a new era in global history, Third World states insisted on holding a special UN session to discuss the structure of the global economy. The meeting resulted in sweeping proposals to give nations total control over natural resources within their borders, assure stable commodity prices, expand market access, and make available larger amounts of development assistance.[37]

These demands touched off a confrontation between industrialized nations, represented above all by the United States, and the Third World that the latter was bound to lose. Part of the problem was that, despite frequent assertions of unity, Third World states themselves had divergent interests on economic questions. The discovery of oil as a potent weapon to use against industrialized nations provides a useful case in point. While Saudi Arabia and other oil-rich nations promised to benefit enormously from their mineral resources, other Third World states such as India were every bit as dependent on foreign sources as were industrialized countries. Price hikes were therefore potentially devastating to countries within the developing world, not just those outside it. Moreover, Saudi Arabia made clear in the late 1970s that it had no intention of using its oil wealth to advance the cause of Third World development. On the contrary, Saudis amassed enormous personal fortunes and invested heavily in the United States and Europe. The oil crisis turned out, then, to be far more significant for widening disparities of wealth among Third World nations than for initiating any sort of advance for the Third World as a whole. Even if Third World nations had been more community-minded, however, the United States and other industrialized nations had little intention of buckling before demands that entailed nothing less than the establishment of a new global order. Reform demands continued to reverberate within the Non-Aligned Movement and the UN General Assembly, where Third World states held a commanding majority, but the industrial nations wielded a more decisive sort of power—power that would only grow as the capitalist world recovered from its nadir and achieved unprecedented dominance in the 1980s and 1990s.[38]

Conclusion

The Non-Aligned Movement survived the end of the Cold War and remains active in the twenty-first century—long after the geopolitical circumstances that engendered it had disappeared. Indeed, as of 2010 the NAM had reached 118 members and 18 observer delegations and was holding summits every three years. Leaders of Asian and African nations marked the fiftieth anniversary of the Bandung Conference in 2005 by convening once again in Indonesia and reaffirming their commitment to the principles enunciated in 1955. Indisputably, however, the Non-Aligned Movement—and more generally the ideas that it embodied at its founding—had faded drastically since its high point in the 1960s. For a time, the movement thrived on the charisma of its founding leaders, commanded headlines around the world as a rising force in international politics, and stirred anxiety among the great powers, which sought to shape, coopt, or blunt the nonaligned project. In many ways, the Non-Aligned Movement's early days captured the mystique of youth, creativity, and dynamism that seemed to emanate from the Third World in those years. The decline came not with the end of the Cold War, though that watershed clearly raised awkward questions about the meaning of nonalignment in a world without rival alliance systems. Rather, the key transition began in the late 1960s and extended over the next decade of profound political and economic changes around the world. Radicalism and economic confrontation seemed like a sound choice for many nonaligned countries in the early 1970s, when the oil crisis and the U.S. failure in Vietnam appeared to signal the decline of the West and the invigoration of the socialist model of development. But it proved a bad bet in the end since the capitalist world, with increasingly powerful nodes in Western Europe, Japan, and (after the mid-1970s) China, bounced back so dramatically as a result of technological innovation and the cluster of trends now known as globalization.

The consequences of the decline of nonalignment—and of Third World solidarity more generally—have become increasingly clear in the opening decades of the twenty-first century. At a moment when poverty, environmental degradation, and disease weigh ever more disproportionately on poor nations, those nations have little traction in international forums. Yet, as numerous authors have made clear in recent years, untended problems in the developing world will increasingly reverberate elsewhere in the form of mass immigration, political instability, and humanitarian catastrophe.[39] The failure to establish an effective body to represent the concerns of developing states also contributes to a desire for new forms of political expression. This yearning does not necessarily portend only harmful results, but at least one major movement to harness the anxieties of marginalized populations—Islamic fundamentalism—clearly carries enormous costs around the world. Whether developing nations exert influence in the future through organized political movements and participation in international forums or through confrontation and catastrophe looms as one of the major questions for the coming years.

NOTES

1. Truman speech, March 12, 1947, in *The Cold War: A History in Documents,* ed. Jussi Hanhimäki and Odd Arne Westad (Oxford: Oxford University Press, 2003), 117.

2. Declaration of the founding of the Communist Information Bureau, September 22, 1947, in *Documents on International Affairs, 1947–1948*, ed. Margaret Carlyle (London: Oxford University Press, 1952), 122.

3. Niall Ferguson et al., eds., *The Shock of the Global: The 1970s in Perspective* (Cambridge, MA: Harvard University Press, 2010).

4. See, for example, Tony Smith, "New Bottles for New Wine: A Pericentric Framework for the Study of the Cold War," *Diplomatic History* 24 (Fall 2000), 551–565.

5. Frantz Fanon, *The Wretched of the Earth*, trans. Constance Farrington (New York: Grove, 1963), 41.

6. Political scientists have written the best surveys of the movement, though most are dated. See G. H. Jansen, *Nonalignment and the Afro-Asia States* (New York: Praeger, 1966); Robert A. Mortimer, *The Third World Coalition in International Politics* (London: Praeger 1980); and A. W. Singham and Shirley Hune, *Non-Alignment in an Age of Alignments* (London: Lawrence Hill, 1986). A recent account by a historian is Vijay Prashad, *The Darker Nations: A People's History of the Third World* (New York: New Press, 2007).

7. Paul Gordon Lauren, *Power and Prejudice: The Politics and Diplomacy of Racial Discrimination* (Boulder, CO: Westview, 1988), chaps. 2–4, and Prashad, *Darker Nations*, 16–30.

8. Robert J. McMahon, *The Cold War on the Periphery: The United States, India, and Pakistan* (New York: Columbia University Press, 1994), 38–39.

9. Quoted in Stanley Wolpert, *Nehru: A Tryst with Destiny* (New York: Oxford University Press, 1996), 448.

10. Richard Wright, *The Color Curtain: A Report on the Bandung Conference* (Cleveland: World Publishing Company, 1956), 135.

11. Quoted in Jason C. Parker, "Cold War II: The Eisenhower Administration, the Bandung Conference, and the Reperiodization of the Postwar Era," *Diplomatic History* 30:5 (November 2006), 877.

12. Christopher Lee, ed., *Making a World after Empire: The Bandung Moment and Its Political Afterlives* (Athens: Ohio University Press, 2010), 15.

13. Sukarno speech, April 18, 1955, http://www.fordham.edu/halsall/mod/1955sukarno-bandong.html (accessed October 8, 2010).

14. Prashad, *Darker Nations*, 52–53; Mortimer, *Third World Coalition*, 10–11.

15. Prashad, *Darker Nations*, 97–99; Mortimer, *Third World Coalition*, 12–13; Richard West, *Tito and the Rise and Fall of Yugoslavia* (London: Sinclair-Stevenson, 1994), 281–283.

16. Singham and Hune, *Non-Alignment in an Age of Alignments*, 89–91.

17. "Non-Aligned Countries Declaration, 1964," in *Encyclopedia of the United Nations and International Agreements*, 3rd ed., ed. Anthony Mango (New York: Routledge, 2003), 1577.

18. Zhou Enlai speech, April 19, 1955, in *China and the Asian-African Conference: Documents* (Beijing: Foreign Languages Press, 1955), 23.

19. Quoted in McMahon, *Cold War on the Periphery*, 46.

20. Nikita S. Khrushchev, *Report of the Central Committee of the Communist Party of the Soviet Union to the 20th Party Congress*, February 14, 1956 (Moscow: Foreign Languages Publishing House, 1956), 23, 27.

21. Peter W. Rodman, *More Precious than Peace: The Cold War and the Struggle for the Third World* (New York: Scribner's, 1994), 57.

22. Aleksandr Fursenko and Timothy Naftali, *Khrushchev's Cold War: The Inside Story of an American Adversary* (New York: Norton, 2006), 293.

23. Piero Gleijeses, *Conflicting Missions: Havana, Washington, and Africa, 1959–1976* (Chapel Hill: University of North Carolina Press, 2002), chaps. 10, 16, and 17.

24. Quoted in McMahon, *Cold War on the Periphery*, 40.

25. Quoted in Thomas Borstelmann, *The Cold War and the Color Line: American Race Relations in the Global Arena* (Cambridge, MA: Harvard University Press, 2001), 113.

26. Rusk speech, December 30, 1961, Department of State Central Files, Record Group 59, Policy Planning Council Subject Files, 1954–1962, box 119, National Archives and Records Administration, College Park, Maryland.

27. For example, Michael E. Latham, *Modernization as Ideology: American Social Science and "Nation Building" in the Kennedy Era* (Chapel Hill: University of North Carolina Press, 2000).

28. See especially Robert Rakove, *Kennedy, Johnson, and the Non-Aligned World* (New York: Cambridge University Press, 2012).

29. Mortimer, *Third World Coalition*, 24–33.

30. Odd Arne Westad, *The Global Cold War: Third World Interventions and the Making of Our Times* (Cambridge: Cambridge University Press, 2007), 202–206.

31. Chen Jian, *Mao's China and the Cold War* (Chapel Hill: University of North Carolina Press, 2001), chap. 3, and McMahon, *Cold War on the Periphery*, chap. 8.

32. Quoted in Mortimer, *Third World Coalition*, 30.

33. Ibid., 29–31.

34. West, *Tito*, 284.

35. Quoted in Basil Perera, *Problems of Non-Alignment* (Colombo: Lanka Trading Co., 1976), 23.

36. Ibid., 23.

37. Declaration of the New International Economic Order, May 1, 1974, http://www.un-documents.net/s6r3201.htm (accessed October 12, 2010).

38. Westad, *Global Cold War*, 334–339.

39. For example, Jared Diamond, *Collapse: How Societies Choose to Fail or Succeed* (New York: Pengin, 2005), and Jeffrey Sachs, *The End of Poverty: Economic Possibilities for Our Time* (New York: Penguin, 2006).

9

CULTURE, THE COLD WAR,
AND THE THIRD WORLD

ANDREW J. ROTTER

Consider three events, broadly speaking, that occurred during the Cold War and involved interaction between, on the one hand, a powerful nation and, on the other, one far less powerful and associated with what would come to be known as the Third World. Begin in the late 1940s, when the administration of Harry S. Truman confronted the possibility that China, the largest country in East Asia and long a target of interest by American diplomats, merchants, and missionaries, would be overtaken by the Chinese Communist Party (CCP) of Mao Zedong and Zhou Enlai. The United States had for years supported the Nationalist (Guomindang, or GMD) government of Chiang Kaishek, but Chiang's troops were by 1948 losing battle after battle to the Communists and his regime was tottering. Under these circumstances, officials weighed their options: should they continue to back Chiang, even increasing military aid and proclaiming their undying support, or should they recognize Chiang as a loser, withdraw quietly their assistance to him, and consider working with the CCP in the hope of moderating its aims and keeping it out of the Soviet sphere of influence? China missionaries—some of them turned politicians—and others of deep religious conviction joined both sides of the debate, but the most persistent voices demanded unwavering support for Chiang. The Methodist bishop Logan Roots wrote Truman that Chiang and his wife were devout Christians and that Chiang "actively seeks Divine Guidance for the affairs of state." Congressman Walter Judd, a former medical missionary, and Senator H. Alexander Smith, who believed he heard daily from God about policy matters, lobbied the administration to bolster the GMD (even when it retreated following its defeat to Formosa) and insisted thereafter that there be no diplomatic recognition of the victorious CCP government. Judd regarded the CCP as a repository of "godless, totally unmoral despotism," and Smith averred, in late 1949, that "non-recognition and Formosa are the two keys we must follow up on to retain a base for ideological advance. All is well. God is guiding us." Indeed, all *was* well for this segment of the Christian China lobby; the United States would not recognize the People's Republic of China for nearly a generation, and support for a Nationalist Chinese Formosa remains a hallmark of American policy to this day.[1]

Jump ahead several years, into the heart of the Cold War, and to Iran. There, in April 1951, Mohammed Mossadeq became prime minister. He almost immediately demanded that his nation capture a greater share, possibly by nationalization, of the wealth generated through the sale of Iranian oil by the Anglo-Iranian Oil Company (AIOC), which had for years siphoned nearly two-thirds of its profits to the British and had wielded significant influence in Iran's politics. The British government, joined in 1953 by the United States, claimed that Mossedeq was irresponsible, eccentric, and radical. Most of all, they said, he was immature or effeminate, either of which disqualified him to lead an oil-rich nation, even an otherwise underdeveloped one. British and American officials derided Mossadeq for receiving them in his pajamas. They described him as "fragile," "impractical," "emotional" rather than "rational," "hysterical," a man who engaged in "negative and feminine tactics" during negotiations. One simply could not deal with a man like that: Who could take him seriously? The Americans helped drive him from the country through a coup in August 1953, to the immense satisfaction of the British. The Americans and British drew his successor from the ranks of the Iranian opposition, where one leading figure showed he could drink "his whisky manfully," someone more manly and Western who would not deny their nations a majority share of Iran's oil profits.[2]

A third scene, one with a broader sweep: Africa during the late 1950s, a time when nations were pulling themselves free of European colonial control and toward independence. About this movement the Americans, and the presidential administration of Dwight D. Eisenhower, were ambivalent. They viewed the end of colonialism as a necessary thing; they had long been critical of what they regarded as its abuses. At the same time, liberation movements in Africa inevitably confronted Americans with their own racial policies and racial attitudes—the persistence of Jim Crow segregation in the southern states, of violence against African Americans, of racial discrimination in jobs and housing throughout the country. Such realities were Cold War embarrassments, undermining U.S. efforts to win the sympathies of people of color around the world and making the United States vulnerable to Soviet propaganda that pointed out the distance between American claims of universal freedom and the oppression of the nation's black underclass. But the racial attitudes of U.S. foreign policy officials were not altogether enlightened. The (once-)influential George Kennan regarded "states with colored populations" as "the neurotic products of exotic backgrounds and tentative Western educational experiences," and the State Department's George McGhee averred that racial "differences really did exist...[as] illustrated by the fact that Africa had always been retarded in its development." At a White House reception, white party-goers surreptitiously pulled on white gloves before shaking hands with dark-skinned visitors. A State Department Africa hand described African freedom fighters as "black baboons." Out of these attitudes emerged a conviction that the black people of Africa were incapable of governing themselves and—given the allegedly genetic basis for their incapability—would never fully stand on their own.[3]

Here are three instances in which religion, gender, or race played a role in shaping U.S. policy toward what was called the Third World after 1945. Religion, gender, and race are categories of analysis that are themselves subsumed by culture. Over the past two decades, the field of diplomatic history has been marked, like other fields of history, by a tendency toward "culturalism." Though a clumsy word and by no means universally accepted, culturalism—which is based on anthropologist Clifford Geertz's identification of culture as "webs of significance" spun by human beings—has established itself, albeit in myriad forms, within a subdiscipline once seen as impervious to methodological innovation and content with its assumptions about what constituted sources and subjects of inquiry. Foreign relations culturalism has become a many-faceted thing, incorporating such categories of analysis as race, gender, religion, maturity, language, and identity— analysands united, if at all, by culturalist scholars' common belief in the constructedness of things, in ambiguity, contingency, and the multiplicity of historical meanings. Its influences include Geertz and other cultural anthropologists; the French poststructuralists Michel Foucault, Jacques Derrida, and Fernand Saussure; feminist theorists, including Joan Scott; and postcolonial theorists, most prominently Edward Said.[4]

While it has by no means displaced other interpretive models used by foreign-relations historians, the culturalist tendency has brought with it several benefits. First, it suggests that the history of foreign relations, or "international" history as it is increasingly called, need not concern itself exclusively with the state. Culturalism is self-reflexive; that is, cultural approaches to foreign affairs help illuminate relations and encounters between nonstate actors. This is true especially in the realm of what is traditionally thought of as culture, or perhaps high culture—art and music, architectural style, the appeal of advertising, fashion, and the transmission of ideas generally across national boundaries. Historians have demonstrated that exchanges of cultural products in these realms affect the way people imagine and act toward each other.[5]

Next, culture requires that scholars think historically. The way the international history of the twentieth century is periodized comes, at it were, from the top down: the end of World War I is the terminus of the long nineteenth century, featuring the collapse of Central European and Ottoman power, modifications of great empires, and the rise of new states in fulfillment of Woodrow Wilson's pledge of their self-determination; the 1920s, in which the powers seemed mainly to hold their breath; the involution of the 1930s, evidently demanded by the Great Depression; World War II; the Cold War; and the unipolar post–Cold War system. This is an organizational scheme that suggests the occurrence of great change everywhere as the most powerful states effect, or are affected by, war and other cataclysmic changes in geopolitics and the global economy. There is logic in this way of seeing history. But the formations of culture lie deeper, shifting in their own time, often more slowly than the political affairs of humans, and often impervious to political rupture or the clash of armies taking place on history's surface. So, for example, the basis for twentieth-century U.S. policy in the Philippines was laid with gendered impulses to fight there in 1898 and racialized perceptions of Filipinos. American policy toward South Asia (India and Pakistan) during the Cold War was predicated on earlier perceptions of the nature of Hinduism and Islam. The war in Vietnam stemmed in part from Western stereotypes of Vietnamese as primitive, lazy, and effeminate. The Cold War in the Third World thus looks different when it is imagined as part of a *longue durée* shaped by culture.[6]

A third benefit of a cultural approach to the study of international history has to do with the fluidity of culture, which corresponds to the shape-shifting realities of human interaction and decision making. Only culture is slippery or supple enough to follow sudden, unexpected twists in human stories, to make necessary detours, to flow with the ambiguities and even contradictions people generate when they try to solve complicated problems. Only culture gets through boundaries, whether physical, conceptual, or psychological—all of them artificial, all placed in the way of understanding how people and the systems they create interact. There is nothing sacrosanct about the conceptual boxes built around nations or nongovernmental organizations (NGOs). The domestic is also the foreign. Selves can form only in the perceived presence of others, and others are made in part of identity fragments that cannot be accepted and thus assimilated by selves. The con-structedness of history invites its deconstruction; culture is the past's most penetrating solvent.

Finally, culture is a shared phenomenon, and one mutually constituted. It does not reside exclusively in "primitive" societies and people, as anthro-pologists once thought; even nations that regard themselves as civilized have cultures. Nor is culture a thing imposed by the strong on the weak. It is impossible to create, for example, a culture of democracy by exporting it as if in a box, and efforts to override one society's cultural practices with another set are inevitably unavailing. Edward Said has argued that culture is "contrapuntal"—that is, for every theme sounded by an imperial power, there was an answer, a counter-theme, sounded by a subaltern. Nor (as Said understood) was this a binary system of call-response: in the very muliti-plicity of sounds, in the entire chorus, lay truth about human and interna-tional relations defined by constant cultural transaction.[7]

All of these features of the cultural approach to foreign relations make it particularly suitable for studying the Cold War in the Third World. The flu-idity and solvent properties of culture effectively erode the barriers that in much social-scientific discourse have artificially separated all three worlds from each other, thus complicating the idea that there was a core and a periphery during the Cold War, and constructively disrupt as well the binary or trilateral oppositions that have long distorted our understanding of the history of that period. That is not to say that all nations participated equally in the Cold War, or that Ghana and Guatemala and Nepal "mattered" as much as did the great powers. I will come presently to the relationship between power and culture. I wish, however, to suggest that looking at the period through cultural lenses compels us to think differently about how we represent it spatially; the Cold War hierarchy implied in the first-to-least numbering of the three worlds is due for some revision.

The term "Third World" (or "le tier monde") was a French coinage of the early 1950s, used ultimately to distinguish "underdeveloped" or (less censo-riously) "developing" nations in Latin America, Africa, and Asia from the developed, liberal capitalist "First World" and the developed, Communist "Second World." The terms thus had both ideological and economic valences. To the United States, the Soviet Union, and their respective allies and subordinates, the Third World was by definition an undifferentiated space. It was filled with vital natural resources but inconveniently wracked by instability, presided over by leaders whom First World and Second World officials generally considered to be racially or civilizationally inferior to themselves. There is no denying that these nations were heavily influenced by Cold War rivalries. Yet, key leaders of Third World nations, particularly Indonesian president Sukarno and India's Jawaharlal Nehru, appropriated the idea of the Third World and claimed it as a source of power. At the Afro-Asian Bandung Conference in April 1955, both men offered definitions of the Third World that denied the inferior status that the label implied. That Third World nations were "developing" economically did not diminish their importance; and to claim that they were "nonaligned" in the Cold War was too negative a description of what they actually stood for, which was (among other things) independence *of* all nations *from* the entanglements of the Cold War. Recourse to military force was unthinkable, argued Nehru, especially in what he called "the unaligned area"; far better was the "moral force of Asia and Africa," which "must, in spite of the atomic and hydrogen bombs of Russia, the U.S.A., count." The nations represented at Bandung were, Sukarno told their representatives, "united by more important things than those which superficially divide us," including the desire for peace, insistence on racial equality, and opposition to colonialism or neocolonialism. Of the meeting, the African-American writer Richard Wright would say: "There was something extra-political, extra-social, almost extra-human about it, it smacked of tidal waves, of natural forces." The Bandung delegates gave a contrapuntal response to the derogatory definition of "Third World" that had been provided them by others. They sought a shared identity that rejected an imposed Cold War.[8]

There are several ways in which consideration of culture demands modification of the traditional Cold War narrative with regard to the Third World. The people and nations in Latin America, Africa, and especially Asia were not merely recipients of initiatives from the so-called West or East but rather participants in events that were partly of their own devising. Recalling the depth of history in culture, and of culture in history, this hearkens back to cultural production of a century ago.

Religion and the Third World

Long before the Cold War but at a time when Americans were contemplating their own identities and others', the Young People's Missionary Movement of the United States and Canada published a musical play, in verse, titled *The Pageant of Light and Darkness*. "Invented and designed" by John Oxenham and Hugh Moss, with music by Hamish MacCunn, the play was staged in Boston in the spring of 1911. It was divided into four "Episodes," each corresponding to a compass point and to a group of people living in each direction: Alaskan Indians to the north; Henry Stanley, David

Livingstone, and "Slaves, African Natives, Armed Escort, Arabs, [and] People" to the south; Asian Indians to the east, including the doomed widow Rhadamani and a "Fanatical mob of natives"; and, to the west, Hawaiians on their coral beach. In each episode, the superstition and ignorance of heathens threaten the innocent with some horrible fate. In each episode the innocents are saved by Christian intervention: a missionary dressed as a hunter, Livingstone himself, a British government official who prevents Rhadamani from immolating herself on her husband's funeral pyre, and Queen Kapiolani, who, having converted to Christianity, defies and routs the evil priest of Pele. In a final, triumphant "Processional," all the characters appear on stage and sing:

> In Christ there is no East or West,
> In Him, no South nor North,
> But one great fellowship of love
> Throughout the whole wide earth....
> Join hands, then, brothers, of the faith,
> Whate'er your race may be!—
> Who serves my Father as a son
> Is surely kin to me.[9]

By 1945, white Americans were somewhat more sophisticated about far-flung peoples, having had more experience of them and having learned at least a bit of decorum in the ways they depicted racial others. In fact, the middlebrow musical entertainments that in part supplanted religious pageants encouraged anti-imperialism and antiracism—in positive terms, as the scholar Christina Klein has called it, a "sentimentally" integrationist vision of the world. What did not change was the religious, Christian basis of American relations with others. Religion is culture because it is meaningful, constructed, fluid, and the basis for the beliefs, attitudes, and practices of U.S. foreign policymakers. It had to do with transmission and interaction, putting American religious beliefs against or alongside those of others—heathen "natives," foreign Catholics, Jews, Hindus, Muslims, and of course atheistic Communists. Religion is, according to historian Andrew Preston, "both the producer and recipient, the shaper and the shaped, of culture." Thus, as historian William Inboden has written, even "though Cold War historians may neglect the spiritual factor" shaping U.S. foreign relations, "Americans in the 1940s and 1950s did not"—nor have Americans since. Inheritors and transformers of the crude Christian exceptionalism of the early twentieth century, the makers of U.S. foreign policy during the

Cold War were frequently men to whom religion mattered, and they made decisions accordingly.[10]

There are several ways in which to understand the influence of religion on the Third World's Cold War. Begin with an obvious point: the Cold War, at its essence, was perceived in America as a contest between believers and unbelievers, between good and evil. The Soviets attacked religious belief at home and sought to spread their "godless materialism" everywhere else. According to Americans, that made the competition for influence in Latin America, Africa, and Asia a contest between faith and cynicism. Framed this way, the United States and its allies took some comfort: State Department papers and British Foreign Office minutes offered reassurance that people in the Third World, religious if not Christian, were likely to reject Soviet attempts to cajole them with an atheistic vision. The Cold War also coincided with a period of religious consolidation in the United States. The Protestant theologian Reinhold Niebuhr advocated for a toughened Protestantism, one intolerant of Communism at home and abroad. The religious commentator Will Herberg helped popularize the belief that the three largest American religions—Protestantism, Catholicism, and Judaism—were not just faiths but elements in the "triple melting pot" that provided separate paths to the common destiny of becoming American. Women and men of faith, they confronted a Third World wherein sharp choices could and must be made.[11]

South Asia was one site of conflict. The Cold War intruded on the postcolonial nations of India and Pakistan, as the competing blocs sought the loyalties of millions of potential producers and consumers. In a totalizing conflict that spared no one, U.S. policymakers believed that everyone must take a stand for right and against wrong; "the world of religion," as religious historian Martin Marty has written, "did not lack people who knew how to apply various toughness tests." This orientation of American Protestantism in particular affected the way the United States approached the two biggest South Asian nations. It is hard to remember it now, but during the Cold War Americans generally had a favorable impression of Muslims, most of whom in South Asia lived in Pakistan. Policymakers regarded Muslims as forthright, honorable, and willing to fight for their beliefs. Above all, they were, like Christians, monotheists, and thus subscribed to the views that there was good (God's word) and evil (all else) in the world, that truth could be distinguished from falsehood, that one side of the Cold War binary was right and the other wrong. Of the Pakistanis, a State Department report concluded in 1952: "Pledged to create a state in harmony with the principles of Islam, they are opposed to the godless ideology of Communism, and they are alert to efforts by subversive elements within their country to undermine the bases of orderly government." Whether or not they agreed with this analysis of them, Pakistani officials were happy to confirm it to Americans who might be in a position to supply them with military aid and take their side against India. Liaquat Ali Khan, Pakistan's prime minister from 1948 to 1951, did a tour of the United States in the spring of 1950 and told audiences that "the people of Pakistan believe in the supreme sovereignty of God." The Americans evidently believed him, and in 1954 created a military alliance with Pakistan.[12]

India, on the other hand, was a Hindu nation—never mind the substantial minorities of Muslims, Sikhs, and Parsis, nor the resolute secularism of Nehru. If Muslims knew where they stood in the right-versus-wrong contest of the Cold War, Hindus, evidently beguiled by a pantheon of gods who offered varying paths to truth, could not reliably say the same. The truth for Hindus, it seemed, was not fixed but relative. There was something to this American belief. The Indian journalist Krishnalal Shridharani observed that Hinduism embodies the "philosophical abhorrence of absolutes," finding human beings mostly on a spectrum between good and evil rather than clustered around either one. In a 1953 interview with the American writer Norman Cousins, Nehru complained about a "narrow religious outlook on politics" abroad in the world that led to "a lack of toleration" for others and "a desire to force your will on the other person or the other nation." As Nehru saw it, that was what the United States was trying to do in South Asia: enforce a Cold War orthodoxy, based in Protestant belief, on nations that wished above all to stay out of conflicts and thus tried to avoid taking sides. Pakistan passed the Americans' litmus test; India failed. U.S. Cold War policy in South Asia was predicated in part on American perceptions of the apparent difference between Muslims and Hindus—perceptions that were shrewdly manipulated by the Pakistanis and less shrewdly by the Indians.[13]

Just at the time when the United States was choosing sides in South Asia, another Cold War dilemma presented itself to the east, in Indochina. Nationalists in the state of Vietnam, led by the Communist Ho Chi Minh, were trying to secure independence from the French. While not entirely enamored of French efforts to retain the colony, the Americans had, by 1954, decided that they could not be selective in their alliances against what they construed as the united Communist adversary, as in the case of Pakistan. But the French grip on Vietnam was loosening, and more and more the Americans found themselves bearing the burden of the conflict. If they were to succeed, U.S. policymakers knew, they would have to find a Vietnamese leader who rejected Communism yet managed to inspire loyalty and stir nationalist passions among his people, a leader who could rival Ho in popularity yet still be susceptible to American advice. By 1954, influential Americans had decided to cast their lot with Ngo Dinh Diem.

It was not an automatic choice. Diem appeared to many Americans as vacillating, inexperienced in governing, and without feeling for the popular pulse. Both President Dwight Eisenhower and Secretary of State John Foster Dulles might have preferred someone more resolute, with greater proven abilities to take the fight to his enemies in southern Vietnam, especially the Communists. Perhaps a French-trained general might have done, or a Saigon strongman, or even a Buddhist leader who would champion the causes dear to his coreligionists. But, as far as the Americans were concerned, Diem had a virtue that none of the others had: he was Catholic. In 1950s America, this made him familiar, part of Will Herberg's triple melting pot consisting of men and women more alike than different, all committed to the battle against atheistic Communism. It gave Diem special appeal to American Catholics, including Francis Cardinal Spellman and Democratic senators Mike Mansfield and John F. Kennedy, all of whom offered support for a man who had in the early 1950s spent time in a New Jersey seminary, meditating and washing dishes alongside the novices. Dulles, while no Catholic, had a predilection for leaders who shared his Christian faith and his stark view of the Cold War. It was a battle between religion and its absence, and Dulles, as Arthur Schlesinger, Jr., put it, was its "high priest." The United States undertook to fight in Korea, according to Dulles, because Communism was "a materialistic creed which denies the existence of moral law." South Korea's Syngman Rhee and the Nationalist Chinese generalissimo Chiang Kaishek were, said Dulles, "Christian gentlemen who have suffered for their faith." So too with Diem, who managed, despite his own indecisiveness and the continued skepticism of some Americans who dealt with him, to defeat rival sects in 1955 and thus impress the editor Henry Luce as "a Roman Catholic and a simon-pure Vietnamese nationalist, thus doubly proof against Communist force." "The fact that Diem was a Christian and his rivals were not proved to be the organizing principle that Dulles and other policymakers seized upon in solving the riddle of Vietnam," concludes historian Seth Jacobs. By the time Diem was ousted (and murdered) in November 1963, the United States had become, through association with him, immersed in the Vietnam War.[14]

Religious thinking also played a role in U.S. Cold War policy in Latin America during the 1980s. President Ronald Reagan, whose view of the Cold War conceded nothing in the way of zeal to Dulles's, undertook to support the forces of anti-Communism in El Salvador and Nicaragua. In the first of these, Reagan gave sustenance to a reactionary government whose associates in the Salvadoran National Guard raped and murdered three American nuns and a lay missionary who had advocated social justice for the country's legions of poor. In the second, the president sought to undermine the government of the Marxist Sandinistas by arming a farrago of oppositionists known as the Contras; he did this surreptitiously, and illegally after 1982. Historian Theresa Keeley has written that "the debate about the meaning of Catholicism in the United States shaped Reagan's foreign policy and responses to it." She argues that supporters and creators of the policy, among them conservative Catholics such as CIA director William Casey, Secretary of State Alexander Haig, and national security advisers Richard Allen and William Clark, reacted sharply, and on the basis of their religious faith, to any threat that seemed to be Communist, such as those posed by the Salvadoran rebels and the Sandinistas. The presence in Latin America of Maryknoll nuns working on behalf of social justice indicated to conservatives that something had gone terribly wrong with American Catholicism since the 1960s. On the other side, supporters of the Maryknollers endorsed a progressive Catholicism that sought to move beyond Cold War binaries. Outraged at the rape and killings of the nuns and the Reaganites' intimations that the women had it coming, Americans flooded the White House with protest letters—many times more than had been sent regarding the Iranian hostages just a few years earlier. In their objections, the nuns' supporters would anticipate the end of the Cold War and give sustenance to a liberal Catholic activism that emerged on college campuses during the 1990s.[15]

Gender and the Third World

Gender analysis has had particular applicability to the study of the colonial experience and the Third World. It has first of all broadened the scope of historical inquiry. No longer confined to what one diplomat said to another, or even to what one nation did to another, the field has been opened by culturalism, and gender analysis more specifically, to include allegedly marginal actors—sex workers, factory workers, wives and families of diplomats, women missionaries, and so forth. Cynthia Enloe has pointed out, for example, that America's military base at Subic Bay, the Philippines, which grew large during the Cold War, created enormous demand for local workers—68,000 were employed at the base in 1987, as domestic workers and concessionaires, and many of these were women. Philippine government estimates at the same time showed that between 6,000 and 9,000 women were registered in nearby Olongapo City as "entertainment workers." Here was a meeting of cultures and the administration of power—sexual power, the power to prevent or convey disease, the power to enhance or disrupt a local economy in ways that would ripple across the country. Companies including Levi, Benetton, and the Gap employed women around the globe to sew jeans and knit sweaters, keeping down the price of labor and clothing by hiring nonunion workers and threatening to relocate if there was any trouble. And the Third World entered the First World, frequently and literally, in the form of domestic servants and nannies who worked in homes in Europe and the United States, often sending substantial remittances back to their families.[16]

It is also true that the way people imagine each other and construct images and stereotypes of others can condition behavior toward them. Following World War II, Americans learned about East Asians from exposure to several Broadway musicals, widely disseminated by phonograph records even to those unable to see the shows in New York. The message of these musicals, as Christina Klein tells us, was one of cooperation, antiracism, and brother- or sisterhood—virtues closely associated with women or the feminine. From the late 1940s to the late 1950s, Richard Rodgers and Oscar Hammerstein collaborated to produce three musicals—*South Pacific, The King and I,* and *Flower Drum Song*—that offered consumers a vision of Asia and Asians and Asian Americans more benign and assimilable than had previous representations of these groups. *South Pacific* conveyed the lesson that Americans should be generous toward others, including racial others, by suggesting that racism was wrong and might be self-defeating in the Cold War. Just as the Arkansas-raised nurse Nelly Forbush can accept as her own her lover's "mixed race" children, "whose skin is a different shade," so should white Americans come to term with dark-skinned people in their midst and overseas. *The King and I* was a thinly veiled metaphor for the American-inspired modernization of Southeast Asia, complete with rejection of authoritarianism (the imperious rule of the king), but softened once more by the interracial and intercultural relationship between the king and the American teacher Anna. In *Flower Drum Song,* Rodgers and Hammerstein made San Francisco's Chinatown a site of an exotic and entertaining American subculture that posed no permanent obstacle to Chinese-American integration into mainstream culture. Hammerstein's song "Chop Suey" features these lyrics:

Chop suey, chop suey!
Living here is very much like chop suey.
Hula hoops and nuclear war,

Doctor Salk and Zsa Zsa Gabor,
Bobby Darin, Sandra Dee, and Dewey,
Chop suey, Chop Suey!

Thus was the Third World lovingly, maternally embraced by the First, maintaining a semblance of its own identity while nevertheless good-naturedly returning the embrace.[17]

In addition to enabling a broad understanding of U.S. relations with the Third World and shaping viewers' understandings of First and Third World encounters through cultural productions, gender also conditioned the way American presidents, especially John F. Kennedy and Lyndon Johnson, approached the Vietnam War during the 1960s. As historian Robert Dean has argued, both Kennedy and Johnson came to political maturity within an "imperial brotherhood," formed by powerful men and sustained by their commitment to a tough, "can-do," manly posture during the Cold War. For Kennedy, all-male boarding schools, university secret societies, men's clubs, and military service instilled a felt need to stand up to the Communists and to deploy in Vietnam James Bond–inspired special forces that were coldly effective counterinsurgency fighters and rather dashing in their berets. They were JFK's male warrior-intellectuals, the "Harvard Ph.D.'s of the Special Forces Art." Lyndon Johnson was a product of rural Texas, where men proved themselves by hunting and fighting, joked casually about sex, and dominated the unmasculine among them, including women and allegedly effeminate men. Johnson envied and feared the Kennedyites, but he also regarded them as "sissies." The Vietnamese who fought him were treacherous in the way of women; Johnson found it galling to be challenged in battle by women fighters and men who held hands and were short statured, smooth skinned, and unwilling, in his view, to stand and fight. He would symbolically castrate Ho Chi Minh—"I didn't just screw Ho Chi Minh," he declared in 1964, "I cut his pecker off."—then seduce him into desisting by "going up his leg an inch at a time." The reason both administrations cited for fighting in Southeast Asia—largely to avoid the "humiliation" they associated with "premature withdrawal"—had a noisily gendered ring. Men don't run away from conflict. Vietnam was thus in part a Third World test of America's Cold War virility.[18]

Though the principal concern of this chapter is First World (U.S.) interaction with the Third World, it was of course true that the Second (Communist) World also involved itself in Latin America, Africa, and especially Asia. Cultural factors were at play in the Soviet Union's failure in Afghanistan from 1979 to 1989. As the United States had in Vietnam, the

Soviets intervened in Afghanistan for many reasons, prominent among them a strategic anxiety far more acute than any felt by the Americans in Southeast Asia fifteen years before: Afghanistan, after all, bordered the Soviet Union, and the chronic instability in the Central Asian state seemed a threat to the Soviet leadership. Yet, students of the Soviet invasion have found incomplete the strategic explanation for Soviet actions. Certainly the implications of the conflict were deeply cultural. There were religious factors involved. The Soviets feared that the rise of Islamic radicalism in Afghanistan would provide dangerous inspiration to the Muslims living in the Soviet republics across the border. The Moscow leadership worried about the rise of Islam throughout the region and imagined the invasion as "the last crusade in the East, a preventive fight of Christians and Muslims before the Muslims' massive final attack." The editor of the newspaper *Izvestia* called the invasion "a holy mission." What seems most to have rankled with Afghans and inspired their resistance—along, of course, with the mass killing from the air, the brutality of Soviet troops, and the destruction of Afghan homes and villages—was the attack on Islam that the Soviets undertook. Local Muslim leaders, the mullahs, were the interpreters of Muslim law and the only figures who held together an otherwise decentralized society. The Soviets singled out the mullahs for capture and harassment, thereby antagonizing large groups of Afghans who might otherwise have avoided identification with the state. The invasion had a gendered element as well. The Soviet military, wrote a journalist, was "anxious to test their strength somewhere," especially in light of apparent American weakness following Vietnam and in Iran, and "Afghanistan happened to be handy." The ailing Soviet leader, Leonid Brezhnev, "wanted to be remembered as a leader who extended the zone of Soviet influence in the East," while none of the men in the circle around him, contending for leadership in the future, "wanted to appear less than tough as the succession to the sick Brezhnev approached." The Afghans, especially the Pashtuns, responded with a masculine toughness of their own, saying they were willing to fight for *"zin, zer,* and *zamin"*— women, gold, and land.[19]

Culture and Power

Culture, it would seem, is handmaiden to tragedy, for when cultural assumptions are misguided the results can be dismal. But is it possible to go beyond that, to an association of culture with power, the hard currency of meaning for foreign relations history? Like Soviet power in George Kennan's famous formulation, the culture concept seems to critics to expand to fill every nook and cranny available to it in the basin of Cold War historiography. Perhaps cultural explanations embroider analyses that get more fully to the core of diplomatic interaction. In fact, culture and power inhere in each other. As three "constructivist" political scientists have put it, "It makes little sense to separate power and culture as distinct phenomena or causes: material power and coercion often derive their causal power from culture." To confine cultural analysis of foreign-relations events to the realm of "context" or "thick description" is thus inadequate, and there are several ways to show that this is so.[20]

The first is to reiterate that language and imagination shape behavior and action. This has special meaning for U.S. relations with the Third World during the Cold War. The symbols, metaphors, tropes, and stereotypes used to describe or depict others influences the policies pursued toward them. Thus, if a First World nation regards the religious practices of a group of Third World people as unorthodox or fanatical, it may assume that there is no ethical basis for a sound relationship, or may try to keep the perceived fanaticism of the other from spreading elsewhere. If a First World nation or people thinks it is more masculine, in some normative, Western sense, and thus considers itself tougher and more logical and reasonable than the people of a Third World nation, it may behave toward the Third World nation paternalistically, in the hope of blunting dangerous feminine emotions or dissolute financial behavior. If Third World nations are described metaphorically as "dominoes," for instance, their essential similarity to each other will be assumed, as will their lack of agency and their inability to think independently or act on their own behalf.[21]

A second way in which to expose the presence of culture in power is by taking up the idea of "strategic culture"—that is, strategy, generally assumed to be the basis for relations between the three Cold War worlds, is itself no fixed category of analysis but one inflected by culture. Two scholars of Chinese foreign relations, Alastair Iain Johnston and Simei Qing, have in different ways made the case for locating the formation of a nation's strategy in cultural "predispositions." Both studies stress the importance of grounding analysis of ideology and policymaking in deep historical soil, and both thus take seriously the cultural differences between China and its peer states, pointing out that strategic postures are influenced by values and visions predicated on culture. These have provided, according to Qing, different "Chinese and American blueprints of the modern economy and polity." A related argument concerns the United States and India. In each state, strategic culture proceeds from profoundly different ideas about space: in the American case, space is an enticement to exploration and expansion;

in (Hindu) India, space is the frightening unknown, a void beyond known boundaries to be protected against, not explored or absorbed. Americans assume their ideas, their institutions, and their bodies should move into territory beyond their own. Indians, who have known frequent invasion from the spaces beyond their borders, are strategically disposed to involution and self-defense. Cold War strategic doctrine was not invented out of thin air; it emerged logically from ways in which societies lived and performed their cultures.[22]

Even as the United States and the Soviet Union developed Cold War empires, it was clear that their extensions of power had cultural consequences, abroad and at home. The American war in Vietnam changed the culture of at least southern Vietnam, creating there great interest in American goods, music, and habits. Poor Vietnamese built shelters out of American beer cans, English appeared on billboards and marquees, bargirls crooned rock 'n' roll in Saigon clubs throughout the war. The United States, too, was changed by the war. Architecture returned to brutalism—low-slung, bunker-like buildings with rough, monochrome exteriors and small windows; returning veterans made Americans aware of the ravages of Agent Orange and reality of fragging hated officers; and the American people felt disillusioned by the prevarications of their government and ashamed of its hubris, at least briefly. Thousands of Vietnamese moved to the United States, transforming the economies and cultural landscapes of Orange County, California; Houston; New Orleans; and Utica, New York. The Soviet invasion of Afghanistan had consequences at least as serious. Fifteen years to the month after their attack on Kabul, the Russians sent troops into the "breakaway" province of Chechnya. They were met by determined Islamic fighters, the mujahideen, many of whom were veterans of the Afghan War. They were united in their hatred of the Russian infidels, whose mission they understood to be the destruction not only of Chechen autonomy but Central Asian Islam. The war in Chechnya absorbed Russian foreign policy for years and deeply vexed its practitioners.

Chalmers Johnson has used the term "blowback" to describe the unintended consequences of overstretch by the United States during and after the Cold War. A CIA coinage, blowback predicts retaliation against America by the victims of the nation's imperial involvements abroad. Blowback brings the Third World jarringly into the First, and bids to even scores. "Given its wealth and power," Johnson wrote in 1999, "the United States will be a prime recipient in the foreseeable future of all of the more expectable forms of blowback, particularly terrorist attacks against Americans... anywhere on earth, including within the United States." It was, of course, the assertion of

American power, especially military power, that caused so much resentment around the world. Even more did the attitudes of Americans at home and abroad, accompanied by the frequent presence of American cultural forms, increase in Third World people and nations a powerful feeling of humiliation and spark movements aimed at ridding politics of such alien influences. In 1948, as the Cold War bore its first frost, a middle-aged Egyptian intellectual named Sayyid Qutb left his country for a sojourn in the United States. During his sea passage, he was evidently propositioned by a young Western woman at the door of his stateroom. Moving between New York, Washington, DC, Colorado, and California, Qutb experienced a full range of American attitudes and customs: kindness and honesty, but, more memorably to him, profanity, open sexuality, drinking, gluttony, and racial prejudice. No one respected Islam. Qutb's encounters with American women left him disgusted: "A girl looks at you," he wrote, "appearing as if she were an enchanting nymph or an escaped mermaid, but as she approaches, you sense only the screaming instinct inside her, and you can smell her burning body, not the scent of perfume but flesh, only flesh. Tasty flesh, truly, but flesh nonetheless." Jazz conveyed the "Negroes'... love of noise and their appetite for sexual arousal." American football was appalling in its violence. More and more, Qutb came to view American and true Egyptian values as incompatible. He returned home in 1950 and took his place among the leaders of the Society of Muslim Brothers, an organization dedicated to the overthrow of secular leadership in Egypt and the purging of secular Western influences from Egyptian society. Imprisoned several times by Gamal Abdel Nasser for radical activities, Qutb refused to make a deal with the government that would have saved his life. He was hanged on August 29, 1966. Immediately afterward, a fifteen-year-old named Ayman al-Zawahiri helped create a cell devoted to the establishment of an Islamist state. Qutb's death and martyrdom, Zawahiri wrote later, inspired "the formation of the nucleus of the modern Islamic jihad movement in Egypt."[23]

Blowback is an exaggerated form of response to perceived cultural encroachment. Still, recalling that one of the strengths of cultural analysis is its insistence on the mutuality of relations between people and nations, it is proper to end on a subtler and more optimistic note. Power, insofar as it embodies culture, can fluctuate over time, and culture can mediate the impact of empire. Cultures are rarely imposed altogether by one group on another; cultures insulate, shift, and change their shape in response to encounters with other cultures. Those in the Third World were not simply "done to" by those in the First and Second worlds. What emerged instead in the Third World during the Cold War was a constant process of synthesis, whereby the seemingly dominant cultures of the First and Second worlds were altered through contact with culture in the Third. Such synthesis occurred in the realm of culture qua culture. The development of musical forms reflected an encounter between the three worlds: American jazz musicians during the early Cold War found their counterparts in Africa, Latin America, and Asia playing versions of their music, and often adapted their compositions to reflect their engagement with the musical styles they discovered elsewhere. On leave in Trinidad during Carnival, U.S. admiral Daniel V. Gallery was captivated by the sound of steel drum bands, whose members made their instruments from fifty-five gallon oil drums left by the Americans after World War II. Gallery made his own drum and started the U.S. Navy Steel Drum Band, based in Puerto Rico and known locally as "The Pandemoniacs." The band undertook popular tours of the Caribbean and the United States, winning such admirers as the folk musician Pete Seeger. Indians and Filipinos were among the most avid consumers of American films during the Cold War years, understanding them as representative of American values and tastes but imparting to them their own interpretations as well: a character in Salman Rushdie's novel *Midnight's Children,* good Hindu that he is, imagines himself in a Western called "Gai Wallah" ("Cow Fellow"), riding the range to free innocent cattle from menacing cowboys. American and European fashion was influenced by Jawaharlal Nehru's jackets and Kwame Nkrumah's dashikis. While religious Americans did not abandon their faith, Cold War encounters with India, Indochina, Tibet, and China raised their awareness of Hinduism and Buddhism especially, and if not always terribly well informed about the tenets of these religions, Americans (and Europeans) nevertheless grew in sympathy for those who practiced meditation, yoga, vegetarianism, and homeopathic medicine, all of which were associated, sometimes accurately, with Hindu and Buddhist practices. And one wonders whether "Western" ideas about gender shifted during the 1960s and 1970s in part because of awareness of others' ways of apprehending human relationships and sexual conduct. In Vietnam, men who are friends hold hands. In India, homosexuality and gender "inversion" are tolerated. Americans tend to deny that they are influenced by the practices of foreigners, regarding their own ways of doing things as superior to those of others. And yet, as we know, culture slips past borders and works in contrapuntal and mysterious and powerful ways. It did not *determine* in every respect what happened in the Third World during the Cold War. But its presence nevertheless intruded constantly on so-called core-periphery relations, complicating any seemingly straightforward narrative concerned only with, say, strategy or economics. "There is no such thing as human nature independent of culture," wrote Clifford Geertz. The Cold War in the Third World was a fully human enterprise.[24]

NOTES

1. William Inboden, *Religion and American Foreign Policy: The Soul of Containment* New York: Cambridge University Press, 2008), 157–225 (quotations at 170, 176, 214).

2. Mary Ann Heiss, "Real Men Don't Wear Pajamas: Anglo-American Cultural Perceptions of Mohammed Mossadeq and the Iranian Oil Nationalization Dispute," in *Empire and Revolution: The United States and the Third World since 1945*, ed. Peter L. Hahn and Mary Ann Heiss (Columbus: Ohio State University Press, 2001), 178–194.

3. Thomas Borstelmann, *Apartheid's Reluctant Uncle: The United States and Southern Africa in the Early Cold War* (New York: Oxford University Press, 1993), 40, 112; Andrew J. Rotter, *Comrades at Odds: The United States and India, 1947–1964* (Ithaca, NY: Cornell University Press, 2000), 159–160.

4. Michael J. Hogan, "'The 'Next Big Thing': The Future of Diplomatic History in a Global Age," *Diplomatic History* 28:1 (January 2004), 1–21; Clifford Geertz, *The Interpretation of Culture* (New York: Basic Books, 1973),

5. Representative titles include the following: On culture generally—Akira Iriye, "Culture and International History," in *Explaining the History of American Foreign Relations* (hereafter *Explaining the History*), ed. Michael J. Hogan and Thomas G. Paterson, 2nd ed. (Cambridge: Cambridge University Press, 2004), 242; and Rotter, *Comrades at Odds*. On race—Thomas Borstelmann, *The Cold War and the Color Line: American Race Relations in the Global Arena* (Cambridge, MA: Harvard University Press, 2001); Gerald Horne, "Race to Insight: The United States and the World: White Supremacy and Foreign Affairs," in *Explaining the History*, 323–335; and Paul A. Kramer, *The Blood of Government: Race, Empire, the United States, and the Philippines* (Chapel Hill: University of North Carolina Press, 2006). On gender—Joan Scott, "Gender: A Useful Category of Historical Analysis," *American Historical Review* 91:4 (December 1986), 1053–1075; Emily Rosenberg, "Gender," *Journal of American History* 77:1 (June 1990); and Kristin Hoganson, *Fighting for American Manhood: How Gender Politics Provoked the Spanish-American and Philippine-American Wars* (New Haven, CT: Yale University Press, 1998). On religion—Seth Jacobs, *America's Miracle Man in Vietnam: Ngo Dinh Diem, Religion, Race, and U.S. Intervention in Southeast Asia* (Durham, NC: Duke University Press, 2004); Andrew Preston, "Bridging the Gap between the Sacred and the Secular in the History of American Foreign Relations," *Diplomatic History* 30:5 (November 2006), 783–812; Andrew Preston, *Sword of the Spirit, Shield of Faith: Religion in American War and Diplomacy* (New York: Anchor, 2012); and Matthew F. Jacobs, "The Perils and Promise of Islam: The United States and the Muslim Middle East

in the Early Cold War," *Diplomatic History* 30:4 (September 2006), 705–739. On maturity—Naoko Shibusawa, *America's Geisha Ally* (Cambridge, MA: Harvard University Press, 2006). On language—Frank Costigliola, "Reading for Meaning: Theory, Language, and Metaphor," in *Explaining the History*, 279–303. On identity—Walter Hixson, *The Myth of American Diplomacy: National Identity and U.S. Foreign Policy* (New Haven, CT: Yale University Press, 2008). On the postcolonial—Edward Said, *Orientalism* (New York: Random House, 1978), and *Culture and Imperialism* (New York: Knopf, 1993).

5. Jessica C. E. Gienow-Hecht, "Cultural Transfer," in *Explaining the History*, 257–278, and *Sound Diplomacy: Music and Emotions in Transatlantic Relations, 1850–1920* (Chicago: University of Chicago Press, 2009); Victoria De Grazia, *Irresistible Empire: America's Advance through Twentieth-Century Europe* (Cambridge, MA: Harvard University Press, 2005).

6. Hoganson, *Fighting for American Manhood*; Andrew J. Rotter, "Christians, Muslims, and Hindus: Religion and U.S.–South Asian Relations, 1947–1954," *Diplomatic History* 24:4 (Fall 2000), 593–613; Mark Philip Bradley, *Imagining Vietnam and America: The Making of Postcolonial Vietnam, 1919–1950* (Chapel Hill: University of North Carolina Press, 2000); Robert D. Dean, *Imperial Brotherhood: Gender and the Making of Cold War Foreign Policy* (Amherst: University of Massachusetts Press, 2001).

7. Said, *Culture and Imperialism*.

8. Odd Arne Westad, *The Global Cold War: Third World Interventions and the Making of Our Times* (Cambridge: Cambridge University Press, 2007), 2–3, 100–101, 110; George McTurnan Kahin, *The Asian-African Conference, Bandung, Indonesia* (Ithaca, NY: Cornell University Press, 1956), 64–72; Cary Fraser, "An American Dilemma: The American Response to the Bandung Conference, 1955," in *Window on Freedom: Race, Civil Rights, and Foreign Affairs, 1945–1988*, ed. Brenda Gayle Plummer (Chapel Hill: University of North Carolina Press, 2003), 115–140 (Wright quoted on 134).

9. John Oxenham and Hugh Moss, *The Pageant of Darkness and Light* (New York: Young People's Missionary Movement of the United States and Canada, 1911).

10. Christina Klein, *Cold War Orientalism: Asia in the Middlebrow Imagination, 1945–1961* (Berkeley: University of California Press, 2003); Preston, "Bridging the Gap"; Inboden, *Religion and American Foreign Policy*, 4. See also Walter A. McDougall, *Promised Land, Crusader State: The American Encounter with the World since 1776* (Boston: Houghton Mifflin, 1997).

11. Inboden, *Religion and American Foreign Policy*, 4, 47; Will Herberg, *Protestant, Catholic, Jew: An Essay in American Religious Sociology* (Chicago: University of Chicago Press, 1955).

12. Martin E. Marty, *Modern American Religion,* vol. 3: *Under God, Indivisible, 1941–1960* (Chicago: University of Chicago Press, 1996), 118; Rotter, *Comrades at Odds*, 233–239. As Jacobs has written, American experts "trying to understand the

Middle East and its significance in global affairs in the late 1940s and early 1950s relied on faulty and essentializing assumptions and common stereotypes about Islam as they focused on it as a dominant feature of regional culture, society, and politics." Jacobs, "Perils and Promise," 708.

13. Rotter, *Comrades at Odds*, 241–242.

14. Ibid., 222; Jacobs, *America's Miracle Man*, 12, 76, 209.

15. Theresa Keeley, "Reagan's Gun-Toting Nuns: The Maryknoll Sisters and Their Influence on U.S. Intervention in Central America," paper given at the conference of the Society for Historians of American Foreign Relations, Madison, WI, June 26, 2010. See also Greg Grandin, *Empire's Workshop: Latin America, the United States, and the Rise of the New Imperialism* (New York: Henry Holt, 2006), 145–150.

16. Cynthia Enloe, *Bananas, Beaches, and Bases: Making Feminist Sense of International Politics* (Berkeley: University of California Press, 1990). In addition to work already cited by Scott, Rosenberg, and Hoganson, see also Glenda Sluga, "Gender," in *Palgrave Advances in International History,* ed. Patrick Finney (Houndmills, UK: Palgrave Macmillan, 2005), 300–319; Geoffrey Smith, "National Security and Personal Isolation: Sex, Gender, and Disease in the Cold War United States," *International History Review* 14:2 (May 1992), 307–337; Mary A. Renda, *Taking Haiti: Military Occupation and the Culture of U.S. Imperialism, 1915–1954* (Chapel Hill: University of North Carolina Press, 2001); Donna Alvah, *Unofficial Ambassadors: American Military Families Overseas and the Cold War* (New York: New York University Press, 2007); Mrinalini Sinha, *Gender and Nation* (Washington, DC: American Historical Association, 2006).

17. Klein, *Cold War Orientalism*, 189, 212–215, 230–231.

18. Dean, *Imperial Brotherhood*, 14, 184–185, 210, 239–240. See also Andrew J. Rotter, "Gender Relations, Foreign Relations: The United States and South Asia, 1947–1964," *Journal of American History* 81:2 (September 1994), 518–542.

19. Artyom Borovik, *The Hidden War: A Russian Journalist's Account of the Soviet War in Afghanistan* (New York: The Atlantic Monthly Press, 1990), 7–10; Henry S. Bradsher, *Afghan Communism and Soviet Intervention* (Oxford: Oxford University Press, 1999), 78, 87; Fredrik Barth, "Cultural Wellsprings of Resistance in Afghanistan," in *Afghanistan: The Great Game Revisited*, ed. Rosanne Klass (New York: Freedom House, 1987), 187–202; Olivier Roy, "The *Mujahedin* and Preservation of Afghan Culture," in *Afghanistan and the Soviet Union: Collision and Transformation*, ed. Milan Hauner and Robert L. Canfield (Boulder, CO: Westview Press, 1989), 40–47.

20. For criticism of the cultural approach, see Bruce Kuklick, "Commentary," *Diplomatic History* 22:1 (Spring 1998), 121–124; Robert Buzzanco, "Where's the Beef? Culture without Power in the Study of U.S. Foreign Relations," *Diplomatic History* 24:4 (Fall 2000), 623–632; Volker Depkat, "Cultural Approaches to International Relations: A Challenge," in *Culture and International History*, ed. Jessica Gienow-Hecht and Frank Schumacher (New York: Berghahn Books, 2003), 181;

Thomas Alan Schwartz, "Explaining the Cultural Turn—Or Detour?" *Diplomatic History* 31:1 (January 2007), 143–147. Quotation is from Ronald L. Jepperson, Alexander Wendt, and Peter J. Katzenstein, "Norms, Identity, and Culture in National Security," in *The Culture of National Security: Norms and Identity in World Politics,* ed. Peter J. Katzenstein (New York: Columbia University Press, 1996), 40.

21. Andrew J. Rotter, "Culture," in *Palgrave Advances in International History,* ed. Patrick Finney (Houndmills, UK: Palgrave Macmillan, 2005), 280; Emily Rosenberg, "Considering Borders," in *Explaining the History,* 176–193.

22. Alastair Iain Johnston, *Cultural Realism: Strategic Culture and Grand Strategy in Chinese History* (Princeton, NJ: Princeton University Press, 1995); Simei Qing, *From Allies to Enemies: Visions of Modernity, Identity, and U.S.-China Diplomacy, 1945–1960* (Cambridge, MA: Harvard University Press, 2007); Rotter, *Comrades at Odds,* 37–76.

23. Chalmers Johnson, *Blowback: The Costs and Consequences of American Empire* (New York: Henry Holt, 2000), 223; Lawrence Wright, *The Looming Tower: Al-Qaeda and the Road to 9/11* (New York: Knopf, 2006), 7–39.

24. Penny M. Von Eschen, *Satchmo Blows Up the World: Jazz Ambassadors Play the Cold War* (Cambridge, MA: Harvard University Press, 2004); Andrew Martin, "Words of Steel: Pete Seeger and the U.S. Navy Steel Band," *Voices* 34 (Spring-Summer 2008); Salman Rushdie, *Midnight's Children* (New York: Penguin, 1991), 50–51; Vicente L. Rafael, "Taglish, or the Phantom Power of the Lingua Franca," *White Love and Other Events in Filipino History* (Durham, NC: Duke University Press, 2000), 162–163; Gita Mehta, *Karma Cola: Marketing the Mysterious East* (New York: Simon and Schuster, 1979); John Frederick Muehl, *Interview with India* (New York: John Day, 1950), 168; Geertz, *Interpretation of Cultures,* 49.

10

THE HISTORIES OF AFRICAN AMERICANS'
ANTICOLONIALISM DURING THE COLD WAR

CAROL ANDERSON

In January 1948, Walter White, executive secretary of the National Association for the Advancement of Colored People (NAACP) wrangled an opportunity to testify before the Senate Foreign Relations Committee on the proposed European Recovery Program, the Marshall Plan.[1] In his testimony, however, White did not mention the growing battle with the Soviet Union for control of Europe. He did not linger on the looming threat of the Communist parties in Italy or France. Instead, he spent the majority of his time outlining the inevitable violence that would occur if racism and colonialism continued. He fully realized that the "European nations which are to benefit from this relief plan . . . receive much of their economic strength from colonies in Africa, the Caribbean, the Pacific, and Asia." But, he explained, "it would be utter folly for the United States to help white Europe" and still "permit it to continue to deny freedom and opportunity to colonial peoples." White noted that the current wars of liberation in Indonesia and Indochina were omens. "Nothing," he noted, "will speed World War III more than attempts to reestablish 'white supremacy'" as the Dutch and French were frantically trying to do. To continue down this path, White warned, "will speed revolt among the hundreds of millions of brown, yellow, and black people who are determined to have freedom also." Marshall Plan dollars, he insisted, must not be used to tighten Europe's hold on its restive empires. Nothing, not even the financial might of the United States, White warned, could stop people of color's quest for freedom.[2]

At those hearings, Walter White gave voice to an important black American perspective on European recovery—one that emphasized the destructive force of colonialism and the unacceptability of white supremacy.

He later asserted that until those who were locked in Jim Crow and those who were decimated by colonialism had "an equal opportunity with other men irrespective of race, creed, color or place of birth…there can be little hope of a lasting peace."[3]

That fusion of race and the Cold War has led historians to examine how Jim Crow complicated U.S. foreign policy.[4] State Department officials complained that when they were trying to deal with the issue of colonialism, inevitably the "maltreatment of negroes in this country receives amazingly wide and detailed attention and stimulates extensive criticism."[5] The U.S. consulate in Lagos, Nigeria, reported, for example, that the liberation newspaper the *West African Pilot* consistently referred to the "persecution," "discrimination," and "segregation" that blacks endured in the United States. The consul lamented that while there was some exaggeration in the report, "it contains a core of undeniable truth." Every racial flare-up, every case of a legal lynching, he continued, "created such ill will for the United States" that the State Department found it "extremely difficult or impossible to counteract."[6] Then-assistant secretary of state Dean Rusk emphasized that "[t]he greatest burden we Americans have to bear in working out satisfactory relations with the peoples of Asia is our minority problems in the United States."[7]

While the focus on the ways that Jim Crow undermined the implementation of U.S. Cold War foreign policy in the Third World is important, the role of African Americans in forging alliances with their Third World counterparts to dismantle white supremacy is equally important.[8] A history from the bottom-up lays open the circuits of informal power that transcended national, racial, ideological, and historical boundaries to take on a system of oppression that had reigned for hundreds of years. It reveals the ways that the seemingly powerless conceptualized their individual and collective strengths to challenge the dominant economic and political regimes. In fact, this battle to dismantle empires of racism in the midst of the Cold War reveals something about the possible. This struggle, frankly, should have been stillborn given the disproportionate financial, political, and technological power arrayed by the Europeans and Americans. It should have been an exercise in futility because of the ideological straitjacket of East and West that construed challenges to that discourse as traitorous. And, it should have been impossible given the geographic dispersion of racial allies spread across three continents with limited access to the technologies that revolutionized communications. Yet, in the end, African Americans found ways to circumnavigate around those challenges and work with and for those whom they saw as waging a similar struggle.[9] In doing so, they scored a series of victories that resulted in delegitimizing racism, colonial rule, and white supremacy as governing principles in a civilized world. In short, the role of African Americans in helping to strip the global system of its urbane veneer to reveal the structures of racist power deepens the story told about the strategies and tactics used by Third World freedom fighters.[10]

There are some limits in the current scholarship, however, that have constrained our knowledge about the role that African Americans played in decolonization. Part of the problem is that, in many instances, black liberals were like stealth fighters who imbibed the strategy pronounced by the first African-American leader of the NAACP, James Weldon Johnson. He noted that "the black man fights passively.... He bears the fury of the storm as does the willow tree."[11] That stealth resistance, to bend like the willow instead of taking the blows and snapping like an oak, has made it difficult to discern what role black liberals played at all in decolonization. That is to say, historians have interpreted the bend as capitulation. Erik McDuffie, for example, summarizing years of scholarship, notes that the "Cold War abruptly ended the close relationships some African Americans cultivated" with anti-imperialists throughout the world. "In the face of anticommunist repression domestically, liberal African American leaders in the NAACP and other black political organizations retreated from any form of militant anticolonialism."[12]

Scholars, therefore, have turned to the most vocal and visible. Those like W. Alphaeus Hunton of the left-wing Council on African Affairs who faced the storm of the anti-Communist witch hunts that seized the United States during the early years of the Cold War. He trenchantly explained:

> Racial oppression and exploitation have a universal pattern and whether they occur in South Africa, Mississippi, or New Jersey, they must be exposed and fought as part of a world-wide system of oppression the fountain-head of which is today among the reactionary fascist-minded ruling circles of white America.[13]

The fire of that pronouncement, the defiance in its words, and the toll that it took on Hunton and so many like him, who were "hounded into oblivion" during the second Red Scare has led scholars to create a seductive narrative arc that runs the radical, martyred gamut from Marcus Garvey, to W.E.B. Du Bois, to Paul Robeson, to Malcolm X, to the Student Nonviolent Coordinating Committee (SNCC), and to the Panthers.[14] In doing so, historians have elevated the role of black radicals in the liberation struggles both at home and abroad with no room to engage a different type of mobilization, one that fought to achieve racial liberation across the globe not from out-side, but from within the institutions that held the power.[15]

Constrained by this narrowed lens, we learn that by the 1960s, after Hunton, Du Bois, and Robeson had been forced into financial, physical, or mental exile, a new wave of radicals took up this battle: the SNCC's "Stokely Carmichael, James Forman…and other youthful leaders from the North brought to the southern movement an explicit Pan-Africanism that perceived the American desegregation struggle as the counterpart of Africa's decolonization struggle."[16] The fight for freedom, however, could not be achieved by moral suasion, lobbying, or passive resistance. One SNCC member particularly singled out the National Association for the Advancement of Colored People as past its prime. "Our parents had the NAACP," he explained, but "[w]e needed something more." For this new generation of freedom fighters, "the NAACP's approach was too slow, too courteous, too deferential and too ineffectual."[17]

That "more" turned out to be more revolutionary. More radical. More global. More confrontational. More violent. It was embodied in Frantz Fanon's *The Wretched of the Earth* (1961).[18] Fanon, a theorist for the Algerian Revolution, argued that colonialism was built on violence, and, therefore, it was going to take unrelenting violence to destroy it. His pre-science about the Algerians' subsequent success in ridding their nation of French rule, culminating with independence in 1962, proved intoxicating and empowering.[19]

There was, of course, a domestic American variant also articulating the need for violence. The omnipresent terror that African Americans faced had led to a long history of self-defense in the black community.[20] In 1959 it rose to the fore in the guise of Robert F. Williams, the leader of the NAACP in Monroe, North Carolina. As he faced down the Ku Klux Klan and a legal system that would not protect black people, Williams, a former marine, argued that African Americans "must meet violence with violence."[21] That is to say, he "had espoused the view that there is no substitute for armed resistance against a recalcitrant and hostile Jim Crow establishment."[22] That utterance put him at odds with the association's national office and shortly thereafter, Williams was relieved of his post. With his ouster from the "overly cautious, politically conservative" NAACP and his subsequent exile to Fidel Castro's Cuba, Williams soon became "a hero to the new wave of black internationalists."[23]

An additional element fueling this revolutionary spirit was Mao Zedong, the leader of the People's Republic of China. Historians Robin Kelley and Betty Esch note that in "Harlem in the late 1960s and early 1970s, it seemed as though everyone had a copy of *Quotations from Chairman Mao Tse-Tung*, better known as the 'little red book.'" The allure to African-American militants was that the "Chinese peasants, as opposed to the European proletariat," had actually launched and executed a successful "socialist revolution." The fact that a people of color had achieved the impossible, "endowed black radicals with a deeper sense of revolutionary importance and power."[24] Indeed, the Black Panther Party (BPP), founded in 1967 on Maoist and self-defense principles, "instructed members to read...[the] *Red Book* but to 'substitute the word communist with the word...revolutionary.'"[25] The BPP took this vision not only to Oakland, California, but to Cuba and Algeria as well.[26]

The SNCC, for its part, articulated an unwavering solidarity with the colonized. John Wilson explained to his "Vietnamese Brothers and Sisters" that the "black militants in the USA believe that there is a necessity for linking our struggle with the liberation struggles in the Third World" because "we have the same enemy...white imperialist America."[27] Similarly, James Forman told the UN Fourth Committee, which handled colonial issues, that African Americans had to fight against apartheid and colonialism because "we are in the same box." Blacks' "experiences in the United States," he continued, "have prepared us to understand the emotional and psychological ordeal of a colonized people."[28]

For the SNCC and Black Panthers, this fight not only in southern Africa, but for people of color throughout the globe could only be won "from the barrel of a gun."[29] Huey Newton, cofounder of the BPP, thus alerted the Communist guerillas in South Vietnam that the Panthers "would...recruit an African American unit to fight with the National Liberation Front,...the Vietcong" against U.S. forces.[30]

But more than that, the SNCC promised to destroy American imperialism by destroying the United States itself. "The fight against racism is a responsibility of all who believe in Human Rights," the SNCC asserted. "We have," therefore, "accepted our responsibility for the attack on the American front."[31] During his 1967 visit to Cuba, for example, SNCC chairman Stokely Carmichael explained that the riot in Newark, New Jersey, that had left twenty-six dead and resulted in more than $10 million in property damage was actually African Americans waging war on the United States. "In Newark," he boasted, "we applied war tactics of the guerilla for our defense in the cities."[32] Similarly, the SNCC later explained to President Houphouet Boigny, president of the Ivory Coast, that "the recent rebellions in Newark and Detroit are just the latest in a long line of slave revolts and resistance to the...degrading condition in the United States."[33] These "black rebellions," the SNCC asserted, were "a dress rehearsal for complete revolution."[34]

John Wilson explained to the Vietnamese:

> We believe that you cannot organize or domesticate a mad dog. You dispose of it. White America throughout history has always been unapproachable and unteachable so there is only one alternative—to destroy it or face genocide.[35]

The war was on, and the SNCC envisioned itself at the forefront of that battle.

Yet, for all of the revolutionary bravado on display, the reality was decidedly more mundane. Detroit, Newark, and the scores of other cities ablaze in the late 1960s were not training grounds for guerillas-in-waiting or boot camps for black commandos on their way to Angola and Vietnam to fight for colonial liberation. Instead, those fiery urban shells were the result of years of policy decisions that trapped African Americans in decaying inner cities with inadequate schools, decrepit housing, bleak economic opportunities, and brutal police forces.[36] Moreover, the physical destruction of blocks and blocks of blighted urban landscapes did not signal the collapse of the United States or the capitalist system; it just meant that many of those areas had even fewer resources to sustain any quality of life for the poor and overwhelmingly black populations who were stranded there.[37]

Nonetheless, many scholars, who are exploring these Cold War connections between Africa and the diasporic communities in the United States, have seized on the rhetoric of militancy to demonstrate the vibrancy and viability of the SNCC's and the Black Panthers' anticolonial efforts.[38] To be sure, the language of revolution and violence was unvarnished and unequivocal. Yet, what these radicals actually accomplished in helping to free Africans and Asians from colonial rule (and not simply raise the global consciousness of black Americans) is not always so clear.[39] When Newton promised to send troops to South Vietnam, for example, he spoke of troops he never had. Carmichael rhapsodized about a full-blown guerilla war in Newark, but it was nothing more than a five-day riot.

Frankly, after a while, the revolutionary governments grew weary of both the bluster and the American-grown radicals who spouted it. Algeria, for example, had become a haven for Eldridge Cleaver, the Black Panthers' minister of information, and a slew of hijackers with ties to the BPP. After a few years, though, President Houari Boumédienne began to limit the Panthers' contact with government officials. Cleaver retaliated with a well-publicized but poorly thought out critique of his host's regime. Not surprisingly, Algerian police raided Panthers' headquarters and Cleaver's home and placed the occupants under house arrest. Then, Boumédienne's government, although it had broken off diplomatic relations with the United States, began to return the ransom collected by the hijackers, although Cleaver frantically pleaded that the Panthers needed that money to finance the revolution.[40]

The saga in Fidel Castro's Cuba was even more brutal. Panthers expected a hero's welcome as they hijacked planes, diverted them to Havana, and hoped to collect hundreds of thousands of dollars to pay for the revolution. Instead, they faced imprisonment and torture.[41] One Panther, after spending eleven years in Castro's prison, "described watching executions and endless beatings." Bearing the scars left by his guards' bayonets, he lamented, "I had believed that Cuba was a revolutionary's paradise. I found a revolutionary's graveyard instead."[42] Another Panther hijacker who landed in Havana also hoped for political asylum, but after facing years "of racial discrimination" in Cuba opted to return to the United States, where he stoically embraced a possible life sentence in prison.[43] What becomes apparent, then, is that it was the aura of militancy not the efficacy of it that captured the imagination of the youth at the time and many historians today.

The result has been to silence the narrative about the ways that African-American liberals fought for the right to self-determination. Without question, black liberals' tactics were more subtle, but that does not mean, as historian Penny Von Eschen asserts, that with the onset of the Cold War the NAACP developed "a new exclusive focus on domestic discrimination and silence on foreign policy issues."[44] Instead, black liberals were bureaucratic infighters, who mastered the arcane rules and power relationships at the State Department, the United Nations, and the White House to undermine the global legitimacy of colonialism and white supremacy. In other words, the fervor of the 1960s and the anti-apartheid movement of the 1970s and 1980s are based on the groundwork laid by black liberals in the early years of the Cold War.

In the late 1940s, for example, the NAACP weighed in decisively in the UN General Assembly to keep Italy from regaining total control of Somalia, Libya, and Eritrea.[45] The future prime minister of Somalia, Abdullahi Issa, openly acknowledged the importance of the NAACP in his people's quest for freedom. He explained to Secretary of State John Foster Dulles that while "the colonial powers controlling almost the entire Continent of Africa...seek the diplomatic support and the economic aid of the United States Government in order to continue their domination of Africa," it was "the National Association for the Advancement of Colored People, which generously offered its moral and material support to the legitimate efforts of the Somali people to secure their unity and independence."[46] Without the "invaluable assistance received from the association," Issa made clear, his delegation to the United Nations "would have faced insurmountable difficulties."[47]

The NAACP also took on South Africa after that nation attempted to annex the international territory of South West Africa (current-day Namibia), a former German colony that the League of Nations assigned to Pretoria in 1919 "as a sacred trust of civilization." When the United Nations created the trusteeship system, all the other Western powers placed their League mandates under the aegis of the United Nations; South Africa, however, patently refused. Instead, in a move that the Indian government could only describe as an "Anschluss," at the first meeting of the United Nations in 1946, South Africa announced that it planned to absorb adjacent South West Africa, thereby placing 350,000 African inhabitants under a white-supremacist state's sovereignty.[48]

The association mobilized. It aligned with the reverend Michael Scott, a heretical, white Anglican priest with Communist ties, who could surreptitiously glide into the mandate and gather data and testimony about the conditions in South West Africa. The NAACP worked with the India League and the Indian government to find ways to circumvent the "security risk" label that the U.S. State and Justice departments had slapped on Scott to prevent him from getting into the United States and testifying before the United Nations. It then secured official UN consultative status for the priest with the International League for the Rights of Man, on whose board top executives from the NAACP sat. The association also provided funding, office space, and secretarial support for the renegade Scott.[49]

With this phalanx of support, Scott submitted documentation to the United Nations about the actual conditions in South West Africa, which were so shocking that it led to an International Court of Justice advisory opinion that South Africa had to report to the United Nations on the economic and political well-being of that mandate's colonized people, the Hereros, Namas, and Berg-Damaras. Scott had also, in a precedent-setting move, testified before the UN's Fourth Committee as a representative of South West Africa's indigenous people, who were "very grateful indeed," for the role the NAACP played in "helping...get their opinions made known."[50]

The pay-off for all of this activity was incremental but essential in transforming the Western perception of South Africa from valued military ally to political ball and chain. The CIA noted that "South African intransigence...has made the country something of a propaganda liability to the U.S. and the Western bloc."[51] Similarly, in a fevered exchange about how to defuse the rancor that South Africa brought to the United Nations, Canadian officials, despite whatever solution Pretoria concocted, all agreed that "South Africa is, admittedly, a handicap to the western world in the struggle of moral supremacy over Communism." Pretoria's regime was "a liability to the white races" because "the behavior of the whites in South Africa…increases the danger that the white world will not have the full support of the coloured peoples in Asia against the Soviet Union."[52]

The tide was shifting, yet the NAACP was not done. Part of its strategy was to find allies within the U.S. delegation to destroy American support, no matter how equivocal, for South Africa's apartheid regime.[53] One of those allies at the fall 1951 UN meeting was an African-American attorney from Chicago, Edith Sampson, whose rose-colored vision of Jim Crow had enraged many in the black community.[54] Even Sampson, however, was appalled that the U.S. delegation was actually planning to shield South Africa from international criticism. Although "she did not speak up often in delegation meetings,…[s]he stood by her guns on the…South West Africa item, insisting that the United States position should be clear-cut and in no sense protective of South Africa."[55]

Sampson laid out her case. South Africa's "virtual slave-system and color discrimination," she argued, "are exhibits of colonialism at its worst, and [are] so identified by the people of Asia, the Middle East and most of Latin America." If the UN backed South Africa and, by implication, its policies, the United States, Sampson concluded, "would be 'damned' from the start" especially in "light of the Union's bad record and obvious steps to integrate SWA into the Union." She asked her colleagues to recognize that the United States could not stand before the United Nations and defend the indefensible. "America's survival is tied up with the amount of confidence we can engender in Asia and the Middle East," she asserted. "We can't buy it; we have to win it by standing for what they and we really believe in: human rights regardless of race or color." Then she came to the reverend Michael Scott. Through Walter White, she had met with the Anglican priest several times throughout the previous year. Scott, she observed, was a "symbol of protest," a voice for the otherwise "gagged natives of South West Africa." If the Americans allowed Pretoria to cover up its human-rights violations in that beleaguered colony, it would "antagonize" the very members of the United Nations that the U.S. government was trying to attract to the West. Sampson was joined in this effort by former first lady and chair of the UN Commission on Human Rights, Eleanor Roosevelt, who had also come to believe in the reverend Michael Scott, even going so far as to anonymously donate funds, through the NAACP, to support his efforts. With this strong ally on her side, Sampson began to turn the tide in the delegation.[56]

It was then up to the chairman of the NAACP Board of Directors, Channing Tobias, who also served as chair of the U.S. delegation in the UN Fourth Committee. *Ebony* magazine had described Tobias as a "tall, scholarly, intensely-spiritual New Yorker...[who] operates in an air of secrecy, steering clear of spectacular high-pressure methods...but somewhere behind the scenes" getting the job done, nonetheless.[57] He would not disappoint. Because Pretoria flatly refused to abide by the World Court's advisory opinion, the Fourth Committee countered that it had every right to go directly to the people most affected to learn what was actually going on in South West Africa. Tobias agreed and made sure that the other U.S. delegates could not provide any support whatsoever to Britain or South Africa as those two nations tried to forestall the United Nations' precedent-setting invitation to the indigenous leadership of South West Africa, the Hereros, Namas, and Berg-Damaras. Although the British and South Africans were furious with Tobias's efforts, the end result was that "shortly after the December 1951 meeting, the UN created a series of committees to investigate the conditions in South West Africa as well as the racial conditions (apartheid) in South Africa, itself." It was the beginning of the transformation of the Union into a pariah nation; it raised the very real possibility of penetrating national sovereignty in the face of systematic human rights violations; and it was a major step on the long, hard road to Namibian independence.[58]

In short, the anticolonial, anti-apartheid struggle was not simply a phenomenon of black radicals in the 1960s. Nor was it solely the province of the Left in the 1950s. Mainstream liberal African Americans had been laboring for decades with their Third World allies to end white minority rule as well. It was this broad coalition that began to shift the terms of debate from East-West to North-global South. It was this coalition that found the cracks in the national sovereignty armor of colonialism and white supremacy to discredit those concepts as governing principles. And, it was this coalition, as South African president Nelson Mandela later noted, "that has fought for the emancipation of black people everywhere."[59]

NOTES

1. Dean Acheson to Walter White, January 5, 1948, box A417, file "Marshall Plan Correspondence, 1947–48," *Papers of the National Association for the Advancement of Colored People*, Library of Congress, Washington, DC (hereafter *Papers of the NAACP*).

2. Senate Committee on Foreign Relations, *European Recovery Program*, 80th Congress, 2d sess. (Washington, DC: Government Printing Office, 1948), 952–953.

3. Broadcast over UN Radio from Paris by Walter White, October 1948, box A635, file "United Nations: General Assembly, Oct., 1948," *Papers of the NAACP*.

4. Mary Dudziak, *Cold War Civil Rights: Race and the Image of American Democracy* (Princeton, NJ: Princeton University Press, 2000); Thomas Borstelmann, *Cold War Color Line: American Race Relations in the Global Arena* (Cambridge, MA: Harvard University Press, 2001); Carol Anderson, "The Cold War in the Atlantic World," in *The Atlantic World, 1450–2000*, ed. Toyin Falola and Kevin D. Roberts (Bloomington: Indiana University Press, 2008), 294–314.

5. Porter McKeever to Warren Austin, memorandum, August 16, 1948, carton V, file "Correspondence: 1948-August," *Papers of Warren Austin*, Bailey-Howe Library, Special Collection, University of Vermont, Burlington.

6. Willard Quincy Stanton to Department of State, dispatch, April 26, 1951, 745h.00/4-2651, box 65, file "Policy Machine—USIA—American Image in Africa," *Papers of Vernon McKay*, Melville Herskovits Africana Library, Northwestern University, Evanston, IL.

7. Dean Rusk to Walter White, January 18, 1951, box A284, file "Foreign Affairs: Asia, 1950–52," *Papers of the NAACP*.

8. Brenda Gayle Plummer, *Rising Wind: Black Americans and U.S. Foreign Affairs, 1935–1960* (Chapel Hill: University of North Carolina Press, 1996).

9. For the factors that created the political space for African American liberals to maneuver in their battle against colonialism, see Anderson, "The Cold War in the Atlantic World," 306–308.

10. Matthew Connelly, *A Diplomatic Revolution: Algeria's Fight for Independence and the Origins of the Post–Cold War Order* (New York: Oxford University Press, 2002), and "Taking off the Cold War Lens: Visions of North-South Conflict during the Algerian War for Independence," *American Historical Review* 105:3 (June 2000), 739–769; Odd Arne Westad, *The Global Cold War: Third World Interventions and the Making of Our Times* (New York: Cambridge University Press, 2005).

11. James Weldon Johnson, *Autobiography of an Ex-Colored Man*, introduction by Arna Bontemps (New York: Hill and Wang, 1960), 75.

12. Erik S. McDuffie, "Black and Red: Black Liberations, the Cold War, and the Horne Thesis," *Journal of African American History* 96:2 (Spring 2011), 241.

13. W. Alphaeus Hunton to A. A. Marks, Jr., July 6, 1950, Reel 1, *Papers of W. Alphaeus Hunton*, Schomburg Center for Research in Black Culture, New York, NY.

14. Frances Njubi Nesbitt, *Race for Sanctions: African Americans against Apartheid, 1946–1994* (Bloomington: Indiana University Press, 2004), 22.

15. An excellent exception is Brenda Gayle Plummer, *In Search of Power: African Americans in the Age of Decolonization, 1956–1974* (New York: Cambridge University Press, 2013).

16. St. Clair Drake, "Black Studies and Global Perspectives: An Essay," *Journal of Negro Education* 53:3 (Summer 1984), 229–230.

17. Cleveland Sellers, quoted in Timothy B. Tyson, *Radio Free Dixie: Robert F. Williams and the Roots of Black Power* (Chapel Hill: University of North Carolina Press, 1999), 145.

18. Drake, "Black Studies and Global Perspectives," 230; Fanon Che Wilkins, "The Making of Black Internationalists: SNCC and Africa before the Launching of Black Power, 1960–1965," *Journal of African American History* 92:4 (Fall 2007), 485.

19. Alistair Horne, *A Savage War of Peace: Algeria, 1954–1962* (New York: New York Review of Books Classics, 2006); Connelly, *A Diplomatic Revolution.*

20. Philip Dray, *At the Hands of Persons Unknown: The Lynching of Black America* (New York: Modern Library, 2003); Alfred L. Brophy, *Reconstructing the Dreamland—The Tulsa Race Riot of 1921: Race, Reparations, and Reconciliation* (New York: Oxford University Press, 2002); Kevin Boyle, *Arc of Justice: A Saga of Race, Civil Rights, and Murder in the Jazz Age* (New York: Henry Holt, 2004).

21. Robin D. G. Kelley and Betsy Esch, "Black Like Mao: Red China and Black Revolution," *Souls* (Fall 1999), 14.

22. Vijay Prashad, "Waiting for the Black Gandhi: Satyagraha and Black Internationalism," in *From Toussaint to Tupac: The Black International since the Age of Revolution*, ed. Michael O. West, William G. Martin, and Fanon Che Wilkins (Chapel Hill: University of North Carolina Press, 2009), 192.

23. Tyson, *Radio Free Dixie*, 110; Kelley and Esch, "Black Like Mao," 14.

24. Kelley and Esch, "Black Like Mao," 7, 8.

25. Yohuru R. Williams, "American Exported Black Nationalism: The Student Nonviolent Coordinating Committee, the Black Panther Party, and the Worldwide Freedom Struggle, 1967–1972," *Negro History Bulletin* 60:3 (July-September 1997), 14.

26. Ibid., 18.

27. Statement by John Wilson, n.d. (ca. July 1967), ibid.

28. Statement of Mr. James Forman, November 17, 1967, ibid.

29. Statement by John Wilson, n.d. (ca. July 1967), ibid.

30. Williams, "American Exported Black Nationalism," 16.

31. "The Indivisible Struggle against Racism, Apartheid, and Colonialism: SNCC Position Paper for the International Seminar on Apartheid, Racial Discrimination, and Colonialism in Southern Africa," 24 July–August 1967, box 7, file 8, Ella Baker Papers, New York Public Library, New York, NY.

32. Williams, "American Exported Black Nationalism," 14.

33. Open telegram to His Excellency Houphouet Boigny from SNCC, August 27, 1967, box 7, file 8, Ella Baker Papers, New York Public Library, New York, NY.

34. Statement by John Wilson, n.d. (ca. July 1967), Williams, "American Exported Black Nationalism."

35. Ibid.

36. Thomas J. Sugrue, *The Origins of the Urban Crisis: Race and Inequality in Postwar Detroit*, 2d ed., (Princeton, NJ: Princeton University Press, 2005), xv–xxiii, 3–11.

37. William Julius Wilson, *When Work Disappears: The New World of the Urban Poor* (New York: Vintage Books, 1997); Douglas Massey and Nancy Denton, *American Apartheid: Segregation and the Making of the Underclass* (New York: Harvard University Press, 1998).

38. See, Peniel E. Joseph, "The Black Power Movement: A State of the Field," *Journal of American History* 96:3 (December 2009), 751–776. An outstanding exception is Sean L. Malloy, "Uptight in Babylon: Eldridge Cleaver's Cold War," *Diplomatic History* (forthcoming).

39. For some of the positive, tangible results of the SNCC's international efforts, see H. Timothy Lovelace, Jr., "Legal History from Below: The Black South and the International Convention on the Elimination of All Forms of Racial Discrimination (ICERD), 1958–1964," Ph.D. diss., University of Virginia, 2012.

40. Benjamin Welles, "U.S. Hears Algerian Police Raided Panthers' Quarters," *New York Times,* August 11, 1972; "Black Panther Villa in Algeria Sealed Off after Raid by Police," *New York Times,* August 12, 1972.

41. Larry Rohter, "25 Years an Exile: An Old Black Panther Sums Up," *New York Times,* April 9, 1996.

42. Eric Pace, "Tony Bryant, Former Hijacker Turned Castro Foe, Dies at 60," *New York Times,* December 26, 1999.

43. "Hijacker of Jet Pleads Guilty to Kidnapping," *New York Times,* December 6, 1986.

44. Penny M. Von Eschen, *Race against Empire: Black Americans and Anticolonialism, 1937–1957* (Ithaca, NY: Cornell University Press, 1997), 116.

45. Carol Anderson, "Rethinking Radicalism: African Americans and the Liberation Struggles in Somalia, Libya, and Eritrea, 1945–1949," *Journal of the Historical Society* 11:4 (December 2011), 385–423.

46. Abdullahi Issa to John Foster Dulles, August 6, 1953, General Correspondence, box 4, file "Somaliland (1953–57)," *Papers of the International League for Human Rights*, New York Public Library, New York, NY.

47. "Somali Leader Thanks NAACP for Aid at UN," press release, May 26, 1949, box A323, file "Italian Colonies, Disposition of Press Releases, Newspaper Clippings and Statements Regarding, 1949, May–Dec," *Papers of the NAACP.*

48. Peter Henshaw, "South African Territorial Expansion and the International Reaction to South African Racial Policies, 1939 to 1948," workshop on South Africa in the 1940s, South African Research Centre, Kingston, September 2003, http://www.queensu.ca/sarc/Conferences/1940s/Henshaw.htm, 4; provisional verbatim record, September 28, 1953, A/PV.448, found in CO 936/97, Public Records Office/National Archives, Kew Gardens, UK.

49. Carol Anderson, "International Conscience, the Cold War, and Apartheid: The NAACP's Alliance with the Reverend Michael Scott for South West Africa's

Liberation, 1946–1952," *Journal of World History* 19:3 (September 2008), 297–320, 323.

50. Ibid., 318–319; Michael Scott to Walter White, June 9, 1948, box A8, file "Southwest Africa, 1947–51," *Papers of the NAACP*.

51. Central Intelligence Agency, "The Political Situation in the Union of South Africa," July 31, 1949, ORE 1–49, box 215, file "Central Intelligence Reports: O.R.E.: 1949: 1–16 [1–3, 6, 9, 11, 14, 16: January 31–August 2]," *Papers of Harry S Truman: Personal Secretary File: Intelligence Reports*, Harry Truman Presidential Library (Independence, MO).

52. From Canadian Department of Foreign Affairs and International Trade, http://www.dfait-maeci.gc.ca/department/history/dcer/details-en.asp?intRefid: memorandum from Commonwealth Division to Deputy Under-Secretary of State for External Affairs, March 23, 1949, no. 199; memorandum by United Nations Division [K. B. Williamson], March 28, 1949, no. 201; memorandum from Deputy Under-Secretary of State for External Affairs [E. Scott Reid] to Commonwealth Division, March 26, 1949, no. 200.

53. Thomas Borstelmann, *Apartheid's Reluctant Uncle: The United States and Southern Africa in the Early Cold War* (New York: Oxford University Press, 1993).

54. Carol Anderson, *Eyes off the Prize: The United Nations and the African American Struggle for Human Rights, 1944–1955* (New York: Cambridge University Press, 2003), 203–206.

55. "Record of Performance," n.d. (ca. November 1951), box 10, folder 210, *Papers of Edith Sampson*, Schlesinger Library, Radcliffe Institute, Harvard University, Cambridge, MA (hereafter *Sampson Papers*).

56. Mary Benson, diary, December 1, 1950, box 78, file "Mary Benson [A. Y. Only]," *Papers of Michael Scott*, Rhodes House, Bodleian Library, University of Oxford, Oxford, UK; notes on UN meeting (Mrs. Edith Sampson: United States Mission to United Nations), n.d., box 10, folder 207, *Sampson Papers*; Edith S. Sampson to Mrs. Roosevelt, et al., memo, November 28, 1951, box 10, folder 210, *Sampson Papers*; "Record of Performance," n.d. (ca. November 1951), *Sampson Papers*.

57. "Mystery Man of Race Relations: Channing Tobias Meets and Influences More Top-Level VIP's Than Any Other Negro," *Ebony* (February 1951), file "Newspaper Clippings and Articles, 1937–1960 [4]," *Papers of the YMCA Biographical File: Channing H. Tobias Collection*, YMCA Kautz Family Archives, University of Minnesota, Minneapolis, MN.

58. Anderson, "International Conscience, the Cold War, and Apartheid," 321–326 (quotation on 326).

59. "Mandela, "We Stand Here Not as Guests, but as Comrades in Arms," *The Crisis* (August/September 1993), 29.

11

THE WAR ON THE PEASANT

The United States and the Third World

NICK CULLATHER

During the pivotal decades of the Cold War the term "Third World" meant the rural world. Until the onset of rapid urbanization in Asia, Africa, and Latin America in the late 1960s and 1970s, the contested zones of Asia, Africa, and Latin America were predominantly agricultural (as many of them still are), with most of their wealth generated by farming and most of their population—usually upwards of 80 percent—residing in the country. In these continents cities were relatively small, distant, isolated, and usually coastal outposts at the edge of vast interior districts teeming with villages. These were, in the language of the time, peasant societies.

Social scientists were anxious that Cold War geopolitics should not obscure this point. "The first and very commonplace observation to be made about the underdeveloped and unprogressive countries is that they are all agricultural," Harvard professor John Kenneth Galbraith stressed in 1951.[1] Peasant farming was associated with a syndrome of social problems— poverty, runaway fertility, resource depletion, and cultural isolation—that impeded state building. Economist Paul N. Rosenstein-Rodan catalogued the characteristics common to all backward societies: "They are all, roughly speaking, agrarian countries engaged in primary production with great density of population per acre of cultivable land, using rather backward methods of cultivation." While antagonisms of race, religion, and ideology lurked in these regions, the "Third World" designated a security problem rooted in the condition of rusticity. When applied to countries, terms like "backward," "underdeveloped," "unindustrialized," "overpopulated," and "low-income" were synonymous with rural, while descriptors such as "advanced" or "modern" connoted urbanity. State Department adviser and social theorist Walt W. Rostow defined modernization as "the transition of a society from a preponderantly agricultural to an industrialized basis."[2]

Early on in the Cold War, U.S. security officials identified the agrarian population as a vulnerable but critical factor. Intelligence officials found in 1946 that the "decisive dividing line" in China corresponded to the rural/urban cleavage. While the Nationalists sided with landlords, "the Communists have clearly identified the Chinese Communist Party as the party of the peasants."[3] China appeared to be a leading indicator of a global trend. After failing to broker a truce, George Marshall foresaw a revolution "of the little people all over the world. They're beginning to learn what there is in life, and learn what they are missing." The swiftness of the Communist victory demonstrated that even these apprehensions had not fully understood danger, and the stoic peasant suddenly emerged as a superman, the decisive factor in a Cold War that was breaking out of Europe. Chiang Kaishek's armies, Secretary of State Dean Acheson explained, had been "brushed aside not by Communist regimes but just by masses of the peasants and people in the country."[4] Chinese strategists also recognized that the Cold War was a clash between rural and urban ways of life. "If North America and Western Europe can be called 'the cities of the world,' then Asia, Africa, and Latin America constitute 'the rural areas of the world,'" General Lin Biao explained. "The contemporary world revolution also presents a picture of the encirclement of the cities by the rural areas."[5] By the beginning of the Kennedy administration underdevelopment had been extensively theorized, but as a strategic problem it could still be reduced to a single issue, how to manage the people in the country. This was "the greatest single challenge to American vision and leadership" in the 1960s, the Policy Planning Staff agreed. "The peasants who control the food supply and constitute a substantial majority of all underdeveloped countries are in a crucially important political position." In another decade "they could form an irresistible revolutionary tide."[6]

Comprehending the Third World as a strategic preoccupation means taking seriously this abstract peril, a threat emanating not from a particular rural place but from the condition of rurality. Historians have analyzed enduring hierarchies of race, class, and gender, but they have been less attentive to other categories of dominance, especially transient ones. One such grouping that flared into geopolitical significance in the first two-thirds of the twentieth century and then practically disappeared was the rural/urban divide. Politicians and the press referred to it as the agrarian problem or, more pointedly, the peasant problem.

As a sociological construct, the peasantry emerged in a specifically European setting centuries before the Cold War, during the transition from an agriculture based on unfree labor to one relying on semi-autonomous freeholders. Eighteenth-century emancipators, faced with the problem of how to liberate serfs, increase output, and still maintain social order in the countryside, saw the family farm as a temporary means of control. Individual homesteads slowed migration to the cities and maintained the domination of landlords during the transition to fully commercial production. Early political economists wrote of the family farm, each with its house and land, as an improvement over feudal modes of bonded labor in terms of efficiency, but as no match for a large mechanized farm using seasonal labor. By 1800, these "modern estates" were already displacing small freeholders and the days when "every rood of ground maintained its man" were passing. Drawing on the elegiac literature of the period, political economists of the Enlightenment distinguished peasants from other rural folk chiefly by the stubborn insularity, fecundity (in all senses), and tightfistedness that set them at odds with the encroaching market system.[7] The small producer first emerged as subject for serious analysis in the first volume of *Kapital* (1867), but Karl Marx and Frederick Engels cast the peasant not as a revolutionary force but as history's victim. The "annihilation" of the peasant, through enclosure, pauperization, and the destruction of household industry launched the process of primitive capital accumulation, the expropriation of wealth from labor and the soil that laid the basis for modern manufacturing. Marx, however, had scant sympathy for the peasants, famously comparing them to "potatoes in a sack," incapable even of constituting themselves as a class. The peasant remained a political subject to be molded by other, dominant classes.[8] With increasing frequency, the term was used loosely to designate small farmers in Latin America or Asia, and as Europeans eradicated their peasantries they increasingly repudiated feudal holdovers as characteristics of an alien, "Asiatic" system.[9]

The perception of a peasant problem arose from the imperatives of rail and steam, which gave cultivators the appearance of collective agency. The consolidation of national grain exchanges in the late nineteenth century gathered local pricing and trading relationships into a single ledger to be read each morning over breakfast in the daily paper. A sudden spike in the price of wheat or a long-declining trend in stocks of cotton or oilseeds could at this aggregate level appear to be the result of a conspiracy. Plowmen were making decisions that affected urban consumers and the nation, essentially unregulated by central authority. To be sure, some peasant actions *were* volitional, and their encounters with uniform prices, standard grades, and taxation sometimes stirred them to action. The first organized peasant strikes that broke out in Spain in the 1880s differed from the brigands, millennialists, and torch-and-pitchfork mobs of earlier ages precisely because of the kinds of collective action available within a modern supply chain.[10] The first half of the twentieth century is rife with peasant activism—strikes in Poland and Russia, unions in Latin America, and uprisings in the Middle East and Southeast Asia—but critically, even where no overt resistance occurred, the introduction of rationalized supply chains created the threat of disruption. Early economists warned that farmers responded to price and tax incentives weakly or "perversely" by hoarding or fallowing and thereby magnifying instability. With little capacity to gauge what was actually happening in the countryside, the state felt a new vulnerability originating not from power in the hinterland, but from weakness at the center. From the urban, industrial vantage point of the state, rural folk came to be regarded not as a political constituency, but as outsiders stubbornly or actively resisting the unifying logic of nation and market. The peasant was the antithesis of the citizen.

The significance of peasant power became apparent as soon as strategists turned their attention from sea power to land power. Writing in 1900, naval theorist Alfred Thayer Mahan warned that assimilating 400 million Asian peasants—"this great mass of beings"—into a system of nation-states was "one of the greatest problems that humanity has yet to solve." The primary work of development, he foresaw, would not be to accelerate but to slow the pace of social change so "that there shall be gained time, and a great element of safety." While British theorist Halford MacKinder was more optimistic about the potential for regimenting large populations, he too recognized the crucial importance of rural peoples. In 1904 and 1905 he articulated his famous "heartland thesis" in an essay generally recognized as the seminal work of geopolitics. The crucial contest, he argued, would be for control of the "geographical pivot," the central part of Eurasia; but while steam power had been the motive force for seaborne empires, the strategic ingredient on land was "man-power." Dominance would belong to the empire that could win the allegiance of the "horse-men, camel-men, and plow-men" who occupied the central Asian plains.[11]

The great state-building experiments of the first half of the twentieth century each centered around programs for "capturing" peasantries and drawing them into projects for national revitalization. Bolsheviks and Mensheviks differed on the type of society they were trying to create, but agreed that peasant culture and institutions had no place in it. Soviet "emergency measures" for grain procurement in the late 1920s, the collectivization of agriculture and the liquidation of the kulaks, the famine of 1932–1933, and the Terror represent successive stages in a process of breaking peasant resistance. The orthodox Marxist program called for a phase of "primitive socialist accumulation" in which the state would squeeze the countryside for resources to build industry. Stalin insisted that to make the Soviet Union "the country of metallurgy, the automobile, and the tractor" required ever-larger grain deliveries, and any official who dared warn of the growing hunger was guilty of "rightist deviation." The party also strove to eradicate remnants of rural "backwardness," such as laziness, hoarding, and religion. Throughout the 1920s, the Red Army's air corps barnstormed the countryside, taking peasants for rides above the clouds to prove there was no God. These "aerial baptisms" anticipated Nikita Khrushchev's hope that Yuri Gagarin's space flight would finally "deal a devastating blow to religious fairy tales about heaven." Implicit in all of this urgent work was the notion that the rural districts, where the majority of the population lived, were alien territory under the sway of values inimical to scientific progress.[12]

By contrast, Nazi ideology venerated the *Bauerntum*, the peasantry, as the essence of German nationhood. The Third Reich's agrarian reforms, directed by party ideologue Richard Walther Darré, aimed to preserve the freehold as "the life source of the people and the breeding ground of the armed forces." But while the state flattered peasants, its policies—breaking up rural political parties, disinheriting the racially impure, and doing away with profit in favor of "reward for work done for the good of the national community"—relegated peasants to a protected but subordinate status.[13] Mexico's land reforms in the 1930s under Lázaro Cárdenas created a system of village communes, *ejidos*, apart from but subordinate to the economy of commercial agriculture. Government-trained technicians, typically young, white, and urban, were dispatched to the countryside as medics, *agronomos*, and teachers to weld Mexico's rural and urban halves into a new national unity. Most of the world experienced the global Depression as an agrarian crisis. Regions dependent on a single crop were hit hardest; in Japan's silk districts, the coffee groves of Brazil, and the Oklahoma panhandle, farmers starved while crops rotted in the fields. Augmented by neglect, natural disasters—floods, droughts, and dust storms—compounded the catastrophe. The League of Nations concluded that the lack of rural purchasing power lay "at the very bottom of the world economic depression" and that the only solution was to rebalance the relationship between city and country on a global level.[14]

Franklin Delano Roosevelt shared the belief that the Depression had been caused by "the dislocation of a proper balance between urban and rural life."[15] While FDR's primary concern was domestic, speeches and editorials in the 1930s made frequent reference to a worldwide "agrarian problem," characterized by low incomes, unrest, and a widening cultural gulf between the traditional village and modern society. Although Soviet and Mexican experiments with collectivization were keenly watched, there was no system, according to foreign correspondent Rebecca West, that could "claim to be able to correct in our own time the insane dispensation which pays the food-producer worst of all workers."[16] Recognizing the international dimensions of the problem, members of FDR's cabinet ruminated on the U.S. response. Vice President Henry Wallace called for a global New Deal, while Secretary of State Henry Stimson wondered if "the capitalist system may not break down on the problem of the peasant." His concern was that "we were developing into great congested populations of people who were not self-supporting but were dependent upon trade and commerce for their supplies of food." While the Great War had exposed this vulnerability, it had not yet been recognized by some states, including Japan, a country ruled by "the militaristic and the peasant elements."[17]

The sectoral division of the economy, a feature of New Deal discourse, foreshadowed the conceptual division of the postwar world into three strategic regions. In 1936, an exiled German statistician, Gerhard Colm, introduced American economists to the distinction between the private and public sectors, each characterized by its own rules (contract vs. regulation) and incentive structures (market vs. budget). In short order a third, the rural or agrarian sector, was added, appearing first in analyses of German and Soviet planning. New Dealers spoke of the agrarian sector as a sphere where neither market nor regulatory mechanisms were wholly adequate to assure productive efficiency. Following the same logic, American social scientists in the 1950s divided "area studies" into an industrialized and non-Communist First World, a socialist Second World, and a largely rural and semicolonial Third World. The "Third World" soon became iconic, and *tiersmondisme* a fashion of the European Left. The classification, Sidney Mintz observes, echoed the French conception of a peasant-based Third Estate and "carries with it ideas of rural life, of agricultural economy, and—of course—of poverty."[18]

Domestic agriculture's conspicuous success during World War II only intensified the perception of social distance between the United States and the rural world. New chemical and machine technologies, coupled with systematic government subsidies, multiplied the harvest while equally dramatically diminishing the need for farm labor. Lured by war industries, millions left the farm never to return, and Americans became conscious of themselves as an urban nation. Historian Richard Hofstadter expressed the consensus:

America had "grown up in the country, but it had moved to the city." To David Riesman, a sociologist, the city-bred American was two stages of personality development removed from the "tradition-directed" peasant, making meaningful communication all but impossible.[19] This estrangement was palpable to diplomat George Kennan as his train passed in 1950 through Mexico's parched and desolate countryside. "Violence seems just around the corner," he wrote in his hotel room that night. "The city sleeps the uneasy sleep of the threatened animal, and its dreams are troubled."[20] But Kennan considered the rural/urban divide even more apparent in China, as Communist armies tightened the noose around coastal cities. "We are deceiving ourselves," he warned, "when we pretend to have answers to the problems which agitate many of these Asiatic peoples."[21]

The January 1949 speech that launched the foreign-aid program, Harry S. Truman's Point IV address, captured this formless dread and gave it a name. The president traced the sources of war and spreading instability to the hunger and ignorance of the "underdeveloped" areas. This was a remarkably expansive category, embracing, *Fortune* magazine guessed, "two-thirds of the world, if not all of it." Truman conflated rurality with danger, linking the erosion of security to the misery and hunger that made these regions a threat.[22] "There are parts of the world where plows can do a better job in maintaining stability and democracy than tanks or warplanes or machine guns," he explained later.[23] Critics scoffed at the idea that security interests were at stake in the boondocks. "'Advanced' nations...have fought the most wars," former ambassador Joseph P. Kennedy pointed out. Aid would only develop "backward nations into warring nations."[24] Congress was staggered by the scope of the plan, which promised an "unlimited opportunity for spending." But a targeted project would never have galvanized the administration and the world the way the Point IV program did. Its vagueness embraced all the trade, relief, and reconstruction projects underway or contemplated. Louis J. Halle remembered how a relieved State Department, with "no philosophy, no theory, no body of applicable principles on which to act," suddenly found a vocation in "development."[25]

As a $35 million appropriation crawled through Congress in 1949, Mao's peasant armies swept into southern China. During the previous year, diplomats had reassured themselves that the Communist drive for power would be overwhelmed by China's immensity, but the southern advance moved as if borne along by a social undertow. Admiral Thomas Inglis, chief of U.S. naval intelligence, gasped at the "superiority and strategic direction of the Communists.... It just doesn't seem Chinese." In postmortems, Americans reproached themselves for underestimating the peasantry's latent power.

Mao had never disguised his strategy of building strength in the countryside and waiting for the cities to fall when they were "ripe." The Communists "rode to victory," Acheson told Congress, on "this great revolutionary movement which is going on throughout all Asia."[26]

The Truman Doctrine cast the Cold War as a choice "between alternative ways of life," but while the Kremlin had a program for revolutionizing stagnant economies, Washington did not. Stalin touted his "plan to transform nature" and to reap "uniform harvests under any conditions," but newly independent regimes were more taken by the Soviet emergence as an industrial powerhouse. Even anti-Communist regimes such as Taiwan and South Korea adopted Soviet-style multiyear economic plans. "Russia was practically an underdeveloped country at the time of the Revolution forty years ago," explained P. C. Mahalanobis, who wrote India's Five-Year plans. The "integrated advance of science and industry" gave the Soviets a "leading position in the whole world." New states envied that position, and Soviet propaganda assured them they would not get it through Point IV. Washington had no intention, the Moscow newspaper *Trud* warned, "of investing their funds in the development of the metallurgical, metal-working, and machine construction industries in backward countries."[27]

While Americans had intervened boldly to restructure Europe's economy and society, they openly doubted their capacity in Asia's alien environment. "The gulf between America and Asia seems so vast, so unfathomable," the globe-trotting Supreme Court justice William O. Douglas observed. "There often seems to be no nexus of understanding."[28] This estrangement disadvantaged only one side in the superpower competition. America's history was not replicable in Asia, and its standard of living was beyond reach. "Our people want social reform and the ownership of their own land," a Chinese official told Republican candidate Thomas Dewey, "but 'the American way of life' has no helpful meaning."[29] The Marshall Plan and Japan's postwar revival relied on an existing, if damaged, social infrastructure. In India and Southeast Asia, Point IV technicians found extensive regions devoid of machinery, engineers, banks, or teachers. There was nothing in America's experience to match the challenges Asian countries faced. "We are not an example that backward peoples can follow," columnist Walter Lippmann affirmed, "and unless we can manage to create an example which they *can* follow, we shall almost certainly lose the Cold War."[30]

Lippmann argued that the United States needed a surrogate, "a very big, very poor country" in which to demonstrate an alternative to Communist force-draft industrialization. In the 1950s, an informal India lobby comprised of Douglas, Galbraith, Eleanor Roosevelt, historian Arthur Schlesinger,

Senator John Kennedy, Ambassador Chester Bowles, and others argued that India's size and poverty made it an ideal setting in which to demonstrate American mastery of the arts of development. *New York Times* columnist Barbara Ward captured this argument in the image of a "development race" between India and China.[31] Kennedy argued that the magnitude of India's deprivation made it the decisive ideological contender with "a world audience" looking on.[32] The development race took its place alongside the space race and the arms race in the Cold War trifecta, but U.S. experts had grave doubts about the worn-out nag they had put their money on.

Even in modern economies farmers responded feebly to market forces, and the Indian village, economists agreed, represented a further degree of market irrationality. Economists distinguished between a "modern" or "progressive" sector of the economy and the "unorganized sector" or the "special situation" in the countryside. They found the interior rife with "disguised" forms of exchange and consumption, habits of sharing food and labor that buried wealth before it could be counted. Development was a process of taking these assets, particularly labor, from the rural areas and putting them to work. S. R. Sen, an economist with the Indian Planning Commission, advised that farming was "a bargain sector, a sector with a large unexploited potential which can produce the requisite surplus with relatively low investment and in a comparatively short time." Prime Minister Jawaharlal Nehru regularly pointed out that the industrial strategy was based on skimming wealth from the countryside to invest in factories. The targets were always overly optimistic, but this never shook his certainty that poor farmers were holding back the capital he needed. If China could wring an extra 30 percent from its surplus rural labor, Jawaharlal Nehru decided, surely free Indians could achieve 15 percent.[33]

Nehru's Five-Year plans leaned heavily on the theory of Jamaican economist W. Arthur Lewis, whose seminal essay "Economic Development with Unlimited Supplies of Labor" (1954) showed how India's overwhelming population could be its salvation. An "enormous expansion of new industries" could be stimulated by putting idle farmhands and women into low-wage factory work and by directing all of the surplus generated by agriculture into capital formation. "It is agriculture which finances industrialization," Lewis explained. It was "essential to get the peasants to produce more," while making sure they are "prevented from enjoying the full fruit of their extra production." This had implications, he acknowledged, for democratic governance in a majority peasant society. "A state which is ruled by peasants may be happy and prosperous, but it is not likely to show such a rapid accumulation of capital."[34] India's great innovations in rural development, the Community Development Program of the 1950s and the green revolution of the 1960s, were schemes designed to extract "surplus" income without provoking a peasant revolt. Neither was completely successful. While they worried about violence, planners were confident that forcing workers out of the rural sector would have no negative *economic* effects.[35]

American officials also worried that "slave economies" were better equipped to engineer the overnight industrial revolution the race required. In February 1955, Rostow published an article designed to set these fears to rest. Pointing to crop failures in China and Russia, he challenged the assumption that Communism could mobilize agriculture more effectively. "Bitter struggle" tactics had not produced the breakaway growth China had hoped for, but only alienated a "smoldering, unproductive peasantry." Turning expert anxieties on their head, he argued that "Marx was a city boy" and his Communist successors were no better at understanding the peasant, who was at heart a capitalist and a consumer. Rostow confidently predicted that victory in the development race would become obvious when China's "chronic starvation" dispelled the notion that "Communism holds the key to rapid economic growth." After the Soviet aid offensive of 1956, envoys and advisers increasingly identified agriculture as an American strength. Nearly all of the $20 billion in nonmilitary aid going to the Asian region between 1956 to 1971 went for rural development, creating an informal division of labor. Soviet and East European engineers built steel mills and stadiums, while Americans sank tube wells and sprayed locusts.

At about the same time, China's Central Committee belatedly recognized its agricultural vulnerability and initiated a series of countermoves. The forced collectivization known as the Great Leap Forward had been founded on a fundamental mistrust of the peasant's acquisitive (and presumptively capitalistic) "dual nature," but Mao recognized that the growing anger of the rural majority could spell disaster. At the Seventh National Party Congress in October 1955, he drew attention to an upsurge in rural unrest and warned that "the alliance we formed with the peasants in the past on the basis of the land revolution no longer satisfies the peasants." The rural sector bore nearly all of the fiscal burden of industrialization, and consequently "the poor peasants don't believe in us."[36] China was already in the throes of a famine that may have killed as many as 22 million. Mao began to articulate, during the next three party congresses, his critique of Soviet economics, which departed from Soviet—and American—theories of modernization in arguing that China could escape the phase of primitive accumulation by equalizing the burden across all social classes and between city and country.

This ideological break led ultimately to the Sino-Soviet split, but also to a reversal of China's sectoral priorities; as investment shifted toward agriculture and agricultural machinery, a food deficit turned into a substantial surplus by 1965.[37]

U.S. officials believed their emphasis on agriculture clearly distinguished "Free World" methods of development. "Wherever Communism goes," Secretary of State Dean Rusk argued, "hunger follows." The pattern of famines confirmed that Western methods of modernization were not simply more humane, they were "technically the efficient way." Barbara Ward, with characteristic poignancy, argued that the countryside was where "the winds of change blow most fitfully, that men are most firmly attached to the ways of their forefathers." India's ability to make headway against these obstacles would determine "whether the open society has any future in Asia at all."[38] In 1963, President Kennedy called for a global "scientific revolution" in agriculture to "rival in its social consequences the industrial revolution."[39]

The American-sponsored "green revolution" had enormous effects on the Asian countryside. Subsistence farming was systematically replaced with commercial agribusiness, and the bonds of village and family with contractual arrangements. Peace Corps volunteers looked for subtle signs—the lowering birthrate, the appearance of a radio in a mud hut—to confirm that the social world of the peasant was breaking down. But the most obvious indicator that the war on the peasantry was being won was the migration of displaced tenant farmers, by the millions, to urban slums. By 1968, the International Labor Office was warning that even the fastest growing economies could not absorb more than a fraction of the refugees. Secretary of Defense Robert McNamara expressed alarm at "the scale of social displacement and the general uprootedness of populations." While the Third World was moving to the city, the First World was fleeing to the suburbs. The 1970 Census showed that 67 percent of the residents of U.S. metropolitan areas lived outside the "inner city," which had become synonymous with crime and social pathology. By 1970, Mexico City, Bombay, Calcutta, and Saigon surpassed the largest U.S. cities in size, with Bangkok and Manila close behind, achieving densities that seemed to risk social breakdown. Henry Kissinger's aides warned that "the great influx into large cities is aggravating the natural obstacles to individual advancement" and heightening social conflict. By 1970, a UN report noted, the development community had come to regard "cities as the symbol of failure."[40]

Without the fearsome embodiment of the peasant, the Third World began to fade from the consciousness of policymakers. The numerical targets for Kennedy's "Development Decade" were actually achieved. India's GNP had risen 5 percent by 1969, but poverty, illiteracy, and infant mortality remained just as prevalent. India claimed self-sufficiency in food, but 80 percent of the pupils in Bombay's public schools had symptoms of chronic malnutrition. "So our horse has won, and it may well win again," economist Hans Singer ruefully observed. "Magnificent—but is it development?"[41] In 1976, modernization theorist Lucian Pye wrote off the development race as if it had all been imagined: "At one time the United States did think that it was helping India in a race against China which would test the relative merits of democracy and communism. With China no longer a threat, it was possible to ask in much more realistic terms what had been accomplished in India as a result of nearly $10 billion of American assistance."[42] Funding was scaled back and redirected toward the Middle East. Détente stalled the arms race temporarily, but it conclusively finished the development race. Nixon's national security adviser, Henry Kissinger, notoriously contemptuous of North Vietnam, "a third-class Communist peasant state," was anxious to liquidate Johnson's war in order to shift the focus of world politics to more vital regions.[43] His realism located the centers of influence in Washington, Moscow, Beijing, Paris, London, and Bonn. "The Third World has not proved to be a decisive arena of great power conflict," he observed. The anticipated dangers, from falling dominoes or a polarization of the poor against the rich, had never materialized. The area, he argued, was "simply too heterogenous" to force a realignment of the power balance.[44]

A decade and a half before the East-West confrontation ended, the North-South confrontation simply evaporated. No walls came down to mark the event, but it ended for the same reason: the fundamental premise that the Third World constituted a bloc, a monolithic system defined by an alternate "way of life" was no longer plausible. The gulf of wealth and understanding dividing the impoverished and still predominantly rural zones from the industrial core remains, of course, but it is framed as a security issue in more selective terms, as a threat from "failed states," narco-terrorism, or Islam. Perhaps even more than "peasant," these formulations conceal more than they illuminate, allowing us once more to dismiss the ramifications for security and justice of the "insane dispensation" that pays the food producer worst of all workers.

NOTES

1. John K. Galbraith, "Conditions for Economic Change in Underdeveloped Countries," *Journal of Farm Economics* 33 (1951), 2:689–696

2. Paul N. Rosenstein-Rodan, "The International Development of Economically Backward Areas," *International Affairs* 20 (1944), 2:157–165; Walt W. Rostow, *The Process of Economic Growth* (New York: Norton, 1962), 19, 104.

3. State Department INR report, "Economy of North China," in *Congressional Record*, July 26, 1946, 79th Cong., 2nd sess., 10224.

4. Sargent Shriver, *Point of the Lance* (New York: Harper and Row, 1964), 9; Senate Committee on Foreign Relations, *Reviews of the World Situation: 1949–1950*, 81st Cong., 1st and 2nd sess. [Historical Series] (Washington, DC: Government Printing Office, 1974), 131.

5. Lin Biao, *Long Live the Victory of People's War!* (Peking: Foreign Languages Press, 1966), 49.

6. Bowles to Rusk, "A Coordinated Approach to Rural Development," August 17, 1961, Department of State Central Files, Record Group 59, PPS, Lot 67D548, box 115, National Archives and Records Administration, College Park, MD.

7. Oliver Goldsmith, "The Deserted Village," *Norton Anthology of English Literature*, ed. M. H. Abrams, 3rd ed. (New York: Norton, 1974), 1:2407; J. J. Rosseau, *The Social Contract and Discourses* (New York: E. P. Dutton, 1913); J. S. Mill, *Principles of Political Economy* (New York: Oxford, 1994); Adam Smith, *The Wealth of Nations* (New York: Penguin, 1999).

8. Karl Marx and Frederick Engels, *Capital* (New York: Modern Library, 1906), 788–805; Claudio J. Katz, "Karl Marx on the Transition from Feudalism to Capitalism," *Theory and Society* 22 (1993), 3; Henri Mendres, "The Invention of the Peasantry: A Moment in the History of Post–World War II French Sociology," *Revue Française de Sociologie* 43 (2002): 157–171.

9. Esther Kingston-Mann, *In Search of the True West: Culture, Economics, and Problems of Russian Development* (Princeton, NJ: Princeton University Press, 1999), 144.

10. E. J. Hobsbawm, *Primitive Rebels* (New York: Norton, 1959), 79–80.

11. Alfred Thayer Mahan, *The Problem of Asia and its Effect on International Politics* (Boston: Little, Brown, 1900), 89–91; H. J. Mackinder, "Man-Power as a Basis of National and Imperial Strength," *National Review* 45 (1905); H. J. Mackinder, "The Geographical Pivot of History," *Geographical Journal* 23 (1904): 421–425.

12. Fabio Bettanin, "Communism," in *A Dictionary of 20th Century Communism*, ed. Silvio Pons and Robert Service (Princeton, NJ: Princeton University Press, 2010), 542–546; Lynne Viola et al., *The War against the Peasantry, 1927–1930: The Tragedy of the Soviet* Countryside (New Haven, CT: Yale University Press, 2005), 176–177; Scott W. Palmer, "Peasants into Pilots: Soviet Air Mindedness as an Ideology of Dominance," *Technology and Culture* 41 (2000), 22; Andrew B. Stone, "Overcoming Peasant Backwardness: The Khrushchev Antireligious Campaign and the Rural Soviet Union," *Russian Review* 67 (2008), 303.

13. Gustavo Corni, *Hitler and the Peasants: Agrarian Policy of the Third Reich, 1930–1939* (New York: Berg, 1990), 18–38.

14. Amy L. S. Staples, *The Birth of Development: How the World Bank, Food and Agriculture Organization, and World Health Organization Have Changed the World, 1945–1965* (Kent, OH: Kent State University Press, 2006), 72.

15. "New Leadership Is Urged," *New York Times*, June 3, 1931, A1; Sarah T. Phillips, "Acres Fit and Unfit: Conservation and Rural Rehabilitation in the New Deal Era," Ph.D. diss., Boston University, 2004, 22, 88–89.

16. Rebecca West, *Black Lamb and Grey Falcon* (New York: Penguin, 1982), 101.

17. Stimson diaries, February 27, 1933, March 26, 1936, *Diaries of Henry Lewis Stimson* (New Haven, CT, [microfilm] 1973), reel 5.

18. Gerhard Colm, "Theory of Public Expenditures," *Annals of the American Academy* 183 (1936), 1–11; Carl E. Pletsch, "The Three Worlds, or the Division of Social Scientific Labor, Circa 1950–1975," *Comparative Studies in Society and History* 23:4 (1981), 565–590; Sidney W. Mintz, "On the Concept of a Third World," *Dialectical Anthropology* 1:4 (1976), 378.

19. Richard Hofstadter, *The Age of Reform* (New York: Knopf, 1955), 23, 328; David M. Potter, *People of Plenty* (Chicago: University of Chicago Press, 1954); David Riesman, *The Lonely Crowd: A Study of the Changing American Character* (New Haven, CT: Yale University Press, 1950), 43, 113.

20. George F. Kennan, *Sketches from a Life* (New York: Pantheon, 1989), 134.

21. George Kennan, "Review of Current Trends: U.S. Foreign Policy," PPS 23, February 24, 1948, in *Containment: Documents on American Policy and Strategy, 1945–1950*, ed. Thomas H. Etzold and John L. Gaddis (New York: Columbia University Press, 1978), 226.

22. Harry S. Truman, inaugural address, 1949, www.presidency.ucsb.edu; "Point IV," *Fortune* (February 1950), 88.

23. Truman, "Radio Address on the Mutual Security Program," March 6, 1952, in *Public Papers of the President, Harry S. Truman, 1952–1953* (Washington, DC: Government Printing Office, 1956), 193.

24. Joseph P. Kennedy, "The U.S. and the World," *Life* (March 18, 1949), 110–112.

25. Louis J. Halle, "On Teaching International Relations," *Virginia Quarterly Review* 40:1 (1964), 11.

26. *Foreign Relations of the United States, 1945–1950: Emergence of the Intelligence Establishment* (Washington, DC: Government Printing Office, 1996), 896; Senate Committee on Foreign Relations, *Reviews of the World Situation: 1949–1950*, 81st Cong., 1st and 2nd sess. [Historical Series] (Washington, DC: Government Printing Office, 1974), 131.

27. "The New Soviet Peasantry," *Sotsialistitcheskoye Zemedelie,* December 10, 1949, in *Soviet Press Translations* (March 1, 1950), 153; P. C. Mahalanobis, *Talks on Planning* (New York: Asia Publishing House, 1961), 56; V. Ivanov, "What Is the American Plan for 'Aid' to Backward Countries?" (August 6, 1949), in *Soviet Press Translations* (February 1, 1950), 78.

28. William O. Douglas, *North From Malaya* (Garden City, NY: Doubleday, 1953), 317.

29. Thomas E. Dewey, *Journey to the Far Pacific* (Garden City, NY: Doubleday, 1952), 109

30. W. Lippmann, "India The Glorious Gamble," *Ladies Home Journal* (August 1959), 48.

31. Barbara Ward, "The Fateful Race Between China and India," *New York Times Magazine* (September 20, 1953), 9–67.

32. John F. Kennedy, "If India Falls," *The Progressive* (January 1958), 8–11.

33. S. R. Sen, "The Strategy for Agricultural Development," *Agricultural Statistics of India* 15:1 (1960), 1068; P. C. Mahalanobis, "The Asian Drama: An Indian View," *Sankhya* 31 (1969), 443; Francine Frankel, *India's Political Economy* (Princeton, NJ: Princeton University Press, 1978), 139–142.

34. W. Arthur Lewis, "Economic Development with Unlimited Supplies of Labour," *Manchester School of Economic and Social Studies* 22 (1954), 174–175.

35. Rosenstein-Rodan, "International Development," 157–165; Theodore W. Schultz, *Transforming Traditional Agriculture* (New Haven, CT: Yale University Press, 1964), 59.

36. Mao, "The Debate over Agricultural Cooperativization and the Present Class Struggle" (October 11, 1955), in *The Writings of Mao Zedong*, ed. John K. Leung (Armonk, NY: M. E. Sharpe, 1992), 1:630; Rebecca E. Karl, "Culture, Revolution, and the Times of History: Mao and 20th Century China," *China Quarterly* 198 (2006), 698–699; Robert Ash, "Squeezing the Peasants: Grain Extraction, Food Consumption, and Rural Living Standards in Mao's China," *China Quarterly* 198 (2006), 959–998.

37. Thomas P. Bernstein, "Mao Zedong and the Famine of 1959–1960: A Study in Willfulness," *China Quarterly* 198 (2006), 421–445; Daniel Kelliher, "Chinese Communist Political Theory and the Rediscovery of the Peasantry," *Modern China* 20 (1994), 396–398.

38. Rusk, "The Tragedy of Cuba," *Vital Speeches* (February 15, 1962), 258–262; Barbara Ward, *India and the West* (New York: Norton, 1961), 181, 227.

39. John F. Kennedy, "Speech at the Opening Ceremony of the World Food Congress" (June 4, 1963), *President John F. Kennedy's Office Files, 1961–1963* (Bethesda, MD: University Microfilms, 1989), part 1, reel 11, frame 1018.

40. Amrit Lall, "India's Urbanization," *Focus* (September 1968), 1–7; Michael Perelman, "Second Thoughts on the Green Revolution," *The New Republic* (July 17, 1971), 21; Osgood to Kissinger, "Overview of World Situation" August 20, 1969, Declassified Document Retrieval System (DDRS), CK3100566100; United Nations, Department of Economic and Social Affairs, *Urbanization in the Second United Nations Development Decade* (New York: United Nations, 1970), 5.

41. "The Undernourished Generation," *Blitz* (December 12, 1970), 13; Hans Singer, "The Riderless Horse," *Internationalist* (November 1972), 26–27.

42. Lucian W. Pye, "Foreign Aid and America's Involvement in the Developing World," in *The Vietnam Legacy*, ed. Anthony Lake (New York: New York University Press, 1976), 379.

43. Walter Isaacson, *Kissinger: A Biography* (New York: Simon and Schuster, 1992), 120.

44. Kissinger to Nixon, October 20, 1969, in *Foreign Relations of the United States, 1969–1976*, vol. 1: *Foundations of Foreign Policy* (Washington, DC: Government Printing Office, 2003), 127; Jeremi Suri, *Henry Kissinger and the American Century* (Cambridge, MA: Harvard University Press, 2007), 235–236; Joan Hoff, *Nixon Reconsidered* (New York: Basic Books, 1994), 158–159.

EPILOGUE

THE COLD WAR AND THE THIRD WORLD

ODD ARNE WESTAD

Is the Third World a place? In North America, and increasingly in Europe, the very question seems preposterous. Just using the term "Third World" is now regarded as deeply politically incorrect; "Third World" has, in the Western public imagery, become a bit similar to "third class" or "failed state"—beyond rescue, derelict, a far-away faint echo of urban slums or immigrant ghettos more nearby. The "developing world" sounds much more upbeat and less injurious. Or, for a vague political edge, the "global South."[1]

This devaluation of the term would have come as a great surprise to those who began using it after the Bandung Conference in 1955. To anticolonial radicals the term was a point of satisfaction: The Third World was the future of the world, as the Third Estate had been the future of France in 1789. It was powerful, plentiful, and proud, and it confronted, self-consciously, both the First World, the aristocrats of the United States, Britain, or France, who wanted to own it, and the Second World, the high priests of the Soviet Union and Eastern Europe (and sometimes also China), who wanted to save it for their own benefit. Out of the postcolonial position would come ideas that would unite the oppressed, destroy all forms of subservience, and free humankind from the threat of obliteration through nuclear war.

So the Third World was an extensive and active project. But was it also a place? That depends on definitions. Frantz Fanon saw it as the postcolonial world, pure and simple: All those who had endured twentieth-century colonialism in any form would have more in common, Fanon believed, than any other transnational group of people, and should therefore form a tightly knit community. Fanon's Third World encompassed Africa, the Caribbean, and Asia (including, inconveniently for the Soviets, the Caucasus and

Central Asia), but not South America, China, or, for that matter, Japan.[2] For Indonesian leader Sukarno, who probably promoted the expression more than anyone, the Third World was an idea waiting to become a geographical reality (though he was always certain it would happen), and it would include all peoples who had been colonized by European powers. In Africa, after the early 1960s, the liberation movements in the Portuguese colonies and in the white-supremacist states of South Africa, South West Africa, and Rhodesia were those who came closest to seeing the Third World as existing geographical space, since for them it created a zone in which they could operate freely and openly. Maybe it is right to conclude that the Third World was a place as long as it fitted someone's political framework, or—if you like—satisfied their mental maps.[3]

Whatever definition you want to give it, the Third World no longer exists today, neither as political project nor as geographical space. It fragmented under economic and political pressures in the 1970s, and it is very unlikely that it can ever be put together again. This concluding chapter discusses two key issues that the contributors to this volume bring up. The first is whether the Third World as a project was a part of the Cold War or was its antithesis—an issue that is central to the concerns held by many of the contributors. The second is why the Third World project collapsed when it did—a question that is understudied by historians (though it has been explored by sociologists, political scientists, and—to some extent—anthropologists).[4]

Positions

The debate about whether the Third World, as a political project, belonged within the Cold War is an old one, laden with tangled political baggage. The position from the "political right" in the United States and Britain was that the Third World was simply another name for left-wing subversion of Western interests, allied de facto to Soviet expansionist urges in Asia, Africa, and Latin America. The view from the European and American Left— especially the so-called New Left of the 1960s—was that the Third World represented a qualitatively new form of socialist democracy, which—in time—would ally itself with radicals in Paris or New York. Both political perspectives turned out to be wrong. Some radical Third World states— Algeria, Ethiopia, Vietnam, and Cuba, for instance—moved ever closer to Soviet-style domestic politics and economics in the 1960s and 1970s, away from the idea of non–Cold War socialist positions. But the bigger story is that almost no Third World country broke with the capitalist world economy as it sought new internal development plans. Except for Cuba and Vietnam, which, for political reasons, were denied access to world trade and finance by the United States, all postcolonial states sought more, not fewer, international market openings in spite of their domestic radicalism.

There were many reasons why "Cold War" was such a laden term among anticolonial leaders. Many defined the term, following Soviet parlance, as an aspect of U.S. foreign policy, not as a description of a bipolar system. Cold War was what the United States used against its enemies. Using the concept of the Cold War in relation to the postcolonial world was, in other words, to heap opprobrium on those who wanted to create a Third World project in and among formerly oppressed nations: It insinuated their lack of agency and their subservience to the Soviet Union. Others saw it as postulating a dichotomous world, in which no position was possible except those of the superpowers. Whatever way it was seen, the "Cold War," as a term, seemed to get in the way of what the Third World promised to be.

In reality, however, there was little escape from the Cold War, however defined. Not only did the United States intervene in various forms against those who tried to assert their independence from U.S. control, but the Soviet Union was, and remained, the only alternative power with a global reach. In practical terms, as far as security was concerned, there was only one game in town: If you did not want to seek accommodation with the United States, then the Soviet Union was the only other power that would provide the kind of security that many postcolonial countries sought. It did not matter whether you defined the world between the end of World War II and 1989 as unipolar or bipolar; as soon as you acted internationally, then those concerns that drove the Cold War impinged on your freedom and, in the end, constrained your options. Many Third World countries tried to break out of the Cold War stranglehold. None succeeded.

For many Western Third-Worldists—intellectuals who believed that the Third World project would defeat the Cold War and build a new global future—the claim of association with the Soviet Union was a particularly galling one. Not only did they oppose the Soviet-linked Communist parties in their own countries; they also often attempted countermanding Soviet influence in their Third World country of choice. In Algeria, French *tiers-mondistes* warned Ben Bella of Soviet perfidy and parsimony. In Nicaragua, Scandinavian leftists spoke of outmoded Soviet models.[5] In every case, their influence was limited. The Soviets offered a concrete alternative in terms of development (which Western Marxists did not). They also offered military supplies and training (which most Third-Worldists steered well clear of).

The attraction of the Soviet model of development up to the 1970s should never be underestimated (although it often is). In spite of the terror (well known but often denied) and the waste (lost in the general figures of growth), the Soviet experience for many Third World leaders offered a way out of the dilemmas of state building under conditions of poverty and international market pressures. It promised modernity *and* justice, technology *and* social progress. While the Soviet Union's main advantage was being a Western country that was not a colonial power, it was also seen as economically successful and—very importantly—a pioneer of central planning. At a time when economic development models were considered prepacked products, the Soviet planning experience counted not only for states that viewed themselves as socialist, but for those—such as India or Nigeria—that wanted to move away from markets to centralized, state-led development.[6]

But in addition to the rather obvious fact that there was much that did not endear postcolonial elites to capitalist forms of development (generations of repression under overseas bourgeois regimes, for one), there were also the links between concepts of national liberation and Bolshevism that went back to the origins of the Russian Revolution. Different from Marx, who had generally viewed colonial rule as progress, Lenin had seen a link between what he called self-determination and socialism; "objectively" the national bourgeoisie were allies of the working class while their country broke free from colonial domination, the Soviet leader taught.[7] Soviet and other Communists helped organize the anticolonial resistance across the globe and, deservedly, made themselves popular among those who were to become postcolonial leaders in the process. As Carol Anderson's chapter reminds us, the emergence of a non-Communist opposition to racial discrimination and colonial oppression abroad was a watershed, which helped set the stage for a rapid decline in Soviet fortunes in the Third World.[8]

Another key link to the Cold War was the category of state-formation chosen by the postcolonial elites. Instead of building on broad identities (Africans, Arabs) or narrow ones (Yoruba, Gujarati), they invariably chose the concept of the nation-state to form the core of their political projects. It was—as Jeffrey Byrne notes—outward from these more or less imagined entities that Third World solidarity was intended to flow. The problem with the implementation, of course, was that not only did it superimpose the wholly European idea of the nation-state on unwilling populations, but it confirmed borders arbitrarily drawn by the imperialist powers. The result was governments lacking in legitimacy, peoples who did not see themselves as one people, and cross-cutting conflicts drawn from both of these deficits, stirring hatred and often violence. It is quite possible, as Salim Yaqub notes, that one of the main roles of the Cold War was to exacerbate conflicts that already existed. But the form that the state itself got—cheered on equally by the United States and the Soviet side in the Cold War—was a key reason for the invalidity of the Third World project as well as an origin for some of the disasters that befell postcolonial states as the first generation of leaders passed from the scene.

A further link worth contemplating—although the literature, especially the comparative literature, so far is weak—is between Cold War strategies and religiously exclusive states. The two main experiments in setting up new states based on religion—Israel and Pakistan—both benefited massively from U.S. Cold War concerns, but at the cost of destabilizing their neighborhoods. As both Yaqub and David Engerman note, U.S. support for Israel and Pakistan brought the Cold War into play in the Middle East and South Asia and helped link other states in these regions to the Soviet Union. But the most important consequence of these U.S. alliances was probably to push local populations—both in the countries the U.S. supported and elsewhere—toward forms of identitarianist politics among Muslims, Hindus, and Jews that fueled long-term conflict. In the case of Pakistan, and throughout the Muslim world, it also linked Washington to authoritarian dictatorships that may have served short-term U.S. security interests but that became less and less legitimate in the eyes of their own populations.

The issue of state and elite legitimacy is the core of the debate on the effects of the Third World project itself. As Nick Cullather notes, regimes across the postcolonial regions—including most of those that saw themselves as part of the Third World—waged war against their own peasant populations in an attempt to force them into the version of modernity that the regime subscribed to.[9] In these brutal efforts they were helped by the Cold War superpowers, which both saw the abolition of the peasantry as a key yardstick for progress. The problem with these campaigns was not only that a lot of people died (although that is bad enough), but that hatreds were sown of a kind that would explode in the face of modern political projects from Algeria to Iraq, from Burma to Cambodia. Cullather is right to argue that the U.S. "battle against poverty" was an intimate accomplice of its Cold War strategies. The success of this "war," however, cannot be measured by the magnitude of U.S. efforts, but by changes in local inequity; as Amartya Sen and others have demonstrated—anti-Malthus—hunger is usually not caused by overpopulation or failed harvests, but by social oppression and failed development plans.[10]

In his excellent contribution to this volume, Greg Grandin deals effectively with one of the big questions: What was the effect of the Cold War on
Latin America, and—going back to definitions—what was that continent's
place in the Third World project? Grandin explains both how U.S. interventionism and dominance in the region predated the Cold War and how there
was a Latin American Cold War that more or less coincided with the global
version. This is important, because both Third World leaders in Asia and
Africa and Latin American radicals were uncertain as to how the struggle in
the Americas fit in with the Third World project. The states in Latin America
had (mostly) been independent for 150 years and were therefore not postcolonial in the same sense as elsewhere. Moreover, the elites (including the
radical elites) were mostly of European origin, something other radicals—
especially those of a nativist bent—found problematic.[11] What came to link
Latin America in with broader Third World developments were concepts of
"dependency" and "structural imperialism," terms that gave the U.S. control
of its southern neighbors a similar *valeur* as the suffering of those who had
been directly colonized elsewhere.[12]

By the late 1960s the Third World had developed a specific set of positions vis-à-vis the Cold War. Its role was problematic, but not hopelessly so.
There were questions of definition and of inclusion that were hard to resolve,
but not more than for the superpower blocs themselves. In spite of its contradictions and its occasional cruelties, the Third World project seemed set
for survival and gradual institutionalization. Its original emphasis on social
justice may have been blunted, but its emphasis on sovereignty and equality among states remained. So did the regime-led modernization model and
the emphasis on planning, which seemed to be spreading outward from the
Third World core during the 1960s. In the United Nations, Third-Worldist
claims and proposals were adopted with increasing frequency. But things
changed.

Collapse

Why, then, did the Third World project collapse as spectacularly as it did
during the 1970s and 1980s? There are, as far as I can tell, four main reasons, all of which are dealt with in this volume. The first one is changes in
global capitalism, which sent the economic situation for Third World countries into free fall. The second is the massive breakdown in legitimacy (and
thereby the ability to govern) within many Third World regimes. The third
is the counterrevolution in China and the unprecedented economic growth

in East Asia. And the fourth is the antirevolutionary offensive of the Reagan administration, which armed rebels in order to overthrow the last holdouts among Third World regimes. It was a kind of perfect storm, which very few international movements could stand against.

The fundamental changes in the global economy that took place at the beginning of the 1970s came, eventually, to privilege an internationalization of U.S. capitalism into what we today call globalization. Ironically, measures that the Nixon administration took in order to deal with rising public indebtedness and inflation, such as floating exchange rates and abolishing capital controls, helped create interactive and international financial markets that strengthened global capitalism (while stimulating its speculative nature) and expanded world trade. By the end of the decade, the United States had begun, on a massive scale, to buy into economic change that happened elsewhere, thereby at least temporarily slowing its own weakening position in the international economy.[13]

Economies that were geared toward selling manufactured goods at low cost internationally benefited from these developments, while those that had emphasized import-substitution and zero-sum central planning did not. Even those who participated to a very great extent in the global economy through raw-material exports did not benefit much, because of the instability of prices. Since all the key countries in the Third World were either central planners or raw-material exporters, their economic development plans suffered and slowed down, especially since many of them were getting increasingly indebted to international financial institutions. And since plans for so-called South-South economic cooperation had mostly failed, loans were the only way in which many states could make up for their economic shortfall.[14]

The Third World project also collapsed because many of the states that represented it became less and less legitimate in the eyes of their own populations. The first generation of leaders—Sukarno, Nasser, Nkrumah—came to base their rule on fiat rather than on popular participation in government, thereby destroying much of the support they had enjoyed when their governments were formed. Human-rights abuses abounded. Electoral support was neglected. Corruption and nepotism became increasingly widespread. The message that the Third World concept had contained—a political and sometimes moral superiority based on the struggle against oppression in the past—became overshadowed by the practices its current representatives engaged in. Although some claim that it was the military regimes that replaced the initial leaders which were the worst sinners in this respect, it was clearly the first generation that set the low standards that others lived down to.

Some historians claim that the Third World project was shattered in the 1970s because of the enormous economic divergence that developed between three groups of postcolonial countries at exactly the moment when the Third World agenda itself was becoming centered on international economic demands. Having its New International Economic Order (NIEO) adopted as a UN resolution in 1974 seemed a high-point for the leading Third World countries—the special session that agreed the resolution had been proposed by Algeria and supported by seventy other states from Africa, Asia, and Latin America. But in reality the NIEO came to exacerbate the already-existing economic tension among the oil-producing countries, the expanding East Asian economies, and the rest. The 1967 Charter of Algiers, which set the framework for NIEO, had underlined how much all nonindustrial economies had in common, especially in terms of economic demands:

> The lot of more than a billion people of the developing world continues to deteriorate as a result of the trends in international economic relations; the rate of economic growth of the developing world has slowed down and the disparity between it and the affluent world is widening.... Although modern technology offers developing countries great possibilities to accelerate their economic development, its benefits are largely by-passing them due to its capital and skill incentive nature, and is drawing away from them such limited skills as are developed.... The international community has an obligation to rectify these unfavorable trends and to create conditions under which all nations can enjoy economic and social well-being, and have the means to develop their respective resources to enable their peoples to lead a life free from want and fear.[15]

But by 1980 the differences among these economies—and therefore their economic interests—were as diverse as those between them and the industrialized economies. The main problem for those who wanted to develop their industrial sectors was unstable energy prices. But the difference between, say, Zambia and Singapore, both members of the Group of 77, which supported the NIEO, had also become enormous in terms of their basic economies. Singapore's prime minister, Lee Kuan Yew, had been to Lusaka the first time for a Third-Worldist nonaligned summit in 1964. He visited again in 1979 and was shocked by what he saw:

> Everything was in short supply. The shops were empty. Imported toiletries were absent and there was little by way of local substitutes. [Mrs. Lee; Kwa Geok] Choo saw women queuing for essentials. The only souvenir she could

buy was a malachite egg, to remind us that Zambia was a single-commodity economy, copper, and its price had not kept up with the prices of oil and other imports. They had no foreign exchange, and their currency was rapidly depreciating. Prime Minister Kenneth Kaunda's major preoccupation was politics, black versus white politics, not the economics of growth for Zambia.... [16]

Matters were made worse in Third World terms by China's wholesale defection from a state-centered development model in the early 1980s. That Lee Kuan Yew saw little to solidarize himself with in Zambia in 1979 was perhaps not a surprise. That Deng Xiaoping—Communist China's powerful new boss—lectured Prime Minister Kaunda the following year on the need for rapid, market-induced development was a shock not just to the Zambian leader, but to other Third-Worldists of the same generation. "It cannot be called socialism while the economy remains stagnant. It cannot be called socialism while people's living standards remain very low," Deng told Kaunda.[17] As Chen Jian points out in this volume, China's defection both in political and economic terms helped split the Third World apart and contributed significantly to the U.S. offensive against radical regimes during the 1980s.

The fourth part of the Third World's collapse was the interventionist offensive that the U.S. administration of Ronald Reagan conducted exactly at the point when many Third World regimes were at their weakest. In Angola, Ethiopia, Afghanistan, and Nicaragua, the Americans supplied materiel and weapons to the opposition, in order to defeat radical regimes. In Cambodia, they supported the Khmer Rouge and its allies in their war against Vietnam. Elsewhere, debt-ridden, politically weakened regimes sought their peace with the United States as a condition for loans and market access. As Brad Simpson points out, this probably had more to do with markets than with threats of armed intervention. But with China and, increasingly, the Soviet Union out of the picture, the Washington-consensus slogan "There Is No Alternative" (to a capitalist economy) began sinking in with many who had earlier supported the Third World project. By the late 1980s Zambia, for instance, was rapidly introducing privatization and market-reform as a condition for debt rescheduling by the International Monetary Fund.[18]

The story of the interaction between the Third World and the Cold War is a complex one. It should be studied, I think, as part of the broader patterns of international and transnational history in the twentieth century, and the present volume is a good starting point for such studies. In many cases it would make sense to see the Third World as a specific project of solidarity among elites who had been oppressed by colonial powers and as an emerging program for undoing the injustices this oppression had created. In this sense it existed for about fifty years in the middle part of the century, roughly between the first League Against Imperialism meeting in Brussels in 1927 up to sometime between the 1966 Tricontinental Conference in Havana and the 1974 UN session on NIEO. It was a project bounded in time and geographical space, with some key states as its representatives.[19]

The Third World's involvement with the Cold War—in the form of the conflict between Communism and its enemies—existed throughout this period. It is therefore right to reintroduce the contested concept of Cold War into key developments in the history of Africa, Asia, and Latin America over the past four generations. In intellectual terms, this is a process long overdue. But in order for it to succeed, historians will have to give up the idea that the Cold War was a narrowly defined battle between the United States and the Soviet Union, often portrayed as the determinant of events elsewhere. The Cold War, even its global form, did not determine everything. But it influenced a lot of things. This, it seems to me, is now the most fruitful perspective: The Cold War was one of many developments that shaped the world of today, and probably the predominant feature of the international system in the latter half of the twentieth century. We may dislike the Cold War, both as a concept and a system, and we may want to de-center it, but we cannot dissolve it.

NOTES

1. For an overview of Third World concepts, see Vijay Prashad, *The Darker Nations: A People's History of the Third World* (New York: New Press, 2007), explored further in my review "The Downtrodden Majority," *The London Review of Books* 30:2 (2008), 30.

2. Fanon talks about Latin America as dominated by fascism "as a dialectical result of the semi-colonial state." Frantz Fanon, *The Wretched of the Earth* (New York: Grove Press, 2005), 117.

3. For a discussion of mental maps and the Cold War, see Jonathan Wright and Steven Casey, eds., *Mental Maps in the Early Cold War Era, 1945–1968* (London: Palgrave Macmillan, 2011).

4. For an early overview of the debate, see Christopher Clapham, "The Collapse of Socialist Development in the Third World," *Third World Quarterly* 13:1 (January 1, 1992), 13–25. For central texts by a key sociologist, see Bertrand Badie, *The Imported State: The Westernization of the Political Order* (Stanford CA: Stanford University Press, 2000), and *La fin des territoires: essai sur le désordre international et sur l'utilité sociale du respect* (Paris: A. Fayard, 1995). For an overview of

anthropological themes, see Ted C. Lewellen, *The Anthropology of Globalization: Cultural Anthropology Enters the Twenty-first Century* (Westport, CT: Greenwood Publishing Group, 2002).

5. On Swedes in Nicaragua, see Linda Berg, "InterNacionalistas: identifikation och främlingskap i svenska solidaritetsarbetares berättelser från Nicaragua," Ph.D. diss., Umeå University, 2007. On Frenchmen in North Africa, see Claude Liauzu, *L'enjeu tiersmondiste: débats et combats*, Logiques sociales (Paris: l'Harmattan, 1987).

6. For Nigeria, see P. N. C Okigbo, *National Development Planning in Nigeria, 1900–1992* (London: James Curry, 1989). For India see *The State and Development Planning in India*, SOAS Studies on South Asia (Delhi: Oxford University Press, 1994). The origins of modern state-led planning, of course, go back to World War I in Europe and North America; see Marc Allen Eisner, *From Warfare State to Welfare State: World War I, Compensatory State-Building, and the Limits of the Modern Order* (University Park: Pennsylvania State University Press, 2000), and the classic Charles S. Maier, *Recasting Bourgeois Europe: Stabilization in France, Germany, and Italy in the Decade after World War I* (Princeton, NJ: Princeton University Press, 1975). Planning and development is discussed in David Engerman, "The Romance of Economic Development and New Histories of the Cold War," *Diplomatic History* 28:1 (January 2004). 23–54, and in Corinna Unger and Stephan Malinowski, eds., "Modernizing Missions: Approaches to 'Developing' the Non-Western World after 1945," *Journal of Modern European History* 8 (2010).

7. V. I. Lenin, "The Socialist Revolution and the Right of Nations to Self-Determination," in *Collected Works*, vol. 22 (Moscow: Foreign Languages Publishing House, 1977), 143–156.

8. Carol Anderson, *Eyes off the Prize: The United Nations and the African American Struggle for Human Rights, 1944–1955* (Cambridge: Cambridge University Press, 2003).

9. This is an argument that goes back to the work of the political scientist and anthropologist James Scott, *Seeing Like a State: How Certain Schemes to Improve the Human Condition Have Failed* (New Haven, CT: Yale University Press, 1998), and is further developed in my *The Global Cold War: Third World Interventions and the Making of Our Times* (Cambridge: Cambridge University Press, 2005).

10. Amartya Sen's argument was first developed in the early 1980s (see his *Poverty and Famines: An Essay on Entitlement and Deprivation* [Oxford: Oxford University Press, 1981]), but is more fully discussed in his *Development as Freedom* (Oxford: Oxford University Press, 1999). See also Nick Cullather, *The Hungry World: America's Cold War Battle against Poverty in Asia* (Cambridge, MA: Harvard University Press, 2010).

11. Such uncertainties were strange parallels to the predominant U.S. racial view of Latin Americans "as white but not white enough"; see Walter D. Mignolo, *The Idea of Latin America* (Malden, MA: Wiley-Blackwell, 2006). 153

12. For origins, see Fernando Cardoso, *Empresàrio industrial e desenvolvimento econômico no Brasil.* (São Paulo: Difusão Européia do Livro, 1964). For an over-

view of the development of terminology in Brazil, see Glaucia Villas Bôas, *A voca-ção das Ciências Sociais no Brasil: Um estudo da sua produção em livros do acervo da Biblioteca Nacional 1945–1966* (Rio de Janeiro: Fundação Biblioteca Nacional, 2007). An excellent discussion of views and attitudes is in Greg Grandin, "Your Americanism and Mine: Americanism and Anti-Americanism in the Americas," *American Historical Review* 111:4 (October 2006), 1042–1066. For the very lively debate on the character of the Cold War in Latin America, see Hal Brands, *Latin America's Cold War* (Cambridge, MA: Harvard University Press, 2010); Greg Grandin and G. M. Joseph, eds., *A Century of Revolution: Insurgent and Counterinsurgent Violence during Latin America's Long Cold War* (Durham, NC: Duke University Press, 2010); G. M. Joseph and D. Spenser, *In from the Cold: Latin America's New Encounter with the Cold War* (Durham, NC: Duke University Press, 2007).

13. For a good overview, see Lauren Benton, "The 1970s in World History: Economic Crisis as Institutional Transition," presented at the "Interactions: Regional Studies, Global Processes, and Historical Analysis" conference, Library of Congress, February 28–March 3, 2001, http://www.historycooperative.org/cgi-bin/citeproc.cgi?=/proceedings/interactions/foltz.html. For a more in-depth discussion, see Duccio Basosi, *Il governo del dollaro: interdipendenza economica e potere statunitense negli anni di Richard Nixon (1969–1973)* (Firenze: Polistampa, 2006). The broader discussion of developments in the 1970s is captured in Niall Ferguson et al., eds., *The Shock of the Global: The 1970s in Perspective* (Cambridge, MA: Harvard University Press, 2010).

14. The best historical discussion of the development concept is in Gilbert Rist, *Le développement: Histoire d'une croyance occidentale*, 3rd ed. (Paris: Les Presses de Sciences Po, 2007).

15. "Charter of Algiers" (Algiers, October 10, 1967), http://www.g77.org/doc/algier~1.htm.

16. Lee Kuan Yew, *From Third World to First: The Singapore Story, 1965–2000*, 1st ed. (New York: HarperCollins, 2000), 366.

17. *Renmin ribao* (People's daily), August 23, 2004.

18. It would of course be entirely wrong to argue that Reagan's interventionism was unprecedented: on Indonesia, see Stig Aga Aandstad, "Surrendering to Symbols: United States Policy towards Indonesia, 1961–1965," master's thesis, University of Oslo, 1999, http://aga.nvg.org/oppgaver/dissertation.html; and on Chile, see Tanya Harmer, *Allende's Chile and the Inter-American Cold War* (Chapel Hill: University of North Carolina Press, 2011).

19. For more on this discussion, see the conclusion in Jeffrey J. Byrne, "The Pilot Nation: An International History of Revolutionary Algeria, 1958–1965," Ph.D. diss., London School of Economics, 2011.

INDEX

CPSIA information can be obtained at www.ICGtesting.com
Printed in the USA
BVOW05s2114160714

359472BV00004B/186/P